Gorgias Reprint Series

Volume 2

The Earliest Life of Christ

The Diatessaron of Tatian

The Earliest Life of Christ

Ever Compiled from the Four Gospels

Being

The Diatessaron of Tatian

Literally Translated from the Arabic Version and containing the Four Gospels woven into One Story

With an Introduction and Notes by

J. HAMLYN HILL

GORGIAS PRESS
2001

First Gorgias Press Edition, November 2001.

 Published in the United States of America by Gorgias Press LLC, New Jersey. From the second abridged edition originally published in Edinburgh by T. & T. Clark in 1910.

ISBN 0-9713097-2-8

GORGIAS PRESS
46 Orris Ave., Piscataway, NJ 08854 USA
www.gorgiaspress.com

Printed in the United States of America
10 9 8 7 6 5 4 3 2 1

TO

THE REVEREND THE MOST NOBLE

THE MARQUIS OF NORMANBY

CANON RESIDENTIARY OF WINDSOR

A KIND FRIEND, A TRUE CHRISTIAN

AND AN EARNEST WORKER IN THE MASTER'S CAUSE

THIS FIRST ENGLISH VERSION

OF THE EARLIEST COMPLETE AND CONTINUOUS

LIFE OF CHRIST

EVER COMPILED FROM THE FOUR GOSPELS

IS INSCRIBED

WITH THE AFFECTIONATE RESPECT AND ESTEEM OF

THE TRANSLATOR

CONTENTS.

	PAGE
Introduction	vii
Introductory Note in the Borgian MS.	xv
The Diatessaron	1
Concluding Note in the Borgian MS.	224

THE DIATESSARON.

INTRODUCTION.

OF the personal history of Tatian, the compiler of the *Diatessaron*, very little is known, and this little is chiefly derived from his extant work called *An Address to Greeks*. He there says: "I was born in the land of the Assyrians, and have been first instructed in your (*i.e.* Greek) doctrines, and afterwards in those which I now undertake to proclaim." Zahn thinks he was born about A.D. 110. He seems to have been a man of birth and fortune, and of exceptional literary powers, and occupied for a time the position of a Sophist. Animated by a keen desire to arrive at the truth respecting God and religion, he visited many countries, studying closely the worship of each. In Greece he obtained admission to the sacred mysteries; and subsequently he visited Rome, arriving there about the middle of the second century. The effect of his intimate study of the heathen religions was a conviction amounting to absolute certainty that there was no truth in them, and that they exercised a corrupting and debasing influence on the soul. This was accompanied by a longing to ascertain the truth, and to be able to worship God in a way acceptable to Him. At Rome Tatian made the acquaintance of Justin; and it was probably he who drew his attention to "certain barbaric writings, too old to be compared with the opinions of the Greeks, and too divine to be compared with their errors."—in other words, the Old Testament Scriptures. Satisfied that he had found the truth at last, Tatian received instruction in the Christian faith, and became a member of the Church at Rome. Here he continued for many years, writing in defence of the faith, exposing vigorously the falseness and licentiousness of the pagan forms of worship, and instructing converts. Here, too, he probably commenced his *Diatessaron*, with the knowledge and approval of Justin. One of his pupils was Rhodon, mentioned by Eusebius, who has preserved some fragments of Rhodon's writings; and in all probability Clement of Alexandria was also his pupil, since Clement tells us that one of his instructors was an Assyrian. Justin and Tatian worked in complete harmony until the martyrdom of the former, which was brought about through the influence of Crescens, who at a much earlier period, Tatian says, had "endeavoured to inflict on Justin, and indeed on me, the punishment of death." It appears to have been after the death of Justin that Tatian, who seems to have been his successor, began to express views which gave offence to the Christians at Rome, and led to his being excommunicated as a heretic about A.D. 172. Shortly afterwards he left Rome for the East, and seems to have resided chiefly in Syria, not far from Antioch; but he is thought to have died at Edessa about A.D. 180. During his stay in Syria he placed himself at the head of a sect called Encratites—a term signifying The Continent, or Self-Controlled; but it is uncertain to what extent, if at all, he was regarded as a heretic in the Churches of that country. The obscurity in which the career of Tatian is involved is largely due to his being branded as a heretic, which led the writers of the Church to concern themselves more with combating his errors than describing his life.

The peculiar views of Tatian may be briefly stated as follows:—(1) He held in some degree the Gnostic theory of Valentinus, that there were certain Aeons, or emanations from the Supreme Deity, the Logos or Word being the chief; (2) Like Marcion he considered the God of this world, or God of the Old Testament, or Demiurge, as distinct from, and inferior to, the God of the New Testament. Origen tells us that he understood the words, "Let there be light," as the *prayer* of the God of this world to His superior, which was granted; (3) Tatian believed in the non-salvability of Adam; (4) He advocated and observed celibacy, condemning marriage as no better than whoredom, believing it to be the work of the inferior God; (5) He advocated abstinence from animal food and also from wine. In this respect he introduced a modification into the celebration of the Lord's Supper, so that water might be used instead of wine.

Tatian wrote many works, of which the names of the following have come down to us: *An Address to Greeks*; The *Diatessaron*; *A Book of Problems*, explaining what seemed obscure in the Old Testament; *Of Perfection according to the Saviour*; *On Animals*; *A Collection of the Epistles of S. Paul.* Lightfoot places his literary activity between A.D. 155 and A.D. 170, but says it may have extended a few years beyond this period either way. Westcott places it between A.D. 150 and A.D. 175. The exact time at which he wrote the *Diatessaron* is uncertain.

In modern times much interest has been awakened in the *Diatessaron*; but all efforts to discover a copy in Syriac, which many believe to be its original language, have failed entirely; and no Greek copy, supposing that to be its language, has been found. But there is in the Vatican Library an Arabic MS., numbered XIV., which originally consisted of 125 leaves; but the 17th and 118th are missing. From its appearance, and the handwriting, it is supposed to have been written in Egypt at some period from the twelfth to the fourteenth century, the latter date being the more probable. On the last page the copyist has written in Latin, "Here endeth, by the help of God, the sacred Gospel, which Tatian collected out of the four Gospels, and which is commonly called the *Diatessaron.*" It was brought to the Vatican about A.D. 1719. Agostino Ciasca, one of the Guild of Writers to the Vatican, wrote an essay upon it, which he published at Paris in 1883. In 1886 Ciasca showed this MS., amongst others, to Antonius Morcos, Visitor-Apostolic of the Catholic Copts, who said he had seen one like it in Egypt, and could obtain it for him. In August 1886 the promised MS. arrived at Rome as a present to the Borgian Museum from its owner, Halim Dos Galî. It is evidently a copy of the same work as MS. XIV., though it contains some important differences of detail. A note at each end plainly asserts that it is Tatian's *Diatessaron.* This work Ciasca selected as the most suitable one for publication in honour of the Jubilee of the priesthood of Pope Leo XIII.; and it was accordingly published at Rome in 1888 in the original Arabic, accompanied by a Latin translation, the wording of the text being based on a careful comparison of the two MSS. of the Vatican Library and the Borgian Museum. The present volume is an attempt to lay before the English reader a literal translation of the *Diatessaron* as published by Ciasca, with a short explanation of its history, contents, and bearing upon modern controversies.

The MS. which reached the Borgian Museum in this singular way, has been the means of explaining the difficulties which prevented the general acceptance of the Vatican MS. as Tatian's work; for, although MS. XIV. closed with a distinct statement that it contained the *Diatessaron* of Tatian, grave doubts rested upon this assertion (which, it was thought, might only express the opinion of the transcriber), because the contents differed in some important respects from those of the *Diatessaron* as described by some of the Fathers. In the first place, MS. XIV. contained the genealogies plainly declared by Theodoret to have been absent from the copies he found in use in his diocese. In the Borgian MS., however, these genealogies are absent from the body of the work, but are put together as an appendix bearing the title, "The Book of the Generation of Jesus." It follows that the Borgian MS. represents an older and more faithful copy of a work which originally did not contain the genealogies at all, but to which they were added in course of time, first of all in an appendix as an acknowledged addition to the original, and then eventually as a part of the text itself. Another obstacle to the acceptance of MS. XIV. was, that it began with the opening words of S. Mark's Gospel instead of those of S. John's, as stated by early writers. Here also the Borgian copy solved the mystery; for it had S. Mark's words: "The Gospel of Jesus, the Son of the living God," separated from the main body of the work, as a *title*, the work itself commencing with, "In the beginning was the Word." It seems safe to conclude, therefore, that the assertion of the copyist in each case is correct, and that we have in these MSS. the *Diatessaron* of Tatian in two of the forms which it assumed after centuries of use. The Arabic text is divided into fifty-five chapters; and these have been subdivided for convenience of reference into verses corresponding as far as possible to those of the Authorised

Version of the Gospels; these will be found to the left of the text. To the right will be found references to the corresponding passages in the four Gospels: these are a revised version of those given in the Vatican MS. We do not get them from Tatian, as verse-divisions were not invented till the sixteenth century.

The advantage of having in one continuous and consecutive story the contents of the four Gospels was found so great that the "compiled" Gospel gradually superseded the "distinct" Gospels in Syria, not only in private use, but in public services, so much so that Theodoret, who became Bishop of Cyrrhus near the Euphrates about A.D. 420, wrote: "I myself found more than two hundred such books held in respect in the churches of our parts; and I collected and put them all away, and put the Gospels of the four Evangelists in their place." Commentaries were also based on this Harmony, such as the Homilies of Aphraates, A.D. 337–345, and the Gospel Commentary of Ephraem, the Deacon of Edessa, and the most famous of the native Syrian Fathers, who died A.D. 373. This latter work is only to be found now in two distinct Armenian MSS. of it, both bearing the date A.D. 1195, one being in the Mechitarist Monastery of S. Lazzaro, near Venice. A careful analysis of its contents shows that S. Ephraem's Harmony followed substantially the same order as the Arabic *Diatessaron*. The reader is referred to *A Dissertation on the Gospel Commentary of S. Ephraem the Syrian*, by the present author (T. & T. Clark, Edinburgh).

Victor, Bishop of Capua, who died A.D. 554, met with an anonymous harmony in Latin, and, after much inquiry as to its authorship, concluded that it was a translation of Tatian's work. Victor published it with a preface of his own; and it was brought to Fulda in the eighth century by Boniface, the apostle of Germany. The work is now known as the *Codex Fuldensis*, and has been edited by Ranke. It is divided into 182 chapters or sections. There is a Table of Contents in barbarous Latin; but the contents themselves are in excellent Latin, evidently copied from the Vulgate. It was probably Victor himself who altered the wording and inserted the first four verses of S. Luke and the genealogies, as they are not mentioned in the Table of Contents. He seems to have also expunged the little explanatory phrases with which Tatian's work in its original form was freely sprinkled. Subject to these variations the appearance of the Arabic version leaves no doubt that what Victor found was really, as he supposed, a Latin version of the *Diatessaron*. The *Codex Fuldensis* was translated into the Eastern Frankish dialect in the ninth century, about the time of Charlemagne, who finally imposed Christianity upon the Saxons. His son, Louis the Pious, caused a poetical version to be made of it for the purpose of supplanting the popular ballads relating to Woden and Thor. This celebrated epic poem is now known as *Hêliand*. It was published at Munich in A.D. 1830 from a comparison of the two known MSS., one of which is in the British Museum and the other at Munich. The poem is alliterative, and gives a life of Jesus harmonised from the four Gospels. It is written in the Old Saxon dialect; and the unknown author has allowed himself some freedom in adopting the popular conceptions of the day.

Eusebius described the *Diatessaron* as "A combination and collection of the Gospels"; and Theodoret, who found so many copies in his diocese, said of Tatian, "He also composed the Gospel called *Diatessaron*, cutting out the genealogies, and whatever other passages show that the Lord was born of the seed of David," the inference being that these things were cut out of the canonical Gospels, the other portions of those Gospels being made use of. Such was the view generally entertained in the Church. But there have been some who on other grounds did not believe that the Fourth Gospel was written at so early a date, or that the three Synoptic Gospels were yet collected and used in common. They contended that *Diatessaron* was a musical term derived from the use of *four notes*, and simply meant a harmony. If, as there seems no doubt, the work published by Ciasca is substantially the *Diatessaron* of Tatian, subject only to such alterations as would naturally be made in it in the course of centuries, to make it conform more in details to the accepted forms of the canonical Gospels, then this controversy is decisively closed in favour of the orthodox view; for beyond all question the book in its present form is a harmony of our four Gospels, and of no others.

And with this is also set at rest, in favour of the same side, the further controversy, as to whether any or all of our four Gospels, in anything like their present form, were known to Justin Martyr, and alluded to by him in his writings. Justin wrote, "In the Memoirs which I say were composed by the Apostles and those who followed with them" . . . (*Dial.* c. 103). Would his friend and disciple, Tatian, leave those Memoirs out?

Now one of the objects sought to be established by those who contended that Justin was ignorant of our present Gospels, was this, that the miracles of healing ascribed to Jesus were a later invention, never heard of in the first century, and even unknown in the time of Justin. I have already pointed out, in my English version of *Marcion's Gospel*,[1] that that Gospel, in which are contained all the miracles of healing found in S. Luke's Gospel except the one performed upon Malchus, was brought by him to Rome about A.D. 140. This fact sufficiently refutes the idea that they were inventions of such a late period, as has been alleged. And now we find it established that Justin Martyr was fully acquainted with and accepted all the four Gospels.

It may be asked, What is the value of the *Diatessaron* as a harmony? and how does it bear comparison with modern harmonies? Are there any indications within it that Tatian was guided by traditional information, enabling him to decide with certainty points which have appeared doubtful in modern times? The last question may be answered in the negative; but the others cannot be dealt with in this short introduction. To understand all the reasons for and against a particular order of harmonisation is the work of a lifetime; and those who have arrived at that knowledge are unable to agree as to the result. The present writer, therefore, does not presume to answer these questions definitely for the reader. But a few general remarks on the subject may be of interest.

We have to consider Tatian's treatment of any subject that is related in more than one Gospel, *e.g.* the Parable of the Sower, from two points of view, the *internal* harmonisation of the several accounts with each other, and the *external* harmonisation of the result, or the place assigned to it in the general narrative. As regards internal harmonisation, the *Diatessaron* leaves little to be desired. It has been carried

[1] Copies may be had from the publishers of this volume.

out in the fullest detail, and the greatest care has been taken not to omit the slightest comment of any one Evangelist, unless it was substantially preserved in the words of another. Taking a general review of the external harmonisation, there seems no reason to doubt that Tatian carefully arranged all the *events* and the *movements* of our Lord in what he believed to be their chronological order, but did not consider it necessary in all cases to record parables and other *discourses* in their strictly historical places, preferring sometimes to insert them where they would best serve to illustrate the narrative, or to bring out points of comparison or contrast in the teaching of Christ. This freedom of treatment seems startling to us; but, if Tatian intended his work to be used along with the Gospels, not to supersede them, the chief objection is removed.

An analysis of this book brings out more and more clearly the fact that its author was a man of a powerful intellect, who saw what was a real need in the Church of his day, and set himself with singular ability to supply that need, devoting to this purpose much time and care. The heretical views which he adopted in his later years, caused the outcome of his labour to be looked upon with suspicion, which, so far as we can judge, it does not appear to have deserved. But in spite of this, its intrinsic merit and the need of such a work made it a great success for centuries in its own country, and led to its use at a later period in a modified form in other countries and in other languages, so that even in this country our Anglo-Saxon forefathers derived their conceptions of Jesus and His life on earth to a large extent from their poetical version of it. It is no small privilege to be permitted to be the first to present to English readers a full and literal translation of this great work, which has been a subject of interest to Christians of every age since it was first written, around which so many controversies have revolved, which has been in its entirety so singularly recovered in our own day, which throws so much light on the information possessed by Christians of the second century, and which at the same time possesses a national interest.

URCHFONT VICARAGE, DEVIZES,
September 1910.

INTRODUCTORY NOTE IN THE BORGIAN MS.

In the name of the one God, the Father, the Son, and the Holy Spirit, to whom be glory for ever.

With the assistance of the Most High God, we begin to transcribe the Holy Gospel and most beautiful garden, entitled *Diatessaron*, the interpretation of which expression is, That which is composed of four, and which Tatian, a Greek, compiled out of the four evangelists, Matthew the chosen, whose sign is M; Mark the selected, whose sign is R; Luke the lovable, whose sign is K: and John the beloved, whose sign is H.

The excellent *and* learned presbyter Abû-l-Faraj Abdullah Ibn-at-Ṭabib,[1] with whom God be pleased, translated it from the Syriac into the Arabic tongue.

And he said as a beginning,

The Gospel of Jesus the Son of the living God.

[1] Ciasca observes that this name is given differently in the notice at the conclusion, and says the latter is the more correct form.

ENGLISH VERSION OF THE ARABIC DIATESSARON.

1 1 In the beginning was the Word, and the Jn.[1] 1 1
Word was with God, and the Word itself is[2]
2 God. The same was in the beginning with „ 2
3 God. All things were made by him; and „ 3
without him not even one existing thing
4 hath been made. In him was life; and the „ 4
5 life is the light of men. And the light „ 5
shineth in the darkness; and the darkness
comprehended[3] it not.
6 There was in the days of Herod the king Lu. 1 5
a certain priest named Zacharias, of the
family of Abijah: and his wife was of the
daughters of Aaron, and her name was Eliza-
7 beth. And they were both righteous before „ 6
God, walking in all the commandments and
8 ordinances of God blameless. And they had „ 7
no child, because that Elizabeth was barren,
and they both were advanced in age.
9 Now while he executed the priest's office „ 8

[1] Throughout this margin the four Gospels are briefly referred to as Mt., Mk., Lu., and Jn. respectively.

[2] Ephraem has "was God," which was probably the original reading. The reader will do well not to assume that all slight departures from the wording of our Authorised Version are due to Tatian. Some arise from the idioms of the different languages into which the work has been translated, and some from the insertions which have been made in it from the Peschito.

[3] Lit. "comprehended."

before God in the order of his ministration,
1 10 according to the custom of the priest's office, Lu. 1 9
his lot was to burn incense, and he entered
11 into the temple of the Lord. And the whole „ 10
multitude of the people were praying with-
12 out at the hour of incense. And there „ 11
appeared unto Zacharias an angel of the
Lord, standing on the right side of the altar
13 of incense. When Zacharias saw him, he „ 12
14 was troubled, and fear fell upon him. But „ 13
the angel saith unto him, Fear not, Zacharias,
because thy supplication is heard, and thy
wife Elizabeth shall bear thee a son, and
15 thou shalt call his name John. And thou „ 14
shalt have joy and gladness; and many shall
16 rejoice at his birth. For he shall be great „ 15
in the sight of the Lord, and he shall drink
no wine nor strong drink; and he shall be
filled with the Holy Spirit while he is yet
17 in his mother's womb. And many of the „ 16
children of Israel shall he turn unto the
18 Lord their God. And he shall go before „ 17
him in the spirit and power of Elijah the
prophet, to turn the heart of the fathers to
the children, and the disobedient to the
knowledge of the just; to make ready for
19 the Lord a perfect people. But Zacharias „ 18
said unto the angel, Whereby shall I know
this? for I am an old man, and my wife
20 advanced in age. The angel answered and „ 19
said unto him, I am Gabriel, that stand in
the presence of God; and I was sent to
speak unto thee, and to announce this unto
21 thee *as good tidings.* From henceforth thou „ 20
shalt be silent and not able to speak, until
the day wherein this shall come to pass,
because thou believedst not this my word,
22 which shall be fulfilled in its season. But „ 21
the people were standing waiting for
Zacharias, and they marvelled because he

1 23 tarried in the sanctuary. And when Lu. 1 22
Zacharias came out, he could not speak
unto them: and they perceived that he had
seen a vision in the sanctuary: and he was
making signs unto them, and remained
24 dumb. And when the days of his ministra- „ 23
tion were fulfilled, he departed unto his house.
25 And after these days Elizabeth his wife „ 24
conceived; and she hid herself five months,
26 and said, This hath the Lord done unto me „ 25
in the days wherein he looked upon me, to
take away my reproach among men.
27 Now in the sixth month the angel Gabriel „ 26
was sent from God into Galilee,[1] unto a city
28 named Nazareth, to a virgin betrothed to a „ 27
man whose name was Joseph, of the house
of David; and the virgin's name was Mary.
29 And the angel came in unto her, and said „ 28
unto her, Hail, *thou that art* full of favour,
our Lord is with thee, O *thou* blessed among
30 women. And when she beheld him, she „ 29
was troubled at his saying, and was con-
31 sidering what this salutation might be. And „ 30
the angel saith unto her, Fear not, Mary;
32 for thou hast found favour with God. Thou „ 31
shalt now conceive, and bring forth a son,
33 and shalt call his name JESUS. He shall „ 32
be great, and shall be called the Son of the
Most High: and the Lord God shall give
unto him the throne of his father David:
34 and he shall reign over the house of Jacob „ 33
for ever; and of his kingdom there shall be
35 no end. Mary said unto the angel, How „ 34
shall this be done unto me since no man
36 hath known me? The angel answered and „ 35
said unto her, The Holy Spirit shall come,
and the power of the Most High shall
descend upon thee: wherefore also that

[1] The Borgian MS. omits "into Galilee." The Vatican MS. above ver. 27 inserts, "The 2nd chapter" (or division) "from the Gospel of Luke."

which shall be born of thee, shall be holy,
1 37 and shall be called the Son of God. And Lu. 1 36
behold, Elizabeth thy kinswoman, she also
hath conceived a son in her old age: and
this is the sixth month with her that is
38 called barren. For nothing shall be difficult „ 37
39 to God. Mary said, Behold, I am the hand- „ 38
maid of the Lord; be it done unto me
according to thy word. And the angel
departed from her.

40 Then Mary arose in those days, and went „ 39
into the hill country with haste, unto a city
41 of Judah; and entered into the house of „ 40
42 Zacharias, and saluted Elizabeth. And „ 41
when Elizabeth heard the salutation of
Mary, the babe rejoiced in her womb; and
Elizabeth was filled with the Holy Spirit;
43 and she cried out with a loud voice, and „ 42
said unto Mary, Blessed *art* thou among
women, and blessed *is* the fruit that is in
44 thy womb. Whence is this to me, that „ 43
the mother of my Lord cometh unto me?
45 When the voice of thy salutation came to „ 44
mine ears, the babe leaped in my womb in
46 great joy. And blessed *is* she that believed; „ 45
for that shall be performed, which was spoken
47 from the Lord. And Mary saith: „ 46

My soul doth magnify the Lord,
48 And my spirit hath rejoiced in God my „ 47
Saviour,
49 Who hath looked upon the low estate of „ 48
his handmaiden:
Behold, from henceforth all generations
shall call me blessed.
50 For he that is mighty hath done to me „ 49
great things;
And holy is his name;
51 And his mercy from a generation to „ 50
generations
Embraceth them that fear him.

1 52 He hath wrought victory by his arm, Lu. 1 51
And he hath scattered the proud in their
opinions.
53 He hath put down the haughty from the „ 52
thrones,
And hath exalted the humble.
54 The hungry he hath filled with good „ 53
things;
And the rich he hath left without anything.
55 He hath holpen Israel his servant, „ 54
And remembered his mercy
56 (As he spake unto our fathers) „ 55
Unto Abraham and unto his seed for ever.
57 And Mary abode with Elizabeth about „ 56
three months, and returned unto her house.
58 Now Elizabeth's time of bringing forth „ 57
was *come;* and she brought forth a son.
59 And her neighbours and kinsfolk heard that „ 58
God had multiplied his mercy towards her;
60 and they rejoiced with her. And on the „ 59
eighth day they came to circumcise the child;
and they called him Zacharias, after the
61 name of his father. And his mother „ 60
answered and said unto them, Not so; but
62 he shall be called John. And they said „ 61
unto her, There is no one among thy kindred
63 that is called by this name. And they made „ 62
signs to his father, How do you wish to call
64 him? And he asked for a writing tablet, „ 63
and wrote, saying, His name is John. And
65 they all marvelled. And his mouth was „ 64
opened immediately, and his tongue *loosed*,
66 and he spake, and praised God. And fear „ 65
fell on all their neighbours: and this was
noised abroad over all the hill country of
67 Judaea. And all that heard *it*, thought in „ 66
their heart saying, What shall this child be?
For the hand of the Lord was with him.
68 And his father Zacharias was filled with „ 67
the Holy Spirit, and prophesied, and said,

1 69 Blessed *be* the Lord, the God of Israel, Lu. 1 68
Who hath regarded his people, and
wrought salvation for them,
70 And hath raised up a horn of salvation „ 69
for us
In the house of his servant David,
71 As he spake from eternity by the mouth „ 70
of his holy prophets,
72 That he would save us from our enemies, „ 71
And from the hand of all that hate us.
73 And he showed mercy towards our fathers, „ 72
And remembered his holy covenant,
74 And the oath which he sware unto „ 73
Abraham our father,
75 That he would grant unto us salvation „ 74
from the hand of our enemies
That we may serve before him without
fear
76 In justice and righteousness all our days. „ 75
77 And thou, child, shalt be called the „ 76
prophet of the Most High;
Thou shalt go before the face of the Lord
to make ready his way,
78 To give knowledge of life unto his people „ 77
Unto the remission of their sins
79 Through the tender mercy of our God, „ 78
Whereby he visits[1] us, rising from on
high
80 To shine upon them that sit in darkness, „ 79
and under the shadow of death,
And to establish our feet in the way of
peace.
81 And the child grew, and waxed strong in „ 80
spirit, and was waiting in the desert till the
day of his showing unto the children of
Israel.
2 1 Now the birth of Jesus Christ was on Mt. 1 18
this wise: When his mother had been betrothed to Joseph, before they came together

[1] Or, "shall visit."

she was found with child of the Holy Spirit.
2 2 And Joseph her husband was a righteous Mt. 1 19
man, and unwilling to make her a public
example, and thought to put her away
3 privily. But while he was thinking of „ 20
this, an angel of the Lord appeared unto
him in a dream, saying, Joseph, son of
David, fear not to take unto thee Mary thy
wife: for that which is begotten in her is of
4 the Holy Spirit. She shall bring forth a „ 21
son; and thou shalt call his name JESUS;
for he shall save his people from their sins.
5 Now all this is come to pass, that it might „ 22
be fulfilled which was spoken by the Lord
through the prophet,
6 Behold, the virgin shall conceive, and „ 23
shall bring forth a son,
And they shall call his name Emmanuel;
which is, being interpreted, Our God is
7 with us. And when Joseph arose from his „ 24
sleep, he did as the angel of the Lord commanded him, and took unto him his wife;
8 and knew her not till she brought forth her „ 25[a]
firstborn son.
9 Now in those days there went out a Lu. 2 1
decree from Caesar Augustus, that all the
people of his dominion should be enrolled.
10 This was the first enrolment made in the „ 2
11 governorship of Quirinius in Syria. And „ 3
all were going into their own city to be
12 enrolled. And Joseph also went up from „ 4
Nazareth, a city of Galilee, into Judaea, to
the city of David, which is called Bethlehem,
because he was of the house and family of
13 David, with Mary his betrothed, who was „ 5
great with child, that he might be enrolled
14 there. And while they were there, the „ 6
days were fulfilled that she should bring
15 forth. And she brought forth her firstborn „ 7
son; and she wrapped him in swaddling

clothes, and laid him in a manger, because
there was no room for them, where they
were staying.
2 16 And there were shepherds staying in that Lu. 2 8
country, who were guarding their flock in
17 the watch of the night. And behold, an „ 9
angel of God came near unto them; and
the glory of the Lord shone round about
them; and they were afraid with a great
18 fear. And the angel said unto them, Be „ 10
not afraid; for I bring you as good tidings a
great joy that shall be to the whole world:
19 there is born to you this day in the city of „ 11
David a Saviour, which is the Lord the
20 Messiah. And this *is* the sign unto you: „ 12
Ye shall find a babe wrapped in swaddling
21 clothes, and laid in a manger. And suddenly „ 13
there appeared with the angels an abundant
heavenly host praising God, and saying,
22 Glory to God in the highest, „ 14
And on earth peace, and good hope to
men.
23 And when the angels went away from them „ 15
into heaven, the shepherds spake one to
another, saying, Let us go to Bethlehem,
and see this saying that is come to pass,
24 even as the Lord hath showed us. And „ 16
they came with haste and found Mary and
Joseph, and the babe laid in the manger.
25 And when they had seen it, they related the „ 17
saying which had been spoken to them about
26 the child. And all that heard it wondered „ 18
at the description, which the shepherds had
27 described to them. But Mary was keeping „ 19
all these sayings, and comparing them in
28 her heart. And those shepherds returned, „ 20
glorifying and praising God for all the things
that they had seen and heard, even as it
was described unto them.
29 And after eight days were fulfilled, that „ 21

the child should be circumcised, his name
was called JESUS; and this is what he was
called by the angel, before he was conceived
in the womb.
2 30 And when the days of their purification Lu. 2 22
according to the law of Moses were fulfilled,
they brought him to Jerusalem to present
31 him before the Lord, as it is written in the „ 23
law of the Lord, Every male that openeth the
32 womb shall be called holy to the Lord, and „ 24
to offer a sacrifice according to that which is
said in the law of the Lord, A pair of turtle
33 doves, or two young pigeons. And there „ 25
was a man in Jerusalem, whose name was
Simeon; and this man was righteous, de-
vout, and looking for the consolation of
Israel: and the Holy Spirit was upon him.
34 And it had been said unto him by the „ 26
Holy Spirit, that he was not going to see
death, until he set his eyes upon the Lord's
35 Christ. And he came in the Spirit into „ 27
the temple: and when his parents brought
in the child Jesus, that they might offer a
sacrifice for him, as it is written in the law,
36 he took him up into his arms, and praised „ 28
God, and said,
37 Now wilt thou loose the bonds of thy „ 29
servant, O Lord,
According to thy word, in peace.
38 For already mine eyes have witnessed thy „ 30
mercy,
39 Which thou hast prepared on account of „ 31
the whole world,
40 A light for the unveiling of the Gentiles, „ 32
And a glory for thy people Israel.
41 And Joseph and his mother were marvel- „ 33
ling at these things which were spoken con-
42 cerning him; and Simeon blessed them, and „ 34
said unto Mary his mother, Behold he is set
for the falling and for the rising again of many

in Israel; and for a sign of contradiction;
2 43 and a sword shall pierce through thine own Lu. 2 35
soul, that the thoughts of many hearts may
44 be revealed. And Anna, a prophetess, the „ 36
daughter of Phanuel, of the tribe of Asher,
she also was advanced in age, and had lived
with her husband for seven years from her
45 virginity; and she remained a widow about „ 37
fourscore and four years, and departed not
from the temple worshipping with fastings and
46 supplications night and day. And she also „ 38
stood up at that hour, and gave thanks unto
the Lord, and spake of him to all that were
looking for the deliverance of Jerusalem.
47 And when they had accomplished all things „ 39
according to what is in the law of the
Lord, they returned into Galilee, to their
own city Nazareth.

3 1 After these things wise men[1] from the Mt. 2 1b
2 east came to Jerusalem, saying, Where is the „ 2
king of the Jews, who has been born? We
have seen his star in the east, and are come
3 to worship him. And when Herod the king „ 3
heard it, he was troubled, and all Jerusalem
4 with him. And gathering together all the „ 4
chief priests and scribes of the people, he
inquired of them, where the Messiah should
5 be born. And they said, In Bethlehem of „ 5
Judah: thus it is written in the prophet,
6 And thou, Bethlehem of Judah, „ 6
Art in no wise least among the kings of
Judah;
For out of thee shall come forth a king,
And he shall rule my people Israel.
7 Then Herod, when he had privily called „ 7
the wise men, inquired of them the time

[1] Arabic, "al majûs." By removing the opening words of S. Matthew, "Now when Jesus was born in Bethlehem of Judaea, in the days of Herod the king," and substituting more vaguely, "After these things," Tatian avoids the difficulty felt by harmonists in assigning a place to Luke ii. 39.

at which the star appeared unto them.
3 8 And he sent them to Bethlehem, and said Mt. 2 8
unto them, Go, and inquire carefully concerning the child; and when ye have found
him, come and bring me word, that I also
9 may come and worship him. And when „ 9
they had heard the king they went their
way; and lo, the star, which they had seen
in the east, went before them, till it came
and stood over the place, where the child
10 was. And when they saw the star, they „ 10
11 rejoiced with exceeding great joy. And „ 11
they came into the house, and saw the child
with Mary his mother; and they fell down
and worshipped him; and opening their
cases, they offered unto him offerings, gold,
12 myrrh, and frankincense. And they saw in „ 12
sleep that they should not return to Herod;
and they departed by another way to go into
their own country.
13 And when they had departed, behold, an „ 13
angel of the Lord appeared to Joseph in a
dream, and said unto him, Arise, and take
the child and his mother, and flee into
Egypt, and be thou there until I tell thee:
for Herod sets about to seek the child to
14 destroy him. And Joseph arose, and took „ 14
the child and his mother by night, and fled
15 into Egypt, and remained there until the „ 15
death of Herod: that it might be fulfilled,
which was spoken by the Lord through the
prophet, saying, Out of Egypt did I call my
16 son. Then Herod, when he saw that he „ 16
was mocked by the wise men, was exceeding wroth, and sent forth, and slew all
the male children that were in Bethlehem,
and in all the borders thereof, from two
years old and under, according to the time
which he had carefully inquired of the
17 wise men. Then was fulfilled that which „ 17

was spoken through Jeremiah the prophet,
saying,
3 18 A voice was heard in Ramah, Mt. 2 18
Weeping and great mourning:
Rachel weepeth for her children,
And is unwilling to be consoled for the
loss of them.
19 But when king Herod was dead, the angel „ 19
of the Lord appeared in a dream to Joseph
20 in Egypt, and said unto him, Arise and take „ 20
the child and his mother, and go into the
land of Israel: for they are dead that sought
21 the child's life. Joseph arose, and took the „ 21
child and his mother, and came into the land
22 of Israel. But when he heard that Archelaus „ 22
was become king in Judaea instead of his
father Herod, he was afraid to go thither;
but he saw in a dream that he should go
23 into the land of Galilee, and that he should „ 23
dwell in a city that is called Nazareth:
that it might be fulfilled which was spoken
through the prophet, He shall be called a
Nazarene.
24 And the child grew, and waxed strong in Lu. 2 40
spirit, filled with wisdom: and the grace of
God was upon him.
25 And his parents[1] went every year to „ 41
26 Jerusalem at the feast of the passover. And „ 42
when he was twelve years old, they went up
27 after their custom to the feast; and when „ 43
the days were fulfilled, they returned; but
the boy Jesus tarried behind in Jerusalem;
and Joseph and his mother knew it not,
28 supposing him to be with the children of „ 44
their company. And when they had made
a day's journey, they sought for him among
29 their kinsfolk and acquaintance: and when „ 45
they found him not, they returned to Jeru-
30 salem, seeking for him again. And after „ 46

[1] Arabic, "kinsfolk."

three days they found him in the temple,
sitting in the midst of the doctors, hearing
3 31 them, and asking them questions: and all Lu. 2 47
that heard him were amazed at his wisdom
32 and sayings. And when they saw him, they „ 48
were astonished: and his mother said unto
him, My son, why hast thou thus dealt with
us? Behold, I and thy father were seeking
33 thee with great anxiety. And he saith unto „ 49
them, How is it that ye sought me? did
ye not know that I must be in my Father's
34 house? And they understood not the say- „ 50
35 ing, which he spake unto them. And he „ 51
went down with them, and came to Nazareth;
and he was subject unto them: and his
mother kept all *these* sayings in her heart.
36 And Jesus advanced in stature and wisdom, „ 52
and in favour with God and men.
37 Now in the fifteenth year of the reign of „ 3 1
Tiberius Caesar, Pontius Pilate being governor
of Judaea, and Herod being tetrarch of Galilee, and his brother Philip tetrarch of the
region of Ituraea and Trachonitis, and Lysanias
38 tetrarch of Abilene, under the high priests „ 2
Annas and Caiaphas, the word of God went
forth unto John, the son of Zacharias, in the
39 wilderness. And he came into all the region „ 3
round about Jordan, preaching the baptism
40 of repentance with remission of sins; and he Mt. 3 1[b]
41 preached in the wilderness of Judaea, and „ 2
said, Repent ye, the kingdom of the heavens
42 is at hand. This is he that was spoken of „ 3[a]
through Isaiah the prophet,

The[1] voice which crieth in the wilderness,
43 Make ye ready the way of the Lord, Lu. 3 4[b]
And establish in the plain a way for our
God.
44 All the valleys shall be filled; „ 5

[1] Omitting Mark i. 2; cf. xiii. 47.

And every mountain and hill shall be
brought low;
And the crooked shall become straight;
And the difficult place easy;
3 45 And all flesh shall see the salvation[1] of Lu. 3 6
God.
46 The same came for a witness, that he might Jn. 1 7
bear witness of the light, that all might
47 believe through him. He was not the light, „ 8
but *came* that he might bear witness of the
48 light, which is the true light, lighting every „ 9
49 man, coming into the world. He was in the „ 10
world, and the world was made through him,
50 and the world knew him not. He came unto „ 11
51 his own, and his own received him not. But „ 12
as many as received him, to them gave he
the power to become children of God, *even* to
52 them that believe on his name: which were „ 13
born, not of blood, nor of the will of the
flesh, nor of the will of man, but of God.
53 And the Word became flesh, and dwelt „ 14
among us (and we saw his glory, as it were
the glory of the only one from the Father),
54 full of grace and truth. John bare witness „ 15
of him, and preached, saying, This is he of
whom I said, He that is about to come after
me is preferred before me: for he was before
55 me. And of his fulness we all received, grace „ 16
56 for grace. For the law was given through „ 17
Moses; truth and grace came through Jesus
4 1 Christ. No man hath seen God at any „ 18
time; the only begotten, God, who is in the
bosom of the Father, he hath declared *him*.
2 And this is the witness of John, when the „ 19
Jews sent unto him from Jerusalem priests
and Levites to ask him, Who art thou?
3 And he confessed, and denied not; and he „ 20
acknowledged that he was not the Messiah.
4 And again they asked him, What then? Art „ 21

[1] Or, "life."

thou Elijah? And he said, I am not. Art
4 5 thou a prophet? He answered, No. They Jn. 1 22
said unto him, Who art thou? that we may
give an answer to them that sent us. What
6 sayest thou of thyself? He saith, I am the „ 23
voice of one crying in the wilderness, Set in
order the way of the Lord, as said Isaiah
7 the prophet. And they that had been sent „ 24
8 were of the Pharisees.[1] And they asked „ 25
him, and said unto him, Why then baptizest
thou, since thou art not the Messiah, nor
9 Elijah, nor a prophet? John answered and „ 26
said unto them, I baptize in[2] water: in the
midst of you standeth one whom ye know
10 not. This is he, of whom I said, that he „ 27
cometh after me, and he was before me, of
whom I am not worthy to unloose the latchet
11 of his shoes. These things were done in „ 28
Bethany beyond Jordan, where John was
baptizing.
12 Moreover John had his raiment of camel's Mt. 3 4
hair, and a leathern girdle;[3] and his food
13 was locusts and wild honey. Then went out „ 5
unto him the people of Jerusalem, and all
Judaea, and all the region round about Jordan;
14 and they were baptized by him in the river „ 6
15 Jordan, confessing their sins. But when he „ 7
saw many of the Pharisees and Sadducees[4]
coming to be baptized, he said unto them,
Ye offspring of vipers, who warned[5] you to
16 flee from the wrath to come? Bring forth „ 8
17 therefore fruits worthy of repentance: and „ 9
do not think, and say within yourselves, We
have Abraham as our father; for I say unto
you, that God is able of these stones to
18 raise up children unto Abraham. Behold, „ 10
the axe is laid unto the root of the tree:

[1] Arabic, "almu 'tazila."
[2] Or, "with."
[3] Omitting "about his loins."
[4] Arabic, "azzanâḏiḳa."
[5] Lit. "guided."

every tree therefore that bringeth not forth
good fruit shall be taken away, and cast into
4 19 the fire. And the multitudes asked him, Lu. 3 10
20 saying, What shall we do? He answered, „ 11
and said unto them, He that hath two coats,
let him give to him that hath none; and he
21 that hath food, let him do likewise. And „ 12
there came also publicans to be baptized,
and they said unto him, Master, what shall
22 we do? He saith unto them, Ask nothing „ 13
more than that which you are commanded
23 to ask. And soldiers asked him, saying, „ 14
What shall we also do? He saith unto
them, Do violence to no man, neither act
unjustly towards him; and be content with
your wages.

24 And as the people were considering, and „ 15
all men were reasoning in their hearts concerning John, whether haply he were the
25 Christ; John answered, and said unto them, „ 16
I baptize you with water; there will come
after me he that is mightier than I, of
whom I am not worthy to unloose the
latchets of his shoes: he shall baptize you
26 in the Holy Spirit and in fire: who, grasp- „ 17
ing a fan in his hand to cleanse his threshing
floor, will gather the wheat into his gar-
ners; but the chaff he will burn up with
unquenchable fire.

27 And other things he taught, and preached „ 18
good tidings unto the people.

28 Then cometh Jesus from Galilee to the Mt. 3 13
Jordan unto John, to be baptized of him.
29 And Jesus was about thirty years of age, Lu. 3 23[a]
and was supposed to be the son of Joseph.
30 Now John saw Jesus coming unto him, and Jn. 1 29
saith, This is the Lamb of God, which taketh
31 away the sin of the world. This is he of „ 30
whom I said, After me shall come a man,
which is preferred before me, for he is

4 32 before me. And I knew him not; but that Jn. 1 31
he may be made manifest to Israel, for this
33 cause am I come baptizing in[1] water. Now Mt. 3 14
John was forbidding him, saying, I have
need to be baptized of thee, and comest
34 thou to me? Jesus answered him, and said, „ 15
Suffer *it* now: thus it becometh us to fulfil
all righteousness. Then he suffered him.
35 And when all the people were baptized, Lu. 3 21[a]
36 Jesus also was baptized;[2] and he went up Mt. 3 16[b]
straightway from the water: and the heaven
37 was opened unto him. And the Holy Spirit Lu. 3 22[a]
descended upon him in the form of a dove's
38 body: and lo, a voice from heaven, saying, Mt. 3 17
This is my beloved Son, in whom I am well
39 pleased. And John bare witness, saying, Jn. 1 32
Furthermore I saw the Spirit descending as
a dove out of heaven; and it abode upon
40 him. And I knew him not; but he that „ 33
sent me to baptize in[3] water, he said unto
me, Upon whomsoever thou shalt see the
Spirit descending and abiding, this is he
41 that baptizeth in[4] the Holy Spirit. And I „ 34
have seen, and have borne witness, that this
is the Son of God.
42 And Jesus, full of the Holy Spirit, re- Lu. 4 1[a]
43 turned from the Jordan, and straightway Mk. 1 12
the Spirit drove[5] him forth into the wilderness, that he might be tempted of Satan; „ 13[b]
44 and he was with the wild beasts; and he Mt. 4 2[a]
fasted forty days and forty nights;[6] and Lu. 4 2[b]
tasted nothing in those days: and he after- Mt. 4 2[b]
45 ward hungered. And the tempter came, „ 3
and said unto him, If thou art the Son of
God, command that these stones become bread.
46 He answered and said, It is written, Man „ 4

[1] Or, "with." [2] Omitting "and praying." [3] Or, "with."
[4] Or, "with." [5] Or, "led."
[6] Both Ephraem and the Curetonian Syriac omit "and forty nights," which therefore may not have been originally in the *Diatessaron*.

liveth not by bread alone, but by every word
that proceedeth out of the mouth of God.
4 47 Then Satan brought him into the holy city, Mt. 4 5
and set him on the pinnacle of the temple,
48 and said unto him, If thou art the Son of „ 6
God, cast thyself down; for it is written,

> He giveth his angels charge concerning thee;[1]
> And in their arms they shall receive thee up,
> Lest haply thou dash thy foot against a stone.

49 Jesus saith unto him, Again it is written, „ 7
Thou shalt not tempt the Lord thy God.
50 And the devil took him up into a high Lu.[2] 4 5
mountain, and showed him all the kingdoms
of the world and the glory of them in a
51 moment of time. And the devil saith unto „ 6
him, To thee will I give all this authority,
and the glory of it, which have been
delivered unto me, that I may give them
52 to whomsoever I will. If therefore thou „ 7
wilt worship before me, all shall be thine.
5 1 Jesus answered and said unto him, Get thee Mt. 4 10
hence, Satan: for it is written, Thou shalt
worship the Lord thy God, and him only
2 shalt thou serve. And when the devil had Lu. 4 13
completed all his temptations, he departed
3 from him until the season; and behold, Mt. 4 11[b]
angels came and ministered unto him.
4 On the next day John was standing, and Jn. 1 35
5 two of his disciples; and he looked upon „ 36
Jesus, as he walked, and said, Behold the
6 Lamb of God! And his two disciples heard „ 37
him speaking; and they followed Jesus.
7 And Jesus turned, and saw them following, „ 38
and said unto them, What seek ye? They
said unto him, Master, where dwellest thou?

[1] Omitting Luke iv. 10, "to keep thee."
[2] Or Matt. iv. 8.

5 8 He said unto them, Come, and see. And Jn. 1 39
they came, and saw the place of his abode;
and they remained with him that day: and
9 it was about the tenth hour. One of the „ 40
two, that had heard from John, and had
followed Jesus, was Andrew, Simon's brother.
10 He first saw his own brother Simon, and said „ 41
11 unto him, We have found the Messiah.[1] And „ 42
he brought him unto Jesus. And Jesus looked
upon him, and said, Thou art Simon, the son
of Jonah: thou shalt be called The rock.
12 On the morrow Jesus wished to go forth „ 43
into Galilee; and he found Philip, and said
13 unto him, Follow me. Now Philip was from „ 44
Bethsaida, the city of Andrew and Simon.
14 And Philip found Nathanael, and said unto „ 45
him, We have found him, of whom Moses in
the law, and the prophets, did write, to be
Jesus, the son of Joseph, from Nazareth.
15 Nathanael said unto him, Can any good „ 46
thing be found from Nazareth? Philip said
16 unto him, Come, and see. And Jesus saw „ 47
Nathanael coming to him, and said of him,
This is indeed a son of Israel, in whom is no
17 guile! Nathanael said unto him, Whence „ 48
knowest thou me? Jesus said unto him,
Before Philip called thee, when thou wast
18 under the fig-tree, I saw thee. Nathanael „ 49
answered, and saith unto him, Master, thou
art the Son of God; thou art king of Israel.
19 Jesus said unto him, Because I said unto „ 50
thee, I saw thee under the fig-tree, thou
believedst: thou shalt see what is greater
20 than this. And he said unto him, Verily, „ 51
verily, I say unto you, Henceforth ye shall
see the heavens opened, and the angels of
God ascending and descending upon the Son
of man.[2]

[1] The clause interpreting "Messiah" is absent.
[2] Lit. "flesh." After commenting on the call of Nathanael Ephraem has

5 21 And Jesus returned in the power of the Lu. 4 14[a]
Spirit into Galilee.
22 And the third day there was a feast in Jn. 2 1
Cana,[1] a city of Galilee; and the mother of
23 Jesus was there: and Jesus also was bidden, " 2
24 and his disciples, to the feast. And when " 3
the wine failed, his mother said unto Jesus,
25 They have no wine. And Jesus said unto " 4
her, Woman, what have I to do with thee?
26 hath not my hour come? But his mother " 5
said unto the servants, Whatsoever he saith
27 unto you, do it. There were six waterpots " 6
of stone set there for the purification of the
Jews, containing two or three firkins apiece.
28 And Jesus said unto them, Fill the water- " 7
pots with water. And they filled them up
29 to the brim. He said unto them, Draw out " 8
now, and bear unto the ruler of the feast.
30 And they did *so*. And when the ruler of " 9
the feast tasted the water, which was
become wine, and knew not whence it was
(but the servants knew, because they had
drawn the water), the ruler of the feast
31 called the bridegroom, and said unto him, " 10
Every man setteth on first the good wine;
and when *men* have drunk freely,[2] he brings
that which is worse: but thou hast kept
32 the good wine until now. This was the first " 11
sign, *namely, that* which Jesus did in Cana
of Galilee, and manifested his glory; and
33 his disciples believed on him. And his fame Lu.[3] 4 14[b]

a heading, "*Ordo et solemnitas Apostolorum Domini,*" followed by remarks upon the class of men chosen for the twelve disciples. Dr. Wace thought this an introduction to the calling of disciples; see later, ver. 44 *et seq.* But is it not rather retrospective, dealing with the call of the first four just related? This heading is only found in one of the two Armenian versions, and there it is in red ink, as if it were a quotation from the *Diatessaron*, which may originally have been divided into sections suitable for instruction. Cf. p. 13.

[1] Arabic, "Qaṭna." The *Codex Fuldensis* puts this "beginning of miracles" after the miraculous draught of fishes, Luke v. 1–11!

[2] Lit. "at the time of drunkenness."

[3] Cf. vii. 8.

was published in all the neighbouring region.
5 34 And he taught in their synagogues, and was Lu. 4 15
glorified by all men.
35 And he came to Nazareth, where he had „ 16
been brought up: and he entered, according
to his custom, into the synagogue on the
36 sabbath day, and stood up to read. And „ 17
there was delivered unto him the book of
the prophet Isaiah. And Jesus opened the
book, and found the place where it was
written,
37 The Spirit of the Lord is upon me, „ 18
Because he anointed me to preach good
tidings unto the poor;
And sent me to heal the bruised in heart;
To[1] proclaim forgiveness to the wicked[2]
and sight to the blind;
To bring the broken into forgiveness,
38 And to proclaim the year acceptable to „ 19
the Lord.
39 And he closed the book and gave it back „ 20
to the attendant; and went away, and sat
down: and the eyes of all, that were standing in the synagogue, were turning upon him.
40 And he began to say unto them, To-day „ 21
hath this scripture been fulfilled, which ye
41 have heard with your ears. And all bare „[3] 22[a]
him witness, and wondered at the words of
grace, which proceeded out of his mouth.
42 From that time began Jesus to preach the Mt. 4 17[a]
gospel of the kingdom of God, and to say,
43 Repent ye, and believe in the gospel. The Mk.[4] 1 15
time is fulfilled,[5] and the kingdom of the
heavens is at hand.

[1] The Vulgate and Ciasca's Latin commence Luke iv. 19 here.
[2] Mr. Rendel Harris thinks the Arabic translator misread the Syriac word for "captives."
[3] For the continuation of this part of S. Luke see xvii. 42, and note thereon.
[4] The internal order of this verse is altered.
[5] Or, "has arrived."

5 44 And walking by the sea of Galilee, he saw Mt. 4 18
two brethren, Simon, who is called Cephas,
and Andrew his brother, casting their nets
45 into the sea; for they were fishers. And „ 19
Jesus saith unto them, Follow me, and I will
46 make you fishers of men. And they im- „ 20
mediately left the nets there, and followed
47 him. And going on from thence he saw „ 21
other two brethren, James the son of Zebedee,
and John his brother, in the boat with
Zebedee their father, mending their nets;
48 and Jesus called them. And they straight- „ 22
way left the boat and their father Zebedee,
and followed him.
49 And when the multitudes were come to- Lu. 5 1
gether unto him, to hear the word of God,
and he was standing by the lake of Gen-
50 nesaret, he saw two boats standing by the „ 2
lake: but the fishermen, who had come up
51 therefrom, were washing their nets. And „ 3
one of them was Simon Cephas's; and into
it Jesus went up, and sat down in it, and
commanded them to put out a little from
the land into the water. And sitting down
he taught the multitudes out of the boat.
52 And when he ceased to speak, he said unto „ 4
Simon, Put out into the deep, and let out[1]
53 your nets for a draught. Simon answered, „ 5
and said unto him, Master, we toiled all
night, and took nothing: but at thy word
54 I will let out[1] the nets. And when they „ 6
had done this, they inclosed an abundant
multitude of fishes; for their net was nigh
55 to be broken; and they beckoned unto their „ 7
partners that were in the other boat, that
they should come and help them. And
when they were come, they filled both the
6 1 boats, so that they were almost sunk. But „ 8
when Simon Cephas saw it, he fell down at

[1] Or "cast."

Jesus' feet, and said unto him, Lord, I
beseech of thee, that thou depart from me,
6 2 for I am a sinful man. For amazement[1] Lu. 5 9
had taken possession of him, and all that
were with him, at the draught of the fishes,
3 which they had taken; so also it had seized „ 10
James and John, the sons of Zebedee, which
were Simon's partners. And Jesus saith
unto Simon, Fear not; from henceforth thou
4 shalt be catching men unto life. And when „ 11
they had brought their boats to land, they
left all, and followed him.
5 After these things came Jesus and his Jn. 3 22
disciples into the land of Judah; and there
he went about with them, and baptized.
6 John also was baptizing in Aennon near to „ 23
Salim, because there was much water there:
and they were coming, and were being
7 baptized. For John had not yet come into „ 24
8 prison. Now there arose a questioning „ 25
between a disciple of John and a Jew about
9 purification. And they came unto John, „ 26
and said unto him, Master, he that was
with thee beyond Jordan, to whom thou
barest witness, behold, he also baptizeth,
10 and many come to him. John answered „ 27
and said unto them, A man can receive
nothing of himself, except it have been
11 given him from heaven. Ye yourselves bear „ 28
me witness, that I said, I am not the
12 Messiah, but one sent[2] before him. He „ 29
that hath the bride is the bridegroom: and
the friend of the bridegroom is he, which
standeth and heareth him attentively, and
rejoiceth with great joy at the bridegroom's

[1] Tatian seems right in putting this incident before Luke iv. 38, 39, as S. Peter would scarcely have felt such "amazement," if he had previously witnessed the miraculous cure of his own mother-in-law. S. Matthew put the latter after the Sermon on the Mount, which position Tatian considered too late.

[2] Lit. "an apostle."

voice: behold, now my joy is already fulfilled.
6 13 He must increase, but I must decrease. Jn. 3 30
14 He that cometh from above is above all: „ 31
he that is from the earth is from the earth,
and from the earth he speaketh: he that
hath come down from heaven is above all.
15 And what he hath seen and heard, of this he „ 32
beareth witness; and no man receiveth his
16 witness. He that hath received his witness, „ 33
hath set his seal to this, that he is truly
17 God. For he whom God hath sent, speaketh „ 34
the word of God: God giveth not the Spirit
18 by measure. The Father loveth the Son, „ 35
19 and hath put all things in his hands. He „ 36
that believeth on the Son hath eternal life;
but he that is disobedient to the Son shall
not see life, but the wrath of God abideth
on him.
20 And Jesus knew that the Pharisees had „ 4 1
heard, that he had admitted, and that he
21 baptized more disciples than John (not that „ 2
Jesus himself was baptizing, but his dis-
22 ciples); and he left Judaea.[1] „ 3[a]
23 Now Herod the governor, when he was Lu. 3 19
reproved by John concerning Herodias his
brother Philip's wife, and concerning all the
24 evil things which he was doing, added this „[2] 20
also above all, that he shut up John in
prison.
25 Now when Jesus heard that John had Mt.[2] 4 12
been delivered up, he withdrew into Galilee;
26 and he entered again into Cana, where he Jn. 4 46
made the water wine. And there was at
Capernaum a certain officer of the king,
27 whose son was sick.[3] When he heard, that „ 47

[1] See note to xxi. 8.

[2] These passages are displaced from their original order, so as to represent Jesus as calling His disciples before the imprisonment of S. John the Baptist.

[3] This narrative is inserted earlier than S. John's setting of it would imply because Tatian places it during the visit to Galilee mentioned in Matt. iv. 12.

Jesus was come out of Judaea into Galilee,
he went unto him, and besought *him*, that
he would come down, and heal his son; for
6 28 he was very near to death. Jesus said unto Jn. 4 48
him, Except ye see signs and wonders, ye
29 do not believe. The officer of the king said " 49
unto him, Sir, come down, lest my child die.
30 Jesus said unto him, Go thy way; thy son " 50
liveth. The man believed the saying, that
Jesus spake unto him, and he went his way.
31 And when he went down, his servants met " 51
him, and announced to him,[1] saying, Thy son
32 liveth. And he inquired of them in what " 52
hour he got better. They said unto him,
Yesterday at the seventh hour the fever left
33 him. And his father knew, that this had " 53
happened at that hour, in which Jesus said
unto him, Thy son liveth: and himself
believed, and the whole family of his house.
34 And this is the second sign, that Jesus did, " 54
when he returned out of Judaea into Galilee.
35 And he was preaching in the synagogues Lu. 4 44
36 of Galilee: and leaving Nazareth he came Mt. 4 13
and dwelt in Capernaum, in the seaside parts,
in the borders of Zebulun and Naphtali:
37 that it might be fulfilled, which was spoken " 14
through Isaiah the prophet, saying,
38 The land of Zebulun, the land of Naphtali, " 15
The way of the sea beyond Jordan
Galilee of the peoples,
39 The people which sat in darkness " 16
Saw a great light;
And to them which sat in the region and
in the shadow of death,
To them did light spring up.
40 And he was teaching them on the sabbaths: Lu. 4 31[b]
and they were astonished at his teaching, " 32
for his speech was as if it had authority.
41 And in the synagogue there was a man, " 33

[1] Or, "gave him the good news."

which had an unclean devil;[1] and he cried
6 42 out with a loud voice, saying, Let me alone, Lu. 4 34
what have I to do with thee, Jesus of Naza-
reth? thou art come to destroy us. I know
thee who thou art, the Holy One of God.
43 And Jesus rebuked him, saying, Shut up thy „ 35
mouth, and go out of him. And the devil
threw him down into the midst, and went
out of him, when he had done him no hurt.
44 And great wonder took hold of all, and they „ 36
spake one with another, saying, What is this
word, which in authority and power commandeth the unclean spirits, and they go
45 out. And a rumour concerning him was „ 37
published into all the neighbouring region.
46 And Jesus going out of the synagogue, „ 38[a]
saw a man sitting among the publicans, Mt. 9 9[b]
Matthew[2] by name; and he saith unto him,
Come after me. And he arose, and followed
him.
47 And Jesus came[3] into the house of Simon Mk. 1 29[b]
48 and Andrew, with James and John. And Lu. 4 38[c]
Simon's wife's mother was weakened with a
great fever; and they besought him for her.
49 And he stood over her, and commanded her „ 39
fever; and it left her; and immediately she
50 rose up, and ministered unto them. And Mt. 8 16[a]
when even was come, they brought unto him
many possessed with devils: and he cast out
51 their devils with a word. And all that had Lu. 4 40[b]
any sick with grievous and divers diseases,
brought them unto him; and laying his hand
52 on each, he healed them; that it might be Mt. 8 17
fulfilled which was spoken, through Isaiah
the prophet, saying, Himself shall take our
53 infirmities, and bear our diseases. And all Mk. 1 33
the city was gathered together unto the door

[1] Lit. "demon," and so in all cases *after this* except xx. 10, xxxv. 55, and xliii. 53.

[2] Cf. note to vii. 9. [3] See note to vi. 2. [4] Lit. "weakened."

6 54 of Jesus; and again he cast out devils from | Lu. 4 41
many, because they cried out, and said, Thou
art the Son of God. And he rebuked them,
and suffered not the devils to speak, because
they knew that he was Christ the Lord.
7 1 And very early in the morning of that day, | Mk. 1 35
he went out, and departed into a desert
2 place, and was there praying. And Simon | „ 36
and they that were with him sought him;
3 and when they had found him, they said unto | „ 37
4 him, All are seeking thee. He saith unto | „ 38
them, Let us go into the next villages and
cities, that I may preach there also; for to
5 this end am I come. And the multitudes | Lu. 4 42[b]
sought after him, and came until they over-
took him; and they laid hold of him, that
6 he should not depart from them. And Jesus | „ 43
said unto them, I must preach as a gospel
the kingdom of God to the other cities also,
because for the sake of this gospel was I
7 sent. And Jesus was going about all the | Mt.[1] 9 35
cities and the villages, and taught in their
synagogues, and preached the gospel of the
kingdom, and healed all diseases and all
8 infirmities, and cast out devils; and his fame | Mk. 1 39[b]; Lu.[2] 4 14[b]
was published abroad, for[3] he taught in | „ 15
9 every place, and was magnified by all. And | Mk. 2 14
as he passed by, he saw Levi,[4] the son of

[1] Repeated almost identically at xii. 40. Tatian may have meant this for Matt. iv. 23, varied; see ver. 10. This is fuller than Luke iv. 44, for which see vi. 35.

[2] Repeated from v. 33; cf. Mark i. 28 and Luke iv. 37.

[3] Or, "that."

[4] Cf. vi. 46 and vii. 25. Tatian seems to have considered that Levi and Matthew were different persons. For a *resumé* of the reasons for and against this view see Alford's *Greek Testament* under Matt. ix. 9. Alford thought the preponderance of testimony was in favour of the distinctness of the persons. It is interesting to find him quoting Clement of Alexandria, who is supposed to have been a pupil of Tatian, as a supporter of the view here taken by Tatian. Ver. 9, 10 are not in the *Codex Fuldensis.* Ephraem, Moes. p. 58, commenting on the disciples baptizing, says, "He chose James the publican," etc., from which some have inferred that his copy had "*James* the son of Alphaeus" here, as D *a b c* and Origen.

Alphaeus, sitting at the place of toll, and he
saith unto him, Follow me. And he arose,
7 10 and followed him. And the report of him Mt. 4 24
was heard in the whole region of Syria: and
they brought unto him all that were sick
with the more serious and divers diseases, and
that were enduring torments, and demoniacs
and lunatics and paralytics; and he healed
them.
11 And Jesus entered again into Capernaum Mk. 2 1
12 after *some* days, and when it was heard, that „ 2
he was in the house, many came together,
so that it would not hold them, not even
at the door; and he announced the word
13 of God unto them. And there were there Lu. 5 17b
certain of the Pharisees and doctors of the
law sitting, which were come out of every
village of Galilee and Judaea and Jerusalem:
and the power of the Lord was present[1] unto
14 healing them. And there came some[2] with „ 18
a couch, whereon there was a man that was
paralytic: and they sought to bring him in,
15 and to lay him before him. And not finding „ 19
a way by which they might bring him in
because of the multitude, they went up to
the roof, and let him down through the tiles
with the couch into the midst before Jesus.
16 And when Jesus saw their faith, he said unto „ 20
the paralytic, My son, thy sins are forgiven
17 thee. And the scribes and the Pharisees „ 21
began to reason in their heart, Why doth
this man speak blasphemies? who can for-
18 give sins but God alone? And Jesus per- Mk. 2 8
ceived in his spirit that they reasoned these
things within themselves, and said unto them,
Why reason ye these things in your heart?
19 Which is easier, to say to the paralytic, Thy „ 9

[1] Lit. "found."

[2] Tatian omits Mark ii. 3, "which was borne of *four*." See also Mark ii. 4. S. Matthew puts this miracle after the Sermon on the Mount.

		sins are forgiven thee; or to say unto him,			
7	20	Arise, and take up thy bed, and walk? That	Mk.	2	10
		ye may know, that the Son of man hath			
		authority on earth to forgive sins (he saith			
	21	to the paralytic), I say unto thee, Arise, take	„		11
		up thy bed, and depart unto thy house.			
	22	And he arose straightway, and took his bed,	„		12[a]
		and went forth in the sight of all, and de-	Lu.	5	25[b]
	23	parted to his house, magnifying God. And	Mt.	9	8[a]
		when the multitudes saw it, they were afraid;			
		for amazement took hold on them, and they	Lu. / Mt.	5 / 9	26[a] / 8[b]
		glorified God, which gave such authority			
	24	unto man, saying, Truly we have already	Lu.	5	26[b]
		seen wonderful things to-day, the like whereof	Mk.	2	12[b]
		we never saw.			
	25	And after these things Jesus went forth	Lu.	5	27
		and saw a publican, named Levi,[1] sitting			
		among the publicans, and saith unto him,			
	26	Follow me. And he forsook all, and rose	„		28
	27	up, and followed him. And Levi made him	„		29
		a great feast in his house; and there was a			
		great multitude of publicans and of others,			
	28	that were reclining *at meat* with him. And	„		30
		the scribes and Pharisees murmured, saying			
		unto his disciples, Why do ye eat and drink			
	29	with the publicans and sinners? Jesus	„		31
		answered, and said unto them, A physician			
		doth not seek the whole, but those that are			
	30	afflicted with evils. I am not come to call	„		32
	31	the righteous but sinners to repentance. But[2]	„		33
		they said unto him, Why do the disciples			
		of John fast continually, and make supplica-			
		tions; likewise also the Pharisees; but thy			
	32	disciples eat and drink? He said unto	„		34

[1] See note to ver. 9. Tatian follows S. Luke in putting this before the Sermon on the Mount.

[2] Omitting Mark ii. 18: "And the disciples of John, and of the Pharisees used to fast; and they come." S. Matthew attributes the question, which follows, to the disciples of John only. Tatian, following S. Luke, attributes it to the scribes and Pharisees.

them, It is not given to you to make the
sons of the bridegroom fast, while the bride-
7 33 groom is with them.[1] The days will come, Lu. 5 35
when the bridegroom shall have been taken
away from them, then will they fast in those
34 days. And he spake a parable unto them: „ 36[a]
No man putteth on a new patch, and seweth Mk. 2 21
it on an old garment; lest the new addition
take from the old, and a great rent be made.
35 And no man putteth new wine into old „ 22
wine-skins; lest the wine burst the skins,
and the skins perish,[2] and the wine be
poured out: but new wine must be put
into new wine-skins, and both are preserved. Lu. 5 38[b]
36 And no man drinking old wine straightway „ 39
asketh for new; for he saith, The old is better.
37 When[3] Jesus was walking through the Mt. 12 1
cornfields on the sabbath day, his disciples
were hungry; and rubbing the ears of corn
38 with their hands they were eating. But „ 2[a]
some of the Pharisees, when they saw them,
said unto him, See, why do thy disciples[4] on Mk. 2 24[b]
the sabbath day that which is not lawful?
39 And Jesus saith unto them, Have ye not „ 25
heretofore read what David did,[5] when he
had need, and was hungry, he, and they that
40 were with him? How he entered into the „ 26
house of God, when Abiathar was high
priest, and did eat the bread of the Lord's
table, which it was not lawful to eat save for
the priests, and gave also to them that were
41 with him? And he said unto them, The „ 27
sabbath was created for man, and man was

[1] Omitting Mark ii. 19: "As long as they have the bridegroom with them, they cannot fast."

[2] Slight change of order.

[3] Tatian follows S. Luke in putting this before the Sermon on the Mount, of which he appears to have considered Luke vi. 17–49 as a part.

[4] Or, "what thy disciples do."

[5] "What of old David did" does not agree so well with the Arabic.

7 42 not created for the sabbath. Or have ye Mt. 12 5
not read in the law, how that the priests in
the temple break the sabbath, and are guilt-
43 less? But I say unto you, that a greater „ 6
44 than the temple is here. If[1] ye knew that „ 7
I love mercy not sacrifice, surely ye would
45 not have condemned the innocent. The Son „ 8
46 of man is lord of the sabbath. And his Mk.[2] 3 21
kindred heard it, and they went out to lay
hold on him: for they said, Truly he is beside
himself.
47[3] And on another sabbath he entered into Lu. 6 6
the synagogue and taught: and there was a
man there, whose right hand was withered.
48 And the scribes and the Pharisees watched „ 7
him, whether he would heal on the sabbath;
that they might find a way to blame him.
49 He knew their thoughts; and he saith to the „ 8
man, whose hand was withered, Rise up, and
come into the midst of the synagogue. And
50 when he had come and stood forth, Jesus „ 9
saith unto them, I ask you, What is lawful
to do on the sabbath day, good or evil? to
save lives, or to destroy them? But they Mk. 3 4b
51 held their peace. Looking round about them „ 5
with anger, and being grieved at the hardness of their heart, he said unto the man,
Stretch forth thy hand. And he stretched
it forth: and his hand was made like *the*
52 *other.* Then he said unto them, What man Mt. 12 11
shall there be of you that shall have one

[1] A similar statement in Matt. ix. 13 is omitted at vii. 30.

[2] It is strange how Tatian removes this verse from the further account, Mark iii. 31, etc., and attributes it to Christ's claim to be lord of the sabbath. It is thus dissociated from the two statements of S. Mark, by which it might be explained, viz.: His neglecting to take food (Mark iii. 20); and the report that he had an unclean spirit (Mark iii. 22 and 30), for which see xiv. 15 and 30; also cf. xvi. 13.

[3] The first leaf missing from the Vatican MS. seems to have extended from this verse to viii. 17 inclusive, this passage being obtained from the Borgian MS. only.

sheep, and if it fall into a well on the
sabbath day, he will not lay hold on it, and
7 53 lift it out? But how much rather is a man Mt. 12 12
better than a sheep! Therefore it is lawful
8 1 to do good on the sabbath days. But the „ 14
Pharisees went out,[1] and took counsel against
2 him, that they might destroy him. But „ 15
Jesus perceiving *it* withdrew from thence:
and great multitudes followed him; and he
3 healed them all, and restrained them, that „ 16
4 they should not make him known: that it „ 17
might be fulfilled which was spoken through
Isaiah the prophet, saying,

5 Behold, my child in whom I am well pleased, „ 18
My beloved in whom my soul hath rested:
I have put my Spirit upon him;
And he shall declare judgment to the nations.
6 He shall not strive, nor cry aloud; „ 19
Neither shall any one hear his voice in the streets.
7 A bruised reed shall he not break; „ 20
And a smoking lamp[2] shall he not put out,
Till he bring forth judgment unto victory.
8 And in his own name shall he preach good tidings unto the nations. „ 21

9 In those days Jesus went out into the Lu. 6 12
mountain to pray; and he was there in the
10 morning *engaged* in prayer to God. And „ 13[a]
when it had become day, he called the
disciples, and withdrew to the sea: and Mk. 3 7[b]
much people from Galilee followed him to
11 pray; and from Judaea, and from Jerusalem, „ 8
and from Idumaea and beyond Jordan, and
from Tyre and Sidon, and from Decapolis:
and a great multitude, hearing what things
12 he did, came unto him. And he spake to „ 9

[1] S. Mark adds: "straightway . . . with the Herodians."
[2] Or, "wick."

his disciples, that they should bring unto
him a boat, because of the crowd, lest they
8 13 should press upon him: and he healed many; Mk. 3 10
so that as many as had plagues were nigh to
throng him on account of their eagerness to
14 touch him. And the unclean spirits, when „ 11
they saw him, fell down, and cried, saying,
15 Thou art the Son of God. And he urgently „ 12
threatened them, that they should not make
16 him known. And they that were troubled Lu. 6 18
17 with unclean spirits were cured. And all the „ 19
multitude sought to touch him; for power
went out from him, and healed *them* all.
18 And Jesus, seeing the multitudes, went Mt. 5 1[a]
19 up into the mountain: and he called his Lu. 6 13[b]
disciples, and chose from them twelve, whom
20 he named apostles: Simon, whom he named „ 14
Cephas, and Andrew his brother, James and
21 John, Philip and Bartholomew, Matthew and „ 15
Thoma, James the son of Alphaeus, and
22 Simon, which is called the Zealot, and Judas „ 16
the son of James, and Judas Iscariot, and
23 this is he that betrayed him. And Jesus „ 17
came down with them, and stood on a level
place, and a crowd of his disciples, and an
24 abundant multitude of the people. And he Mk. 3 14
selected these twelve, that they might be
with him, and that he might send them
25 forth to preach, and that they might have „ 15
the power of curing diseases, and casting out
devils.
26 Then he lifted up his eyes on them, and {Lu. 6 20[a] / Mt. 5 2}
opened his mouth, and taught them, saying,
27 Blessed are the poor in spirit: for theirs Mt. 5 3
is the kingdom of the heavens.
28 Blessed are the mournful: for they shall „ 4
be comforted.
29 Blessed are the meek: for they shall „ 5
possess the earth.[1]

[1] Aphraates gives, "the land of life."

8 30 Blessed are they that hunger and thirst Mt. 5 6
after righteousness: for they shall be filled.
31 Blessed are the merciful: for they shall „ 7
obtain mercy.
32 Blessed are the pure in heart: for they „ 8
shall see God.
33 Blessed are the peacemakers: for they „ 9
shall be called sons of God.
34 Blessed are they that are cast out for „ 10
righteousness' sake: for theirs is the kingdom
of the heavens.
35 Blessed shall ye be, when men shall hate Lu. 6 22[a]
you, and when they shall separate you, and
cast you out, and reproach you, and say Mt. 5 11[b]
every evil word against you, speaking falsely,
36 for my sake. Then rejoice, and be exceed- „ 12
ing glad; for your reward is abundant in the
heavens: for so cast they out the prophets,
that were before you.
37 But woe unto you that are rich! for ye Lu. 6 24
have received your consolation.
38 Woe unto you that are full! ye shall „ 25
hunger.
Woe unto you that laugh now! ye shall
mourn and weep.
39 Woe unto you, when men shall praise you! „ 26
for so did their fathers to the false prophets.
40 I say unto you which hear, Ye are the {Lu. 6 27 / Mt. 5 13}
salt of the earth: but if the salt lose its
savour, wherewith shall it be salted? it is
good for nothing; but it shall be cast out,
41 and trodden down by men. Ye are the Mt. 5 14
light of the world. A city built upon a
42 mountain cannot be hid. Neither do *men* „ 15
light a lamp, and put it under the bushel,
but on the lamp-stand, that it may shine
43 upon all that are in the house. So let your „ 16
light shine before men, that they may see
your good works, and glorify your Father,
44 which is in the heavens. For there is Mk. 4 22

nothing secret, except it shall be also
manifested; nor hidden, except it shall be
8 45 also known. He that hath ears to hear, let Mk. 4 23
him hear.
46 Think not that I came to destroy the law Mt. 5 17
or the prophets: I came not to destroy, but
47 to fulfil. Verily I say unto you, Till heaven „ 18
and earth pass away, one point or one letter
shall not pass away from the law, till all of
48 it be accomplished. Whosoever therefore „ 19
shall break one of these least commandments,
and shall teach men so, shall be called least
in the kingdom of the heavens: whosoever
shall do and teach them, he shall be called
49 great in the kingdom of the heavens. For „ 20
I say unto you, Except your righteousness
shall exceed *the righteousness* of the scribes
and Pharisees, ye shall not enter into the
kingdom of the heavens.
50 Ye have heard that it was said to them „ 21
of old time, Thou shalt not kill; for whosoever shall kill shall be accountable[1] to the
51 judgment: but I say unto you, that every „ 22
one who is angry with his brother without a
cause shall be accountable[1] to the judgment;
and whosoever shall say to his brother, O!
horrid one,[2] shall be accountable to the
council; but whosoever shall say to him,
Thou fool, shall be accounted worthy of the
52 Gehenna of fire. If therefore thou shalt „ 23
be offering thy gift upon the altar, and there
shalt remember, that thy brother hath con-
53 ceived any hatred against thee, leave thy „ 24
gift upon the altar, and go thy way first,
and be reconciled to thy brother, and then
54 return, and offer thy gift. Agree with thine „ 25[a]
adversary quickly: whilst thou art still Lu. 12 58[b]
with him in the way, give a ransom and be

[1] Lit. "accounted worthy of."
[2] The word "Raca" is not retained in the Arabic.

8 55 freed from him; lest haply the adversary Mt. 5 25[c]
deliver thee to the judge, and the judge
deliver thee to the officer,[1] and thou be cast
56 into prison. Verily I say unto thee, Thou „ 26
shalt not go out thence, till thou payest the
last mite.[2]
57 Ye have heard that it was said, Thou „ 27
58 shalt not commit adultery: but I say unto „ 28
you, that whosoever looketh on a woman,
lusting after her, hath committed adultery
59 with her there already in his heart. If thy „ 29
right eye injureth thee, pluck it out, and cast
it from thee: for it is expedient for thee that
one of thy members should perish, rather
than that thy whole body should go into
60 Gehenna. And if thy right hand injureth „ 30
thee, cut it off, and cast it from thee: for it
is better for thee that one of thy members
should perish, than that thy whole body
61 should fall into Gehenna. It was said, „ 31
Whosoever shall put away his wife, let him
62 give her a certificate of divorcement: but I „ 32
say unto you, Whosoever shall put away
his wife, without the cause of fornication,
maketh her already commit adultery; and
whosoever shall marry one who is put away,
committeth adultery.

9 1 Again, ye have heard that it was said to „ 33
them of old time, Thou shalt not forswear
thyself; but call thou upon God in thy
2 faith: but I say unto you, Swear not at „ 34
all; not by the heaven, for it is the throne
3 of God; nor by the earth, for it is the „ 35
foot-stool under his feet; nor even by Jeru-
4 salem, for it is the city of the great king.
Neither swear by thy head, for thou canst „ 36
5 not make one hair black or white. But „ 37
let your speech be either, Yes, or No; but

[1] Lit. "Exactor of fines."

[2] Arabic, fals, *i.e.* $\frac{1}{48}$ of a dirhem = half a farthing.

what is more abundant than this, is of the
evil *one*.
9 6 Ye have heard that it was said, An eye Mt. 5 38
7 for an eye, and a tooth for a tooth: but I „ 39
say unto you, Resist not an evil *man:* but
whosoever smiteth thee on thy right cheek,
8 offer him the other also. And to him that „ 40
wisheth to strive at law with thee, and take
away thy coat, to him give up thy cloke also.
9 And whosoever shall impress thee to go a „ 41
10 mile, go with him two. Give to him that „ 42
asketh of thee, and from him that wisheth
to borrow of thee withhold it not: and do Lu. 6 30b
not restrain[1] him that taketh away the
11 things that are thine. And as ye wish „ 31
that men should do to you, do ye also to
them likewise.
12 Ye have heard that it was said, Love thy Mt. 5 43
13 neighbour, and hate thine enemy: but I say „ 44
unto you, Love your enemies, bless them
that curse you, do good to them that hate
you, and pray for them that receive[2] you
14 harshly and drive you out; that ye may be „ 45
sons of your heavenly Father, who maketh
his sun to rise on the good and the evil,
and sendeth his rain on the just and the
15 unjust. If ye love them that love you, „ 46a
what reward shall ye have? for publicans Lu. 6 32b
and sinners likewise love those that love
16 them. And if ye do good to them that do „ 33
good to you, where is your superiority?
17 since even sinners do so. And if ye give „ 34
a loan to him, of whom ye expect repay-
ment, where is your superiority? for even
sinners lend to sinners, expecting as much
18 from them. But love your enemies, and do „ 35
them good, and give a loan, and cut off no
man's hope, that your reward may be great,
and that ye may be sons of the Most High:

[1] Or, "punish." [2] Or, "seize."

for he is kind toward the evil and the un-
9 19 thankful. Be ye merciful, even as your Lu. 6 36
Father also is merciful.
20 And if ye salute your brethren only, what Mt. 5 47
do ye more *than others?* do not even the
21 publicans the same? Be ye therefore per- „ 48
fect, as your heavenly Father also is perfect.
22 Take heed that ye do not your alms „ 6 1
before men, to be seen of them: otherwise
ye shall have no reward with your Father,
23 which is in the heavens. When therefore „ 2
thou doest alms, sound not a trumpet before
thee, as the hypocrites do in the synagogues
and in the streets, that they may be praised
of men. Verily I say unto you, They have
24 received their reward. But when thou „ 3
doest alms, let not thy left hand know
25 what thy right hand doeth: that thine alms „ 4
may be secret; and thy Father which seeth
in secret shall recompense thee openly.
26 And when thou prayest, be not as the „ 5
hypocrites, who love to stand and pray in
the synagogues and in the corners of the
streets, that they may be seen of men.
Verily I say unto you, They have received
27 their reward. But thou, when thou prayest, „ 6
enter into thy bedchamber, and having shut
the door, pray to thy Father *which is* in
secret, and thy Father which seeth in secret
28 shall recompense thee openly. And in pray- „ 7
ing speak not much, as the heathen *do:*
for they think that they shall be heard in
29 much speaking. Be not therefore likened „ 8
unto them, for your Father knoweth your
30 petition, before ye ask him. One[1] of his Lu. 11 1[b]
disciples said unto him, Lord, teach us to
pray, even as John taught his disciples.
31 Jesus saith unto them, After this manner „ 2[a]
32 then pray ye: Our Father which art in the Mt. 6 9[b]

[1] This interruption during the Sermon on the Mount is noticeable.

9 33 heavens, hallowed be thy name. Thy king- Mt. 6 10
dom come. Thy will be done, as in heaven
34 so on earth. Give us the sustenance[1] of to- „ 11
35 day. And forgive us our faults, as we also „ 12
forgive those who commit faults against us.
36 And bring us not into temptation, but de- „ 13
liver us from the evil *one.* For thine is
the kingdom, and the power, and the glory,
37 unto the ages of ages. If ye forgive men „ 14
their trespasses,[2] your Father which is in the
38 heavens will forgive you. But if ye forgive „ 15
not men, neither will your Father forgive
you your trespasses.
39 When ye fast, become not, as the hypo- „ 16
crites, mournful: for they disfigure their
faces, that they may appear unto men as
fasting. Verily, I say unto you, They have
40 received their reward. But thou, when „ 17
thou fastest, wash thy face, and anoint thy
41 head, that thou appear not unto men as „ 18
fasting, but unto thy Father which is in
secret: and thy Father, which seeth in
secret, shall recompense thee.
42 Fear not, little flock, for it hath pleased Lu. 12 32
your Father well to give you the kingdom.
43 Sell what ye possess, and give alms; make „ 33[a]
for yourselves purses which wax not old.
44 Lay not up[3] for yourselves treasure upon[4] Mt. 6 19
the earth, where moth and rust[5] doth corrupt, and where thieves dig through and
45 steal: but lay up for yourselves treasure in „ 20
heaven, where neither moth nor rust doth
corrupt; and thieves do not dig through, nor
46 steal: for where thy treasure is, there is „ 21
47 thy heart also. The lamp of the body is „ 22

[1] Lit. "power"; cf. ver. 36, an error for "food."
[2] Or rather, "folly," and so in ver. 38.
[3] Lit. "Treasure not," and so in ver. 45.
[4] Or, "in." [5] Or, "woodworm."

the eye: for if thine eye be unimpaired, thy
9 48 whole body shall be full of light. But if Mt. 6 23
thine eye be worthless, thy whole body shall
be full of darkness. If therefore the light
that is in thee be darkness, how great will
49 thy darkness be! Beware, lest the light Lu. 11 35
50 that is in thee be darkness. For if thy „ 36
whole body be full of light, not having any
part dark, it shall be wholly full of light, as
a lamp lightens thee with its bright shining.
10 1 No man can serve two masters: for he is Mt. 6 24
obliged to hate one of them, and love the
other; and to honour one, and despise the
other. Ye cannot serve God and riches.
2 Therefore I say unto you, Be not anxious for „ 25
your lives, what ye shall eat, and what ye
shall drink; nor for your bodies, what ye
shall put on Is not the life more than the
food, and the body more than the raiment?
3 Consider attentively the birds of the „ 26
heaven, which sow not, nor reap, nor gather
into barns; and your Father, which is in the
heavens, feedeth them. Are not ye of more
4 value than they? And which of you, when „ 27
he tries, shall be able to add one cubit unto
5 his stature? If then ye are not able *to do* Lu. 12 26
even that which is least, why are ye anxious
6 concerning the rest? Consider the lilies of Mt. 6 28[b]
the field, how they grow, though they toil
7 not, nor spin. And I say unto you, that „ 29
even Solomon in the magnificence of his glory
was not arrayed even as one of these.
8 But if God doth so clothe the grass of the „ 30
field, which to-day is, and to-morrow is cast
into the oven, how much rather shall it be
9 done to you, O ye of little faith. Be not „ 31
therefore anxious, saying, What shall we
eat? or, What shall we drink? or, Where-
withal shall we be clothed? nor let your Lu. 12 29[b]
10 mind be troubled because of this. All Mt. 6 32

these things do the nations of the world
seek after; and your Father, which is in
the heavens, knoweth that ye have need of
10 11 all these things. Seek ye first the kingdom Mt. 6 33
of God, and his righteousness; and all these
12 things shall be added unto you. Be not „ 34
anxious for the morrow: for the morrow
will be anxious for what is its own.[1] Its
own evil is sufficient for the day.
13 Judge not, that ye be not judged: con- {Mt.[2] 7 1 / Lu. 6 37[b]}
demn not, that ye be not condemned:
14 forgive, and ye shall be forgiven: release,[3] Lu. 6 38
and ye shall be released: give, and it shall
be given unto you; good measure, pressed
together and full, shall they thrust into
your bosom. With the same measure wherewithsoever ye measure, it shall be measured
15 to you. Take heed what ye hear: with Mk. 4 24[b]
whatever measure[4] ye measure, it shall be
measured to you again, and it shall be
added to you. I say unto these, which hear,
16 He that hath,[5] to him shall be given: and „ 25
he that hath not, even that which he can
have, shall be taken away from him.
17 And he spake a parable unto them: Can Lu. 6 39
a blind man guide a blind man? do they
18 not both fall into a pit? The disciple is „ 40
not superior to his master: but every per-
19 fect man shall be as his master. Why „ 41
lookest thou at the mote[6] that is in thy
brother's eye, but considerest not the beam
20 that is in thine own eye? Or how canst „ 42
thou say to thy brother, Brother, let me cast
out the mote from thine eye, when thou
thyself beholdest not the beam in thine own
eye? Thou hypocrite, cast out first the beam

[1] Or, "peculiar to it."
[2] Or, Luke vi. 37[a].
[3] This clause appears to be an addition.
[4] Unnecessary repetition.
[5] Repeated from Matt. xiii. 12 at xvi. 33.
[6] Or, perhaps, "stalk," a bit of wood like the "beam," but extremely small.

from thine own eye, and then shalt thou see
to draw out the mote from thy brother's eye.
10 21 Give not that which is holy unto the Mt. 7 6
dogs, neither cast your pearls before swine,
lest haply they trample them with their feet,
and turn and rend you.
22 And he saith unto them, Which of you Lu. 11 5
shall have a friend, and shall go unto him
at midnight, and say to him, Friend, lend
23 me three loaves; for a friend is come to me „ 6
from a journey, and I have nothing to offer
24 him; and the friend from within shall „ 7
answer and say unto him, Trouble me not:
the door is now shut, and my children are
with me in bed; I cannot rise and give unto
25 thee? Verily I say unto you, Though he „ 8
will not give[1] unto him because of friend-
ship, yet because of his importunity he will
arise and give unto him what he asked of
26 him. And I say unto you, Ask, it shall „ 9
be given you; seek, ye shall find; knock,
27 it shall be opened unto you. Every one „ 10
that asketh receiveth; and he that seeketh
findeth; and to him that knocketh it shall
28 be opened. What father among you, whose „ 11
son asketh of him a loaf, do you think, will
give him a stone? and if he ask of him a fish,
will he, do you think, for a fish give him a
29 serpent? and if he ask of him an egg, will he, „ 12
30 think you, hold out to him a scorpion? If „ 13
ye then, whilst ye are evil, know good gifts,
and give them unto your sons, how much more
shall your Father, which is in the heavens,
give the Holy Spirit to them that ask him!
31 All things whatsoever ye wish that men Mt. 7 12
should do unto you, do ye also unto them:
this is the law and the prophets.
32 Strive earnestly[2] at the narrow gate: for „ 13

[1] Omitting "rise and."
[2] The root is the same as in ver. 25, "importunity."

a wide gate, and a broad way leadeth to
destruction; and they are many that go
10 33 therein. How narrow is the gate,[1] and Mt. 7 14
confined the way, that leadeth unto life!
and they are few that find it.
34 Beware of false prophets, which come to „ 15
you in lambs' clothing, whilst inwardly they
are ravening wolves: but by their fruits ye „ 16[a]
35 shall know them. For each tree is known Lu. 6 44
by its own fruit. For not of thorns do
they gather figs, nor of a bramble-bush do
36 they gather grapes. Even so every good tree Mt. 7 17
bringeth forth good fruit; but an evil tree
37 produceth evil fruit. A good tree cannot „ 18
bring forth evil fruit, nor an evil tree pro-
38 duce good fruit. The good man out of Lu. 6 45
the good treasure, which is in his heart,
bringeth forth good things; and the evil
man out of the evil treasure, which is in
his heart, bringeth forth evil things: for
out of the abundance of the heart the lips
39 speak. Every tree that produceth not good Mt. 7 19
fruit shall be hewn down, and cast into
40 the fire. Therefore by their fruits ye shall „ 20
41 know them. Not every one that saith unto „ 21
me, Lord, Lord, shall enter into the kingdom
of the heavens; but he that doeth the will
of my Father, which is in the heavens.
42 Many will say unto me in that day, Lord, „ 22
Lord, did we not prophesy in thy name, and
in thy name cast out devils, and in thy name
43 do many mighty works? Then will I say „ 23
unto them, I never knew you: depart from
44 me, ye servants of iniquity. Every one that Lu. 6 47
cometh unto me, and heareth my words, and
doeth them, I will show you to what he is

[1] In Addai, though absent from some of the Greek MSS. Addai, however, does not give it as an exact quotation, but in his speech he says: "Because that the gate of life is straight, and the way of truth is narrow, therefore few are the believers of truth," etc.

10 45 like. He is like a wise man, that built a — Lu. 6 48[a]
house, and digged, and went deep, and laid
46 the foundations upon the rock: and the — Mt. 7 25
rain descended, and the floods overflowed,
and the winds blew, and shook that house;
and it fell not: for its foundations had been
47 laid upon the rock. And every one that — „ 26
heareth these words of mine, and doeth them
not, shall be like a foolish man, which built
his house upon the sand without a founda-
48 tion: and the rain descended, and the floods — „ 27
overflowed, and the winds blew, and burst
into that house; and it fell: and great was
the fall thereof.

11 1 And when Jesus had ended these words, — „ 28
the multitudes were astonished at his teaching:
2 for he taught them as *one* having authority, — „ 29
not as their scribes and the Pharisees.
3 And when he was come down from the — „ 8 1
mountain, great multitudes followed him
4 And when Jesus had entered into Caper- — „ 5[a]
naum, the servant of a certain distinguished — Lu. 7 2
officer, *who was* dear unto him, was sick, and
5 was already very near to death. And he — „ 3[a]
heard concerning Jesus, and came[1] unto him
6 with the elders of the Jews, and besought — Mt. 8 5[b]
him, and said, Lord, my boy lieth in the house — „ 6
paralytic,[2] and he is grievously tormented.
7 And the elders besought him earnestly, — Lu. 7 4[b]
saying, He is worthy that this should be
8 done for him: for he loveth our nation, and — „ 5
9 he built us even the synagogue. Jesus saith — Mt. 8 7
unto him, I will come and heal him. The
10 officer answered, and saith, Lord, I am not — „ 8
worthy that my roof should overshadow thee:[3]

[1] According to S. Matthew, he came himself; but according to S. Luke, he *sent* the elders. Ephraem has "elders of the people."

[2] Or, "crippled."

[3] Omitting Luke vii. 7, "Wherefore neither thought I myself worthy to come unto thee." Cf. note to ver. 5.

but it is enough that thou speak the word,
11 11 and my boy shall be healed. For I also Lu. 7 8
am a man under obedience to authority,
having under me soldiers: and I say to this
one, Go, and he goeth; and to another,
Come, and he cometh; and to my servant,
that he should do this, and he doeth it.
12 And when Jesus heard this, he marvelled, „ 9a
and turned, and said unto the multitude that
were coming with him, Verily I say unto Mt. 8 10b
you, I have not found such faith in Israel.
13 I say unto you, that many shall come from „ 11
the east and the west and shall lie down
with Abraham, and Isaac, and Jacob, in the
14 kingdom of the heavens: but the sons of „ 12
the kingdom shall be cast forth into the
outer darkness: there shall be the weeping
15 and gnashing of teeth. And Jesus said „ 13
unto the officer, Go thy way; and as thou
hast believed, *so* be it done unto thee. And
16 the boy was healed in that hour. And the Lu. 7 10
officer returned home, and found that sick
servant already whole.
17 And the day after he went to a city, „ 11
which is called Nain, and with him his
18 disciples and an abundant multitude. Now „ 12
when he drew near to the gate of the city,
he saw people that were attending one that
was dead, the only son of his mother, and his
mother was a widow: and a great multitude
19 of the city was with her. And when Jesus „ 13
saw her, he was moved with compassion on her,
20 and said unto her, Weep not. And he went, „ 14
and came near to the bier: and they that
were bearing him, stood still. And he saith,
21 Young[1] man, I say unto thee, Arise. And „ 15

[1] Aphraates has "Young man" twice, and in Mark v. 41 also he has "Maid, maid." Cf. "Martha, Martha," Luke x. 41; "Simon, Simon" (not in the Arabic), Luke xxii. 31; also "Saul, Saul," Acts ix. 4. These passages suggest a tendency to reduplication in Christ's words.

he that was dead sat up, and began to speak.
11 22 And he gave him to his mother. And fear Lu. 7 16
took hold on all: and they magnified God,
saying, A great prophet is arisen among us:
23 and, God hath visited his people. And this " 17
report was spread abroad into the whole of
Judaea concerning him, and into all the
region round about.
24 Now when Jesus saw great multitudes Mt. 8 18
about him, he gave commandment to go
25 across. And[1] as they were departing in Lu. 9 57[b]
the way, one scribe came near, and saith Mt. 8 19
unto him, Master, I will follow thee whither-
26 soever thou goest. Jesus said unto him, " 20
The foxes have holes, and the birds of the
heaven *have* nests; but the Son of man
hath not a place, where he may lay his
27 head. And he saith unto another, Follow Lu. 9 59
me. But he said, Lord, suffer me first to go
28 and bury my father. Jesus said unto him, " 60
Leave the dead to bury their own dead; but
follow thou me, and announce the kingdom
29 of God. And another saith unto him, I will " 61
follow thee, Lord; but suffer me first to go
and bid farewell to my household, and I
30 will come. Jesus said unto him, No man,[2] " 62
putting forth his hand to the plough, and
looking back, is fit for the kingdom of God.
31 And[3] on that day, when it was become late, Mk. 4 35[a]
he saith unto them, Let us cross over the Lu. 8 22[c]
lake.
32 And sending away the multitudes, Jesus {Mk. 4 36[a] / Lu. 8 22[b]}
went up into a boat, and sat down, himself

[1] If the two accounts are to be identified, S. Luke's seems a better setting, when Jesus was about to leave Galilee finally, and it was a question, who would leave Galilee for his sake, and accompany Him. So Schleiermacher and Tischendorf.

[2] Addai remarks, "A husbandman, who puts his hand to the ploughshare, if he looks behind, the furrows before him cannot be straight."

[3] Continuing S. Matthew's order.

11 33 and his disciples. And other boats were Mk. 4 36b
with them. And a great tumult was stirred Mt. 8 24a
up in the sea by[1] a whirlwind and a wind;
and the boat was nigh to be sunk through Lu. 8 23
34 the abundance of the waves. But Jesus was Mk. 4 38a
in the stern, asleep on the cushion: and his Mt. 8 25
disciples came to him, and awoke him, say-
35 ing, Lord, save us, behold, we perish. But Lu. 8 24b
he arose, and rebuked the wind and the
waves of the water, and said unto the sea, Mk. 4 39b
Be still, for thou art rebuked. And the
wind was silent; and a great calm took
36 place. And he saith unto them, Why are „ 40
ye so fearful? and why have ye not faith?
37 And they feared with a great fear; and they {Mk.[2] 4 41a; Lu. 8 25b}
marvelled, saying one to another, Who, think
you, is this, that commandeth even the wind
and waves and sea, and they obey him?
38 And they departed, and came to the Lu. 8 26
country of the Gadarenes,[3] which is beyond
the sea over against the land of Galilee.
39 And when he was come forth from the ship „ 27a
to the land, there met him out of the tombs Mk. 5 2b
a man[4] that had a devil now for a long time, Lu. 8 27c
and was wearing no garment, and abode not
40 in a house but in the tombs. And no man Mk. 5 3b
could bind him with chains; for as often as „ 4a
he was confined with chains and fetters, he
rent asunder the chains, and brake in pieces
41 the fetters: and he was driven by the devil Lu. 8 29b
into the desert: and no man was able to Mk. 5 4b
42 tame him. And always day and night he „ 5a
was in the tombs and in the mountains, so Mt. 8 28b
that no man could pass by that way; and Mk. 5 5b
he was crying out, and cutting himself with

[1] Or, "owing to."

[2] Included with ver. 40 in the Arabic, which follows the numbering of the Vulgate, in which there is no ver. 41.

[3] Arabic, "Ḥadarenes" throughout.

[4] One only, as at Mark v. 2; not two, as at Matt. viii. 28.

11 43 stones. And when he saw Jesus from afar, Mk. 5 6
44 he ran and worshipped him; and crying out „ 7[a]
with a loud voice, he said, What have we to Lu.[1] 8 28[b]
do with thee, Jesus, thou Son of the Most
High God?[2] I adjure thee by God, torment Mk. 5 7[c]
45 me not. And Jesus commanded the unclean Lu. 8 29[a]
spirit to go out from the man: for for a long
46 time he was in captivity to it. And Jesus „ 30
asked him, What is thy name? He said
unto him, Legion: for many devils had
47 entered into him. And they intreated him „ 31
that he would not command them to go into
48 the abyss. Now there was there a herd of „ 32
many swine feeding on the mountain: and
those demons intreated him that he would give
them leave to enter into the swine. And he
49 gave them leave. The devils therefore went „ 33
out of the man, and entered into the swine:
and the herd ran to the summit, and fell into Mk. 5 13[b]
the middle of the sea, about two thousand;
50 and they were choked in the water. And Lu. 8 34
when the herdsmen saw what had happened,
they fled, and told it to them that were in
51 the cities and in the villages. And some „ 35
went out to see what was come to pass; and
they came to Jesus, and found the man,
from whom the devils were gone out, sitting,
clothed and ashamed,[3] at the feet of Jesus:
52 and they were afraid. And they related „ 36
what they had seen, and how that man, in
whom there had been a devil, had been
made whole, and also concerning the swine. Mk. 5 16[b]
12 1 And all the multitude of the Gadarenes Lu. 8 37[a]
besought him to depart from them; for they
were holden with great fear.

2 And Jesus went up into a boat, and Mt. 9 1

[1] Or, Mark v. 7[b] nearly.

[2] Omitting Matt. viii. 29, "Art thou come hither to torment us before the time?"

[3] Probably derived from σωφρονοῦντα.

crossed over, and came into his own city.
12 3 And the man, from whom the devils were Lu. 8 38
gone out, besought him that he might remain
with him: but Jesus sent him away, and
4 said unto him, Return to thy house, and „ 39
declare what things God hath done for thee.
5 And he went his way, and began to publish Mk. 5 20
in Decapolis how great things Jesus had
done for him: and all men did marvel.
6 And when Jesus had passed over in the „ 21[a]
boat across the sea, a great multitude wel- Lu. 8 40[b]
comed him; for they were all waiting for
7 him. And a certain man, whose name was „ 41[a]
Jaïrus, a ruler of the synagogue, fell down at
8 Jesus' feet, and prayed him much, saying, I Mk. 5 23[a]
have one daughter, and she is already very
near death: but come, lay thy hand upon Mt. 9 18[b]
9 her, and she shall live. And Jesus arose, „ 19
10 and his disciples, and followed him. And a Mk. 5 24[b]
great multitude came to him; and they were
pressing upon him.
11 And a woman, in whom there was an „ 25
12 issue of blood for twelve years, and who had „ 26
suffered many things of many physicians, and
had spent all her *means*, and had made no
13 progress, but even grew worse;[1] when she „ 27
had heard concerning Jesus, came in the
press of the crowd behind, and touched his
14 garment. For she said secretly within her- „ 28
self, If I touch his garment, I shall live.
15 And straightway the fountain of her blood „ 29
was dried up; and she felt in her body that
16 she had been healed of her plague. And „ 30
straightway Jesus perceived in himself, that
power had gone out from him, and he turned
round to the crowd, and said, Who touched
17 my garments? And when all denied, Simon Lu. 8 45[b]
Cephas and they that were with him, said
unto him, Teacher, the multitudes press thee

[1] Lit. "her injury even increased."

4

and crush thee, and sayest thou, Who touched
12 18 me? But he said, Some one did touch me: Lu. 8 46
for I perceived that power had gone out[1]
19 from me. And[2] when the woman saw that „ 47[a]
she was not hid from him, fearing and Mk. 5 33[a]
trembling, because she knew what had been
20 done in her, she came, and falling down, she Lu. 8 47[b]
worshipped him, and declared in the presence
of all the people for what cause she touched
him, and how she was healed immediately.
21 And Jesus said unto her, Daughter, be „ 48
of good cheer, thy faith hath made thee
whole; go in peace, and be whole from thy Mk. 5 34[b]
plague.[3]
22 While he yet spake, there came one from Lu. 8 49
the ruler of the synagogue's house, and said
unto him, Thy daughter is dead: trouble not
23 the Teacher. But Jesus hearing it, said „ 50
unto the father of the maid, Fear not: but
24 believe only, and she shall be saved. And Mk. 5 37
he suffered no man to go with him, save
Simon Cephas, and James, and John the
25 brother of James. And they came into the „ 38
house of the ruler of the synagogue; and
he saw them excited,[4] weeping and wailing.
26 And when he had entered in, he saith unto „ 39
them. Why are ye excited,[4] lamenting? the
27 maid is not dead, but sleepeth. And they Lu. 8 53
laughed at him, knowing that she was dead.
28 But he, having put them all forth, took the Mk. 5 40[b]
father and the mother of the maid, and
Simon, and James, and John, and went into
29 the room, where the maid was lying.[5] And „ 41
taking the hand of the maid, he saith unto

[1] Or, "went forth."

[2] Omitting Mark v. 32, "And he looked round about to see her, that had done this thing;" but cf. ver. 16.

[3] Omitting Matt. ix. 22, "and the woman was made whole from that very hour;" but cf. ver. 15.

[4] Or, "terrified."

[5] Or, "laid."

her, Maid,[1] arise. And her spirit returned; Lu. 8 55[a]
12 30 and she rose up immediately, and walked: she Mk. 5 42[b]
was about twelve years *old*. And he com- Lu. 8 55[b]
manded that something should be given her
31 to eat. And her father was amazed with „ 56
great amazement; and he charged them to
32 tell no man what had been done. And this Mt. 9 26
report went forth into all that land.
33 And as Jesus passed by from thence, two „ 27
blind men followed him, crying out, and
saying, Have mercy on us, thou son of David.
34 And when he was come home, the two blind „ 28
men came to him: and Jesus said unto them,
Believe ye that I am able to do this? They
35 said unto him, Yea, Lord. Then touched „ 29
he their eyes, and said, Even as ye have
36 believed, be it done unto you. And im- „ 30
mediately their eyes were opened. And
Jesus warned them, saying, See that no man
37 know it. But they went forth, and published „ 31
abroad the news in all that land.
38 And when Jesus had gone forth, they „ 32
brought to him a dumb man that had a devil.
39 And when the devil was cast out, the dumb „ 33
man spake: and the multitudes marvelled,
saying, It was never so seen in Israel.
40 And Jesus went about all the cities and „[2] 35
villages, teaching in their synagogues, and
preaching the gospel of the kingdom, and
healing every sickness and disease. And
41 many followed him. And when Jesus saw the „ 36
multitudes, he was moved with compassion
for them, because they were wearied out and
forsaken, as sheep not having a shepherd.
42 And he called his twelve disciples,[3] and {Mt. 10 1[a]; Lu. 9 1[b]}
gave them power and great authority over

[1] Aphraates had "Maid, maid;" cf. note on xi. 20. The original words, "Talitha cumi," being Syriac, needed no interpreting clause in a *Diatessaron* for Syrian readers; hence the absence of such a clause in our text.

[2] Cf. vii. 7.

[3] Cf. note to xv. 16.

12 43 all devils and sickness. And he sent them Lu. 9 2
two and two to preach the kingdom of God,
44 and to heal the sick. And he charged them, Mt. 10 5[b]
saying, Into the way of the heathen depart
not, and into the cities of the Samaritans
45 enter not: attend chiefly to the sheep, that " 6
have perished, of the children of Israel.
46 And as ye go, preach, saying, The kingdom " 7
47 of the heavens is at hand. Heal the sick, "[1] 8
cleanse the lepers, cast out devils: freely ye
48 received, freely give. Possess no gold, nor " 9
49 silver, nor brass in your girdles;[2] nor carry " 10[a]
anything on the way, save a wand[3] only; Mk. 6 8[b]
no wallet, nor bread, neither have two coats, Lu. 9 3[b]
50 nor shoes, nor staff; but be shod with {Mt. 10 10[b] / Mk. 6 9[a]}
sandals: for the labourer is worthy of his Mt. 10 10[c]
51 food. And into whatsoever city or village Mt. 10 11
ye shall enter, inquire who in it is worthy;
52 and there abide till ye go forth. And as ye " 12
53 enter into the house, salute it. And if the " 13
house be worthy, your peace shall come upon
it: but if it be not worthy, your peace shall
54 return to you. And whosoever shall not " 14[a]
receive you, nor hear your words, as ye go
forth out of that house, or out of that city,
shake off the dust that is under your feet Mk. 6 11[b]
55 upon them for a testimony. Verily I say Mt. 10 15
unto you, There shall be rest for the land of

[1] Omitting "raise the dead." [2] Or, "purses."

[3] The distinction which Tatian here draws between "wand" and "staff," receives no support from the Greek, where we find the same word for what was allowed according to S. Mark, and for what was forbidden according to the other synoptists. The actual Greek phrases are: Matt. μηδὲ ῥάβδον; Mark, εἰ μὴ ῥάβδον μόνον; Luke, μήτε ῥάβδον.

Ephraem has this distinction; but it is not in the *Codex Fuldensis*, where the "wand" alone is mentioned, and is forbidden. According to the Armenian the word "staff" seems more applicable to what was allowed; whilst what was forbidden was a rough stick. The Peschito has the same word throughout. The Curetonian (Luke only) has also that word. The Jerusalem Syriac (Luke only) has a different word, which occurs in the Peschito of Mark xiv. 43. There can be little doubt that Tatian first drew the distinction in his Syriac.

Sodom and Gomorrah in the day of judgment
in preference to that city.
13 1 I send you forth as lambs in the midst of Mt. 10 16
wolves: be ye therefore wise as serpents,
2 and spotless[1] as doves. Beware of men,[2] „ 17
who will deliver you up to councils, and
3 scourge you in their synagogues; and before „ 18
governors and before kings shall they bring
you for my sake, for a testimony to them
4 and to the Gentiles. But when they „ 19
deliver you up, do not premeditate and
consider what ye speak: but it shall be
given you in that hour what ye must speak.
5 For it is not ye that speak; but the Spirit „ 20
6 of your Father speaketh in you. A brother „ 21
shall deliver up his brother unto death, and
a father *his* son; and sons shall rise up
against their parents, and put them to death.
7 And ye shall be hated of all men for my „ 22
name's sake: but whosoever endureth to the
8 end, the same shall live. When they shall cast „ 23
you out of this city, flee into another. Verily
I say unto you, Ye shall not complete all the
cities of the people of Israel, till the Son of
man come.
9 A disciple is not superior to his master, „ 24
10 nor a servant to his lord. For it is enough „ 25
for the disciple that he be as his master,
and for the servant *that he be* as his
lord. If they have called the master of
the house Beelzebub,[3] how much more *shall*
11 *they call* them of his household! Fear them „ 26
not therefore: for there is nothing covered,
that shall not be revealed; nor hidden, that
shall not be shown forth, and made known.
12 What I tell you in the darkness, speak ye in „ 27[a]
the light: and what ye have spoken secretly Lu.[4] 12 3[b]

[1] Or, "peaceable." [2] Cf. xli. 43, etc. [3] Lit. "Beelzebul."

[4] Tatian probably meant this as a continuation of Matt. x. 27; as he brings this in later at xli. 20[b].

in the ears in the bedchambers, shall be
13 13 proclaimed upon the housetop. I say unto Lu. 12 4[a]
you, my friends, be not afraid of them, which
kill the body, but are not able to kill the Mt. 10 28[b]
14 soul. I will show you whom ye shall fear: Lu. 12 5[a]
him, who is able to destroy both soul and Mt. 10 28[c]
body into Gehenna: yea, I say unto you, Lu. 12 5[c]
15 Fear him especially. Are not two sparrows Mt. 10 29
sold for a mite[1] in a noose,[2] and not one of
them falleth to the ground without your
16 Father: but in what relates to you, even " 30
17 the hairs of your head are numbered. Fear " 31
not therefore: ye are better than many
18 sparrows. Every one therefore, who shall " 32
confess me before men, him will I also confess before my Father, which is in the
19 heavens. But whosoever shall deny me " 33
before men, him will I also deny before my
Father, which is in the heavens.
20 Think ye that I am come to send peace Lu. 12 51
unto the earth? I am not come to send
21 peace but division: there shall be from " 52
henceforth five in one house; three of them
shall be divided against two, and two against
22 three. They shall be divided, the father " 53
against his son, and the son against his
father; the mother against the daughter,
and the daughter against her mother; the
mother-in-law against her daughter-in-law,
and the daughter-in-law against her mother-
23 in-law: and a man's foes shall be they of his Mt. 10 36
24 own household. He that loveth father or " 37
mother more than me, is not worthy of me:
and he that loveth son or daughter with a
deeper love than me, is not worthy of me.
25 And every one that doth not take his cross, " 38
26 and follow me, is not worthy of me. He " 39

[1] Arabic, "fals"; cf. viii. 56. From Syriac for ἀσσαρίου.
[2] The same Syriac word mistranslated and added.

that findeth his life, shall lose it; and whosoever loseth his life for my sake, shall find it.
13 27 He that receiveth you, receiveth me; and Mt. 10 40
he that receiveth me, receiveth him that sent
28 me. And he that receiveth a prophet in the „ 41
name of a prophet, shall receive a prophet's
reward: and he that receiveth a righteous
man in the name of a righteous man, shall
29 receive a righteous man's reward. And who- „ 42[a]
soever shall give as a drink unto one of these
very little ones a cup of water only, in the
name of a disciple, verily I say unto you, He Mk.[1] 9 41[b]
shall not lose his reward.
30 And when Jesus had ended his commands Mt. 11 1
to his twelve disciples, he passed over from
thence to teach and preach in their cities.
31 And as they went on their way, they entered Lu.[2] 10 38
into a certain village: and a woman named
32 Martha entertained him in her house. And „ 39
she had a sister named Mary, who came[3] and
sat at the Lord's feet, and listened to his
33 word. But Martha was distracted about „ 40
much serving; and she came, and saith unto
him, Lord, dost thou not care that my sister
hath left me to serve alone? bid her that
34 she help me. Jesus answered, and said unto „ 41
her, Martha, Martha, thou art anxious and
35 troubled about many things: and that which „ 42
is needed is one: but Mary hath chosen for
herself a good part, which shall not be taken
away from her.
36 And the apostles went out, and preached Mk. 6 12
37 unto men, that they should repent. And „ 13

[1] Or conclusion of Matt. x. 42.

[2] A singular displacement from S. Luke's order. It may have been put here to illustrate ver. 27–29 above. Tatian makes the sisters reside apparently in Galilee, not at Bethany. This is the natural impression conveyed by S. Luke, and it was adopted by Greswell; but the idea prevails that S. Luke has intentionally placed it *too early*.

[3] So Ephraem, the Curetonian, and the Peschito.

they cast out many devils, and anointed with
oil many sick *men*, and healed them.
13 38 And the disciples of John told him of Lu. 7 18
39 all these things. And John, when he had Mt. 11 2[a]
heard in the prison the works of the Christ,
called two of his disciples, and sent them to Lu. 7 19
Jesus, saying, Art thou he that cometh,
40 or look we for another? And they came „ 20
unto Jesus, and said, John the Baptist hath
sent us unto thee, and said, Art thou he
41 that cometh, or look we for another? Now „ 21
in that hour he cured many of diseases,
and of plagues of an evil spirit; and on
42 many blind *men* he bestowed sight. Jesus „ 22
answered, and said unto them, Go, and
relate to John all things which ye have seen
and heard; the blind receive their sight, the
lame walk, the lepers are cleansed, the deaf
hear, the dead rise again, the poor have
43 good tidings preached to them: and blessed „ 23
is he whosoever shall not be made to stumble
in me.

44 And when the disciples of John were „ 24
departed, Jesus began to say unto the
multitudes concerning John, What went ye
out into the wilderness to see? a reed
45 shaken with the wind? Otherwise, what „ 25
went ye out to see? a man clothed in soft
raiment? Behold, they which are in a
costly robe and luxuries, are in king's
46 houses. Otherwise, what went ye out to „ 26
see? a prophet? Yea, I say unto you, and
47 more than a prophet. This is he of whom „ 27
it is written,

Behold I send my messenger before thy
face,
To prepare a way before thee.

14 1 Verily I say unto you, Among them that Mt. 11 11
are born of women there hath not arisen a
greater than John the Baptist: yet he that

is less in the kingdom of the heavens, is
14 2 greater than he. And all the people that Lu. 7 29
were listening, and the publicans, justified
God, for they had been baptized with the
3 baptism of John. But the Pharisees and „ 30
the scribes treated unjustly the counsel of
God among themselves, for they had not
4 been baptized by him. But[1] from the days Mt. 11 12[a]
of John the Baptist until now the kingdom
5 of the heavens is seized with violence. The Lu. 16 16
law and the prophets *were* until John: from
thenceforth the kingdom of God is announced
as good tidings, and all men push themselves forward, that they may enter; and Mt. 11 12[b]
those who strive hard, take it by force.
6 All the prophets and the law prophesied „ 13
7 until John. And if ye are willing, receive „ 14
it that he is Elijah, which is about to come.
8 He that hath ears to hear let him hear. „ 15
9 It is easier for heaven and earth to perish, Lu. 16 17
than for one point to fall[2] from the law.
10 Unto whom then shall I liken the men of „ 7 31[b]
this generation, and to whom are they like?
11 They are like unto children sitting in the „ 32
market place, which summon their com-
panions, and say, We chaunted unto you,
and ye did not dance; we mourned unto
12 you, and ye did not weep. John the Baptist „ 33
came eating no bread nor drinking wine;
13 and ye said, He hath a devil. But the Son „ 34
of man came eating and drinking; and ye
said, Behold, a gluttonous man, and a wine-
bibber, and a friend of publicans and sinners!
14 And wisdom was justified by all her children. „ 35
15 And when he had said this, they came Mk. 3 19[b]
into the house. And the multitudes came „ 20
together unto him again, so that they

[1] The discourse of Jesus is resumed here without remark, ver. 2, 3 being explanatory on the part of some person recording what took place.

[2] Or, "cease."

14 16 could not even eat bread. And he was Lu. 11 14
casting out a devil, which was dumb.[1] And
when he had cast out that devil, the dumb
man spake, and the multitudes marvelled.
17 But when the Pharisees heard it, they said, Mt. 12 24
This man doth not cast out devils, except in
Beelzebub,[2] the prince of the devils, who is
18 in him. And others, tempting him,[3] sought Lu. 11 16
19 of him a sign from heaven. But Jesus, Mt. 12 25
knowing their thoughts, said unto them in
parables, Every kingdom divided against
itself will be brought to desolation: and
every house or city divided against itself
20 will not stand: and if Satan casteth out „ 26[a]
Satan, he is divided against himself, and Mk. 3 26[b]
will not be able to stand, but his end will
21 be. How then shall his kingdom stand? Mt. 12 26[b]
because ye say that I cast out devils in Lu. 11 18[b]
22 Beelzebub.[2] And if I in Beelzebub[2] cast Mt. 12 27
out devils, by what do your sons cast them
out? therefore shall they be your judges.
23 But if I in the Spirit of God cast out devils, „ 28
then is the kingdom of God come near unto
24 you. Or how can any one enter into the „ 29
house of a strong *man*, and rob his goods,[4]
except he first render himself safe from the
strong man? and then he will spoil his
25 house. When the strong *man* armed Lu. 11 21
guardeth his own court, those things which
26 he possesseth are in peace: but if a stronger „ 22
than he come upon him, he will overcome
him, and will take from him his whole
armour wherein he trusteth, and divide his
27 spoils. He that is not with me is against „ 23
me; and he that gathereth not with me

[1] Tatian does not identify with this miracle the cure of a demoniac "*blind and* dumb," prefixed (Matt. xii. 22) to the same discourse, but puts the latter afterwards. Tischendorf identifies the former with Matt. ix. 32–34.

[2] Lit. "Beelzebul."

[3] Or, "that he might be put to the test."

[4] Lit. "garments."

14 28 surely scattereth. Therefore I say unto you, Mk. 3 28
All sins shall be forgiven unto men, and
the blasphemies, wherewithsoever they shall
29 blaspheme; but whosoever shall blaspheme „ 29
against the Holy Spirit shall never have
forgiveness, but shall be accounted worthy
30 of eternal punishment. Because[1] they said, „ 30
that there was in him an unclean spirit,
31 he said again, Whosoever shall speak a word Mt. 12 32
against the Son of man, it shall be forgiven
him; but whosoever shall speak against the
Holy Spirit, it shall not be forgiven him,
neither in this world[2] nor in the world[2] to
32 come. Either ye make the tree good, and „ 33
its fruit good; or ye make the tree evil, and
its fruit evil: since the tree is known by its
33 fruit. Ye offspring of vipers, how can ye, „ 34
since ye are evil, speak good things? out
of the abundance of the heart the mouth
34 speaketh. The good man out of the good Lu.[3] 6 45[a]
treasure, which is in his heart, bringeth forth
good things; and the evil man out of the
evil treasure, which is in his heart, bringeth
35 forth evil things. I say unto you, that every Mt. 12 36
idle word that men shall speak, there shall
be exacted from them an account of it in
36 the day of judgment. For out of thy words „ 37
thou shalt be justified; and out of thy words
37 thou shalt be condemned. And he said to Lu. 12 54
the multitudes, When ye see a[4] cloud rising

[1] This clause is made to begin the new sentence instead of closing the old.

[2] Or, "age."

[3] Apparently meant by Tatian for Matt. xii. 35, making the passage continuous. Luke vi. 45 he has before identified with the Sermon on the Mount; cf. x. 38.

[4] Or, "the." It is very remarkable that, whereas both S. Matthew (xii. 38) and S. Luke (xi. 29) continue the preceding discourse with the demand for a sign from heaven, Tatian postpones that until xvi. 1, and inserts instead the signs of coming weather. Many commentators think the former ought to be postponed and the visit of Christ's brethren inserted here, followed by the series of parables, as in Mark iii. 31, etc.

from the west, straightway ye say, The rain
14 38 cometh; and so it cometh to pass. And Lu. 12 55
when it bloweth a south wind, ye say, There
will be a scorching heat; and it cometh to
39 pass. And when it is evening, ye say, It Mt.[1] 16 2^b
40 will be fair: for the heavens are dull. And " 3
in the morning ye say, To-day there will be a
storm: for the redness of the heavens is dull.
Ye hypocrites, ye know how to judge the face
of the heaven and the earth; but ye know
not how to discern the signs of this time.
41 Then[2] was brought unto him one that had Mt. 12 22
a devil, dumb and blind; and he healed him,
so that the dumb and blind man spake and
42 saw. And all the multitudes were amazed, " 23
and said, Is this, think you, the son of David?
43 And the apostles returned[3] unto Jesus, Mk. 6 30
and recounted unto him all things, which
44 they had done, and wrought. And he saith " 31
unto them, Come, let us go apart into a
desert place,[4] and rest a little. For there
were many going and returning; and they
had no leisure even to eat bread.
45 After these things came a certain man of Lu. 7 36
the Pharisees, and asked him to eat bread
with him. And he entered into the Phari-
46 see's house, and reclined *to meat.* And there " 37
was in that city a woman, a sinner; and
when she knew that he had reclined *to meat*
in the Pharisee's house, she took a flask of
47 ointment, and standing behind at his feet, " 38
weeping, she began to wet his feet with
tears, and wiped them with the hair of her
head, and kissed his feet, and anointed them

[1] Cf. xxiii. 13, where Matt. xvi. 1^a is made to introduce Mark viii. 11^b, followed by Matt. xvi. 4^b, etc.

[2] Cf. note to ver. 16.

[3] Put before Mark vi. 14–29 (death of S. John), because S. Matthew, who does not mention this return, puts that death at a later period of the history.

[4] Tatian omits Luke ix. 10, "belonging to the city called Bethsaida."

14 48 with the ointment. Now when the Pharisee, Lu. 7 39
which had bidden him, saw it, he thought
within himself, saying, This man, if he were
a prophet, would certainly know who she is,
and of what sort her character is, since the
woman, that touched him, was a sinner.
15 1 Jesus answered, and said unto him, Simon, „ 40
I have somewhat to say unto thee. Then
2 he saith, Master, say on. Jesus said unto „ 41
him, A certain creditor had two debtors:
the one owed five hundred pence, and the
3 other owed fifty pence. When they had „ 42
not from whence to pay, he forgave them
both. Which ought to love him the more?
4 Simon answered, and said, He, I suppose, to „ 43
whom he forgave the more. Jesus said unto
5 him, Thou hast rightly judged. And, turn- „ 44
ing to the woman, he said unto Simon, See
this woman. I entered into thine house;
and water for washing my feet thou gavest
not: but she hath wetted my feet with
6 tears, and wiped them with her hair. A „ 45
kiss thou gavest me not: but she, since the
time she came in, hath not ceased to kiss
7 my feet. My head with oil thou didst not „ 46
anoint: but she hath anointed my feet with
8 ointment. On account of which I say unto „ 47
thee, Many sins are forgiven her; for she
loved much: but to whom little is forgiven,
9 *the same* loveth little. And he said unto „ 48
the woman, Thy sins are forgiven thee.
10 And they that were bidden began to say „ 49
within themselves, Who is this that even
11 forgiveth sins? And Jesus said unto the „ 50
woman, Thy faith hath saved thee; go in
peace.
12 And many believed on him, beholding Jn.[1] 2 23[b]

[1] Tatian having removed these remarks of the evangelist from their setting, has found it necessary to omit the first part of this verse, which applied them to a particular occasion.

15 13 the signs which he did. But Jesus did not Jn. 2 24
trust himself with them, for that he knew
14 all men, and he had no need that any one „ 25
should bear witness unto him concerning a
man; for he himself knew what was in the
man.
15 Now[1] after these things Jesus appointed Lu. 10 1
out of his disciples seventy[2] others, and sent
them two and two before his face[3] into
every country and city, whither he himself
16 was about to come. And he said unto them, „ 2
The[4] harvest is plenteous, but the labourers
are few; pray ye therefore the Lord of the
harvest, that he may send forth labourers
17 into his harvest. Go your ways: behold, I „ 3
send you forth as lambs in the midst of
18 wolves. Take with you no purses,[5] nor „ 4
wallet, nor shoes: and salute no man on the
19 way. Into whatsoever house ye enter, first „ 5
20 salute that house. And if a son of peace be „ 6
there, your peace shall rest upon him: and
if he be not *there*, your peace shall turn to
21 you again. And in the same house remain, „ 7
eating and drinking of their substance: for
the labourer is worthy of his hire. And
22 cross not from house to house. And into „ 8
whatsoever city ye enter, and they receive

[1] See note to ver. 27.

[2] The *Codex Fuldensis* and the *Doctrine of Addai* have "seventy-two." Ephraem implies the same in two places (Moesinger, pp. 59 and 160).

[3] Ephraem has, "after his own likeness," instead of "before his face."

[4] The *Codex Fuldensis*, cap. 68, goes on here with ver. 32, "He that heareth," etc.; and Ephraem omits all comment on the instructions to the Seventy as such, but seems to refer to them in connection with the Mission of the Twelve (xii. 42 to xiii. 29). It seems likely that Tatian *harmonised* the two sets of instruction at the earlier place, and these verses have been inserted here since.

[5] Addai, who is represented as one of the seventy-two, says, "That which was ours we have forsaken, as we were commanded by our Lord to be without purses and without scrips, and carrying crosses upon our shoulders we were commanded to preach His gospel to the whole creation."

you, eat the things which are set before
15 23 you: and heal the sick that are therein, and Lu. 10 9
say unto them, The kingdom of God is come
24 nigh unto you. But into whatsoever city ye „ 10
enter, and they receive you not, go out into
25 the street, and say, Even the dust from your „ 11
city, that clave to our feet, we do wipe off
against you: howbeit know this, that the
26 kingdom of God is come nigh unto you. I „ 12
say unto you, There shall be ease for Sodom
in the day of judgment but not for that city.
27 Then began Jesus to upbraid[1] the cities, Mt. 11 20
wherein many mighty works had been done,
28 and they had not repented. And he said, „ 21
Woe unto thee, Chorazin! woe unto thee,
Bethsaida! if the signs had been done in
Tyre and Sidon, which were done in thee,
they would peradventure have repented in
29 sackcloth and ashes. Howbeit I say unto „ 22
you, There shall be rest for Tyre and Sidon
in the day of judgment, rather than for you.
30 And thou, Capernaum, which art exalted „ 23
even unto heaven, thou shalt sink down into
the abyss: for if the gifts had been made to
Sodom, which were made to thee, it would
surely have remained even until this day.
31 And now I say unto thee, that there shall „ 24
be ease for the land of Sodom in the day of
judgment, rather than for you.
32 He said again to the apostles, He that Lu. 10 16
heareth you, heareth me; and he that heareth
me, heareth him that sent me; and he that
rejecteth you, rejecteth me; and he that
rejecteth me, rejecteth him that sent me.

[1] Tatian has identified this passage with Luke x. 13–15; this appears to be his reason for placing Luke x. 1–12, which cannot well be dissociated from the latter, so much earlier than S. Luke did; for the evangelist clearly intended it to belong to the final departure from Galilee; and surely no time could be more appropriate for this upbraiding, than when Jesus was about to quit the country of these ungrateful cities.

15 33 And those seventy returned with great Lu. 10 17
joy, and said unto him, Lord, even the devils
34 are made subject unto us in thy name. He „ 18
saith unto them, I saw Satan as lightning,
35 falling from heaven. Behold I have given „ 19
you authority to tread upon serpents and
scorpions, and over every kind of enemies,
36 and nothing shall hurt you. Howbeit ye „ 20
need not to rejoice, that the spirits are
subject unto you; but rejoice, because your
names are written in heaven.
37 And in the same hour Jesus rejoiced in „ 21
the Holy Spirit, and said, I acknowledge
thee, O Father, Lord of heaven and earth,[1]
that thou didst hide these things from the
wise and understanding, and didst reveal them
unto children: yea, Father, so was thy will.
38 And he turned unto his disciples,[2] and said „ 22
unto them, All things have been delivered
unto me of my Father: and no one knoweth
who the Son is, save the Father; and who
the Father is, save the Son, and he to whom-
39 soever the Son willeth to reveal *him*. Come Mt. 11 28
unto me, all ye that are wearied and heavy
40 laden, and I will give you rest. Carry my „ 29
yoke upon you, and learn of me; for[3] I am
meek and lowly in my heart: and ye shall
41 find rest for your souls. For my yoke is „ 30
pleasant, and my burden light.
42 And when great multitudes were going Lu. 14 25
forth with him, he turned, and said unto
43 them,[4] He that cometh unto me, and hateth „ 26
not his father, and his mother, and brethren,
and sisters, and wife, and children, yea, and
his own life also, cannot be my disciple.

[1] Ephraem's copy left out "and earth."

[2] This additional clause is found in several MSS.

[3] Or, "that."

[4] Similarity of subject with the preceding seems to be the cause of the insertion of this passage here.

15 44 And he that doth not bear his own cross, Lu. 14 27
and follow me, cannot be my disciple.
45 Which of you, desiring to build a palace, „ 28
doth not first sit down and count his
expenses, and whether he have *wherewith*
46 to complete it? Lest after he lays the „ 29
foundations, and is not able to finish, all
47 that see him say, This man began to build, „ 30
48 and was not able to finish. Or what king, „ 31
about to go to commit war against another
king, doth not first consider, whether he is
able with ten thousand to meet him that
cometh against him with twenty thousand?
49 And if he is not equal to it, while he is yet „ 32
a great way off, he sendeth an embassy unto
50 him, and asketh for peace. So let every one of „ 33
you, that wisheth to be my disciple, consider:
for if he renounce not all that he possesseth,
he cannot be my disciple.
16 1 Then[1] certain of the scribes and Phari- Mt. 12 38
sees answered *him*, that they might tempt
him, saying, Master, we wish to see a sign
2 from thee. And he answering saith, This „ 39
evil and adulterous generation seeketh after
a sign; and there shall no sign be given to
3 it but the sign of Jonah the prophet: for Lu. 11 30
even as Jonah was a sign unto the Nine-
vites, so shall also the Son of man be to
4 this generation. And even as Jonah was Mt. 12 40
three days and three nights in the belly of
the whale, so shall the Son of man be three
days and three nights in the heart of the
5 earth. The queen of the south shall rise Lu. 11 31
up in the judgment against the men of this
generation, and shall condemn them: for
she came from the ends of the earth to
hear the wisdom of Solomon; and a better
6 than Solomon is here. The men of Nineveh Mt. 12 41
shall rise up in the judgment against this

[1] Cf. xxiii. 13-15. See note to xiv. 37.

generation, and shall condemn it: for they
repented at the preaching of Jonah, and a
16 7 greater than Jonah is here. When the un- Lu 11 24
clean spirit goeth out of the man, it
walketh and goeth about through waterless
places to find rest for itself; and when
it findeth it not, it saith, I will turn back
8 unto my house, whence I went out. And if „ 25
it come, and find it adorned and arranged,
9 then it goeth, and taketh with itself seven „ 26
other spirits more evil than itself; and they
enter in and dwell therein: and the last state
of that man becometh worse than the former.
10 So shall it be unto this evil generation. Mt. 12 45[b]
11 And as he said these things, a certain Lu. 11 27
woman out of the multitude lifted up her
voice, and said unto him, Blessed is the
womb that bare thee, and the breasts which
12 gave thee milk. But he said unto her, „ 28
Blessed is he that heareth the word of God,
and keepeth it.
13 While he was yet speaking to the multi- Mt. 12 46[a]
tudes, there came to him his mother and Lu. 8 19[a]
14 brethren; and they sought to speak to him, Mt. 12 46[b]
and they could not for the crowd; and {Lu. 8 19[b] / Mk. 3 31[b]}
standing without, they sent to call him to
15 them. A certain man said unto him, Be- Mt. 12 47
hold, thy mother and thy brethren stand
16 without, and seek to speak to thee. He „ 48
answered him that told him, Who is my
17 mother? and who are my brethren? And „ 49
motioning with his hand outstretched
towards his disciples, he said, Behold, my
18 mother, and behold, my brethren! For „ 50
whosoever shall do the will of my Father,
which is in the heavens, he is my brother,
and sister, and mother.
19 And after these things Jesus went round Lu. 8 1
the cities and villages, preaching and
announcing as good tidings the kingdom of

16 20 God, and with him the twelve, and the Lu. 8 2
women which had been healed of infirmities
and of evil spirits, Mary that is called
Magdalene, from whom he had cast out
21 seven devils, and Joanna the wife of Chusa, „ 3
Herod's steward, and Susanna, and many
others, which ministered unto them of their
substance.
22 And after these things Jesus went out Mt. 13 1
of the house, and sat on the seashore.
23 And there were gathered unto him great „ 2
multitudes; and when the press of men
around him was great, he went up, and
sat in a boat; and all the multitude were
24 standing on the seashore. And he spake „ 3
unto them many things in parables, saying,
25 He that soweth went forth to sow; and „ 4[a]
when he sowed, some[1] fell by the wayside,
and were trodden under foot, and the birds Lu. 8 5[b]
26 devoured them: and others fell upon a Mt. 13 5
rock: and others,[2] where they had not much
earth: and straightway they sprang up, because they had no deepness in the earth:
27 and when the sun was risen, they were „ 6
scorched; and because they had no root,
28 they withered away. And some fell among Lu. 8 7
the thorns; and the thorns sprang up at the
same time, and choked them; and they Mk. 4 7[b]
29 yielded no fruit. And others fell into Lu. 8 8[a]
ground good and beautiful, and came up, Mk. 4 8[b]
and grew, and brought forth fruit, some
thirty, some sixty, and others a hundred.
30 When he had said these things, he cried, Lu. 8 8[c]
He that hath ears to hear, let him hear.
31 And when they were alone, his disciples Mk. 4 10
came near, and asked him, and said unto him,
What is this parable? and why dost thou

[1] In the Arabic idiom "some" and "others" and the words dependent on them are given in the singular form throughout this parable.
[2] "And others" added.

16 32 speak unto them in parables? He answer- Mk. 4 11
ing saith unto them, Unto you is given the
knowledge of the secrets of the kingdom of
God: but it is not given unto them that
33 are without. He that hath, to him shall be Mt. 13 12
given, and he shall have increase: but he
that hath not, from him shall be taken
34 away even that which he hath. Therefore „ 13
speak I to them in parables; because seeing
they see not, and hearing they hear not,
35 nor understand. And in them is fulfilled „ 14
the prophecy of Isaiah, saying,

By hearing they shall hear,[1] and shall not understand;
And seeing they shall see, and shall not learn thoroughly:
36 For the heart of this people is waxed gross, „ 15
And in their ears their hearing hath become dull,
And their eyes they have closed;
Lest they should see with their eyes,
And hear with their ears,
And understand with their heart,
And should turn again,
And I should heal them.

37 But ye, blessed are your eyes, which see; „ 16
38 and your ears, which hear. Blessed *are* the Lu. 10 23[b]
eyes, which see the things which ye see.
39 Verily I say unto you, Many prophets and Mt. 13 17
righteous men desired to see the things
which ye see, and saw them not; and to
hear the things which ye hear, and heard
40 them not. If ye know not this parable, Mk. 4 13[b]
41 how shall ye know all the parables? Hear Mt. 13 18
42 ye the parable of the sower. The sower, Mk. 4 14
that soweth, soweth the word of God.
43 Every one that heareth the word of the Mt. 13 19
kingdom, and understandeth it not, the evil

[1] *I.e.* "They shall surely hear."

one cometh, and snatcheth away the word
sown in his heart. This is he[1] that was
16 44 sown by the wayside. And he[1] that was Mt. 13 20
sown upon a rock, this is he that heareth
the word, and straightway with joy receiveth
45 it; yet, since he hath no root in himself, Mt. 13 21[a]
46 but his faith in it is for a time, when { Lu. 8 13[b] / Mt. 13 21[b] }
tribulation or persecution ariseth because of
the word, straightway he is made to stumble.
47 And he[1] that was sown in the thorns, this Mt. 13 22[a]
is he that heareth the word; and the care
of this world, and the deceitfulness of riches,
and the remaining lusts enter in, and choke Mk. 4 19[b]
the word, and it is rendered unfruitful.
48 And that which was sown into the good Lu. 8 15
ground, he it is that in a pure and excellent
heart heareth my word, and understandeth,
and holdeth it fast, and bringeth forth fruit
in patience, and produceth either a hundred- Mt. 13 23[b]
fold, or sixtyfold, or thirtyfold.
49 And he said, So is the kingdom of God Mk. 4 26
even as a man that should cast seed into
50 the earth, and should sleep and rise night " 27
and day; and the seed should sprout and
51 grow while he knoweth not. For the earth " 28
bringeth it through into fruit; first there
will be the blade, afterwards the ear, and at
52 length the full corn in the ear. And when " 29
the fruit ripeneth,[2] straightway he bringeth
the sickle, because the harvest is here.
17 1 Another parable set he before them, saying, Mt. 13 24
The kingdom of heaven is likened unto a
2 man that sowed good seed in his field: but " 25
while men slept, his enemy came and sowed
tares amidst the wheat, and went away.
3 But when the blade had sprung up, and " 26
brought forth fruit, then appeared the tares
4 also. And the servants of the householder " 27
came, and said unto him, Sir, didst thou not

[1] Or, "that which," as ver. 48. [2] Lit. "fatteneth."

sow good seed in thy field? whence are the
17 5 tares in it? He saith unto them, An enemy Mt. 13 28
hath done this? The servants said unto
him, Wilt thou that we go, and pick them
6 out? He saith unto them, Would you not „ 29
perchance, when you picked out the tares,
7 root up also the wheat with them? Let „ 30
both grow together until the harvest, and at
the time of the harvest I will say to the
reapers, Pick out first the tares, and bind
them into bundles for burning with fire:
but gather the wheat into my barns.
8 And another parable set he before them, „ 31[a]
9 saying, Unto what is the kingdom of God Lu. 13 18[b]
like? and whereunto shall I liken it? and Mk. 4 30[b]
10 with what parable shall I compare it? It Lu. 13 19[a]
is like unto a grain of mustard seed, which Mt. 13 31[c]
11 a man took, and sowed in his field: and Mk. 4 31[b]
which of all things that are sown in the
earth, is less than all the things that are
12 sown, that are upon the earth; but when it Mt. 13 32[b]
hath sprung up, it is greater than all the
herbs, and maketh great branches; so that the Mk. 4 32[b]
birds of the heaven build nests in its branches.
13 And another parable set he before them. Mt. 13 33[a]
14 Whereunto shall I liken the kingdom of God? Lu. 13 20[b]
15 It is like unto leaven, which a woman took, Mt. 13 33[b]
and kneaded in three measures of meal, till
the whole was leavened.
16 All these things spake Jesus in parables „ 34[a]
unto the multitudes, as they were able to Mk. 4 33[b]
hear *them:* and without parables spake he Mt. 13 34[b]
17 not unto them: that it might be fulfilled, „ 35
which was spoken by the Lord through the
prophet, saying,

I will open my mouth in parables,
And I will utter things hidden before the
foundation of the world.

18 But privately to his disciples he expounded Mk. 4 34[b]
all things.

17 19 Then Jesus sent the multitudes away, and Mt. 13 36
came into the house: and his disciples came
near unto him, and said unto him, Explain
unto us the parable of the tares and the
20 field. He answered and saith unto them, „ 37
He that sowed the good seed is the Son of
21 man; and the field is the world; the good „ 38
seed are the sons of the kingdom; and the
22 tares are the sons of the evil *one;* and the „ 39
enemy that sowed them is Satan: but the
harvest is the end of the world; and the
23 reapers are angels. And even as the tares „ 40
are picked out, and burned with fire; so
24 shall it be in the end of this world. The „ 41
Son of man shall send forth his angels, and
they shall pick out of his kingdom all things
that cause stumbling,[1] and all the workers
25 of iniquity, and shall cast them into the „ 42
furnace of fire: there shall be the weeping
26 and gnashing of teeth. Then shall the „ 43
righteous shine forth as the sun in the
kingdom of their Father. He that hath
ears to hear, let him hear.
27 Again, the kingdom of heaven is like unto „ 44
a treasure hidden in the field; which the
man that findeth, hideth; and for joy thereof goeth and selleth all that he hath, and
buyeth that field.
28 Again, the kingdom of heaven is like unto „ 45
a merchant-man seeking pearls of great
29 price: and having found one pearl of great „ 46
price, he went and sold all that he had, and
bought it.
30 Again, the kingdom of heaven is like unto „ 47
a net cast into the sea, and gathering of
31 every kind: which, when it was filled, they „ 48
drew up on the seashore; and sat down to
pick them out, and they cast the good into
vessels, but the bad they threw away out-

[1] Or, "injure."

17 32 side. So shall it be in the end of the world: Mt. 13 49
the angels shall go forth, and sever the
wicked from the midst of the righteous,
33 and shall cast them into the furnace of fire: " 50
there shall be the weeping and gnashing of
teeth.
34 Jesus saith unto them, Have ye understood " 51
all these things? They said unto him, Yea,
35 Lord. He saith unto them, Therefore every " 52
scribe, *that is* a disciple of the kingdom of
the heavens, is like unto a man that is a
householder, which bringeth forth out of his
treasure things new and old.
36 And when Jesus had finished all these " 53
37 parables, he passed over from thence, and " 54a
came into his own city, and taught them in
their synagogues, insomuch that they were
38 astonished. And when the sabbath was Mk. 6 2
come, Jesus began to teach in the synagogue:
and many of those that heard him were
astonished, and said, Whence are these things
39 done unto this man?[1] And many envied
him, and did not apply their mind to him,
but said, What is this wisdom that is given
unto this man, so that such mighty works
40 are wrought by his hands? Is not this the Mt. 13 55
carpenter, the son of the carpenter? is not
his mother called Mary? and his brethren,
James, and Joses, and Simon, and Judas?
41 And his sisters, are they not all with us? " 56
Whence hath this man all these things?
42 And they were suspicious of him. But { Mt. 13 57a / Lu.[2] 4 23 }
Jesus, knowing their thoughts, saith unto

[1] Or, "hath this man these things?"

[2] It is noticeable how Tatian has cut off part of a continuous account of a visit to Nazareth, beginning at Luke iv. 16, in order to harmonise it with parallel passages in S. Matthew and S. Mark belonging to a later portion of Christ's ministry. The reason for this may have been the mention of a previous visit to Capernaum not recorded earlier in S. Luke, and which had not been placed in the *Diatessaron*, when the first portion of this narrative was inserted at v. 35.

them, Peradventure ye will say unto me
this parable, Physician, heal thyself first:
all things that we have heard that thou
hast done in Capernaum, do also here in
17 43 thine own city. And he saith, Verily I say Lu. 4 24
unto you, No prophet is accepted in his own
44 country, nor among his own brethren: for a Mk. 6 4[b]
prophet is not without[1] honour save in his
own country, and among his own kin, and in
45 his own house. Verily I say unto you, There Lu. 4 25
were many widows among the children of
Israel in the days of Elijah the prophet,
when the heaven was shut up three years
and six months, and a great famine was in
46 all the land; and unto none of them was „ 26
Elijah sent, but only to Sarepta of Sidon,
47 unto a widow woman. And there were „ 27
many lepers among the children of Israel in
the days of Elisha the prophet; and no one
of them was cleansed, but only Naaman the
48 Nabathaean.[2] And he could not do many Mk. 6 5
mighty works there, because of their unbelief,
save that he laid his hands upon a few sick
49 folk, and healed them. And he marvelled „ 6[a]
50 at their lack of faith. And when they that Lu. 4 28
were in the synagogue had heard, they were
51 all filled with wrath; and they rose up and „ 29
brought him forth out of the city, and led
him unto the brow of the hill whereon their
city was built, that they might cast him
52 from its summit. But he, passing through „ 30
the midst of them, went away.
53 And he went about the villages around Mk. 6 6[b]
Nazareth, and taught in their synagogues.
18 1 At that time Herod the tetrarch heard Mt. 14 1
the fame of Jesus, and all things that were Lu. 9 7[b]
done by his hand: and he marvelled, for Mk. 6 14[b]
2 his fame had firmly stood. And some said, Lu. 9 7[c]

[1] Or, "despised."
[2] The Peschito has "Aramæan."

John the Baptist is risen from the dead; Lu. 9 8[a]
18 3 but others said, Elijah hath appeared; but Mt.[1] 16 14[b]
others, Jeremiah; and others, A prophet out Lu. 9 8[b]
4 of the ancient prophets is risen; and others Mk. 6 15[b]
said, He is a prophet, just as one of the
5 prophets. Herod said unto his servants, „ 16
This is John the Baptist, whose head I cut
off: he is risen from the dead, therefore Mt. 14 2[b]
6 mighty works are wrought by him. For Mk. 6 17
Herod had sent forth, and laid hold upon
John, and cast him into prison for the sake
of Herodias, his brother Philip's wife, whom
7 he had married. For John said unto Herod, „ 18
Thou hast no right to have thy brother's
8 wife. And Herodias avoided him, and desired „ 19
9 to kill him; and she could not; for Herod „ 20
feared John, knowing that he was a righteous
man, and a holy; and he used to keep him
safe, and hear him much, and do, and obey
10 him gladly. And when he wished to put Mt. 14 5
him to death, he feared the people, because
11 they counted him as a prophet. And there Mk. 6 21
occurred a festival; for Herod on his birth-
day made a feast to his great men and to
the officers and the chief men of Galilee;
12 and the daughter of Herodias came in and „ 22
danced in the midst of the assembly, and
fascinated Herod and them that reclined *at*
meat with him; and the king said unto the
damsel, Ask of me what thou wilt, and I
13 will give it thee. And he sware unto her, „ 23
Whatsoever thou shalt ask of me, I will
14 give it, unto the half of my kingdom. And „ 24
she went out, and said unto her mother,
What shall I ask of him? She said unto
15 her, The head of John the Baptist. And „ 25
she came in straightway with haste unto the

[1] Tatian seems to have added the words, "but others Jeremiah," to the opinions which Herod heard about Jesus, copying them from the opinions which the disciples had heard about Him. Cf. xxiii. 33.

king, and said unto him, I will that in this
hour thou give me in a dish the head of
18 16 John the Baptist. And the king was exceed- Mk. 6 26
ing sorry; but for the sake of the oath, and
17 of the guests, he would not deny her. But „ 27
straightway the king sent forth an execu-
tioner, and commanded that the head of
John should be brought: and he went and
18 cut off the head of John in the prison, and „ 28
brought it upon a dish, and handed it to
the damsel; and the damsel gave it to her
19 mother. And when his disciples heard „ 29
thereof, they came and took up his body, and
buried it: and they came to tell Jesus what Mt. 14 12[b]
20 had happened. For this cause Herod had Lu. 9 9
said, John I beheaded: who is this, about
whom I hear these things? and he wished
21 to see him. Now Jesus when he had heard Mt. 14 13[a]
it, withdrew from thence in a boat to a desert
place apart,[1] to the other side of the sea of Jn. 6 1[b]
Galilee of Tiberius.
22 And many saw them going, and recognised Mk. 6 33
them; and hurrying on foot from all the cities
went thither before them; because they saw Jn. 6 2[b]
23 the signs which he did on the sick. Jesus „ 3
therefore went up into the mountain, and
24 there he sat with his disciples. Now the feast „ 4
of the passover of the Jews was very near.
25 And Jesus lifted up his eyes, and saw a „ 5[a]
great multitude coming unto him; and he Mk. 6 34[b]
had compassion on them, because they were
26 as sheep not having a shepherd: and he Lu.[2] 9 11[b]
welcomed them, and spake to them of the
kingdom, and them that had need of healing,
27 he healed. And when even was come, the Mt. 14 15[a]
disciples came to him, saying, The place is
28 desert, and the time is already past; send Mk. 6 36
away the multitudes of men, that they may

[1] Or, "by himself;" cf. ver. 46.
[2] Cf. xxxii. 23. This seems the right place for the extract.

go into the surrounding farms and villages,
and buy themselves bread, for they have
18 29 nothing to eat. But he said unto them, Mt. 14 16
They have no need to go away; give ye
30 them to eat. They said unto him, We have „ 17[a]
none here. He said unto Philip, Whence Jn. 6 5[b]
may we buy bread, that these may eat?
31 And this he said proving him: for he him- „ 6
32 self knew what he was about to do. Philip „ 7
said unto him, Two hundred pennyworth of
bread is not sufficient for them, that every
33 one may take a little. One of his disciples, „ 8
to wit Andrew, the brother of Simon Cephas,
34 said unto him, There is a lad here, which „ 9
hath five barley loaves, and two fishes: but
35 this amount, what is it for all these? but Lu. 9 13[b]
wilt thou that we go and buy for all the
people what they may eat? for we have no
more than these five loaves and two fishes.
36 Now there was much grass in that place. Jn.[1] 6 10
Jesus said unto them, Arrange them all, so
that they may sit upon the grass by companies of fifty each. And the disciples did
37 so. And they all reclined by companies, a Mk. 6 40
38 hundred each, and fifty each. Then Jesus Mt. 14 18
saith unto them, Bring hither those five
39 loaves and the two fishes. And when they Mk. 6 41
had brought them, Jesus took the loaves and
the fishes, and looking up to heaven, he
blessed, and brake, and gave to his disciples
40 to set before them; and the disciples set Mt. 14 19[b]
before the multitudes the bread and the
fish. And they did all eat and were filled. „ 20[a]
41 And when they were filled, he said to his Jn. 6 12
disciples, Gather up the broken pieces which
42 remain over, that nothing be lost. And „ 13
they gathered them up, and filled twelve
baskets with the broken pieces, which remained over from them that had eaten out

[1] And parallel passages.

of the five barley loaves and the two fishes.
18 43 And they that had eaten were five thousand Mt. 14 21
men, besides the women and children.
44 And straightway he constrained his dis- Mk. 6 45
ciples to go up into the boat, and to go
before him across the sea to Bethsaida, while
45 he himself sent the multitudes away. Now Jn. 6 14
those men that had seen the sign which
Jesus had done, said, This is of a truth a
prophet that hath come into the world.
46 And Jesus, knowing of their intention to „ 15
come to take him by force, and make him
king, left them, and went up into the mountain, himself alone, to pray.
47 And when it was become late, his dis- „ 16
48 ciples went down unto the sea, and sitting „ 17
in a boat they came across the sea unto
Capernaum. And darkness prevailed, and
49 Jesus had not come to them. Now the sea „ 18
was swelling against them on account of a
50 violent wind blowing: and the boat was Mt. 14 24
many furlongs[1] distant from the land, and
they were much tossed about[2] by the waves;
19 1 *for* they had a contrary wind. And in the „ 25
fourth watch of the night Jesus came unto
2 them, walking upon the water. After they Jn. 6 19[a]
had with difficulty made way about five and
twenty or thirty furlongs, and when he had
3 come nigh unto their boat, his disciples saw Mt. 14 26
him walking on the water; and they were
troubled, thinking that it was an apparition;[3]
4 and they cried out for fear. And straight- „ 27
way Jesus spake unto them, saying, Be of
5 good cheer; it is I; be not afraid. And „ 28
Cephas answered, and said unto him, Lord, if
it be thou, bid me come unto thee upon the

[1] So in some versions, including the Curetonian and Peschito; but cf. John vi. 19, from which Tatian may have taken it. Cf. also the margin of the Revised Version.

[2] Lit. "distressed."

[3] Lit. "delusive appearance."

19 6 waters. And Jesus said unto him, Come. Mt. 14 29
And Cephas went down from the boat, and
walked upon the water, to come to Jesus.
7 But when he saw the wind was strong, he „ 30
was afraid; and when he was near to sink,
he lifted up his voice, and said, Lord, save
8 me. And immediately the Lord stretched „ 31
forth his hand, and took hold of him, and
said unto him, O thou of little faith, where-
9 fore didst thou doubt? And when Jesus „ 32
had come near, he went up into the boat,
himself and Simon, and immediately the
10 wind ceased. And they that were in the „ 33
boat came, and worshipped him, saying, Of
11 a truth thou art the Son of God. And Jn. 6 21[b]
straightway the boat arrived at the land,[1] to
12 which they were going. And when they Mk. 6 54[a]
were come out of the boat unto the land,
they marvelled greatly one with another, and „ 51[b]
13 were amazed among themselves; for they „ 52
had not understood concerning that bread,
because their heart was hard.
14 And when the people of that country „ 54[b]
perceived the arrival of Jesus, they ran „ 55
about that whole land, and began to bring
on their beds those that were sick, where
15 they heard that he was. And whithersoever „ 56
he entered into villages and into cities, they
laid the sick in the streets, and besought
him that they might touch even the fringe
of his garment: and as many as touched
him were made sound and whole.
16 On the next day the multitude that stood Jn. 6 22
on the other side of the sea, beheld, and
there was no other boat there save that,
into which the disciples had gone up; and
they beheld that Jesus had not gone up with

[1] Tatian seems to have omitted the mention of Gennesareth (Mark vi. 53 and Matt. xiv. 34) as superfluous after the mention of Bethsaida in xviii. 44. He slightly transposes S. Mark for better order of the combined narrative.

19 17 his disciples into the boat; but there were Jn. 6 23
other boats from Tiberias nigh unto the
place, where they had eaten the bread, when
18 Jesus blessed *it*. When the multitude there- „ 24
fore saw that Jesus was not there, nor his
disciples, they went up into those boats, and
19 came to Capernaum, and sought Jesus. And 25
when they had found him on the other side
of the sea, they said unto him, Master, when
20 camest thou hither? Jesus answered, and „ 26
said unto them, Verily, verily, I say unto
you, Ye have not sought me, because ye saw
the signs, but because ye ate of the bread,
21 and were filled. Work not for the food „ 27
which perisheth, but for the food which
abideth unto[1] eternal life, which the Son
of man shall give unto you: him God the
22 Father hath sealed. They said unto him, „ 28
What shall we do, that we may work the
23 work of God? Jesus answered, and said „ 29
unto them, This is the work of God, that ye
24 believe in him whom he hath sent. They „ 30
said unto him, What sign hast thou done,
that we might see and believe in thee? what
25 hast thou wrought? Our fathers ate the „ 31
manna in the wilderness, as it is written,
He gave them bread out of heaven to eat.
26 Jesus said unto them, Verily, verily, I say „ 32
unto you, Moses gave you not the bread out
of heaven; but my Father gave you the
27 true bread out of heaven. The bread of „ 33
God is that which came down out of
heaven, and giveth life unto the world.
28 They said unto him, Lord, give us this bread „ 34
29 always. Jesus said unto them, I am the „ 35
bread of life: he that cometh to me shall
not hunger, and he that believeth in me
30 shall never thirst. But I said unto you, Ye „ 36
31 have seen me, and have not believed. Every- „ 37

[1] Or, "in."

thing which my Father hath given me shall
come unto me; and him that cometh to me
19 32 I will not cast out. For I am come down Jn. 6 38
from heaven not to do mine own will, but to
33 do the will of him that sent me. And this „ 39
is the will of him that sent me, that I should
lose nothing of what he hath given me, but
34 should raise it up in the last day. This is „ 40
the will of my Father, that every one that
seeth the Son, and believeth in him, should
have eternal life; and I will raise him up in
the last day.
35 The Jews therefore murmured concerning „ 41
him, because he had said, I am the bread
36 which came down out of heaven. And they „ 42
said, Is not this Jesus, the son of Joseph,
whose father and mother we know? how
then doth this man say, Surely I am come
37 down out of heaven? Jesus answered, „ 43
and said unto them, Murmur not with one
38 another. No man can come to me, unless „ 44
the Father which sent me draw him: and I
39 will raise him up in the last day. It is „ 45
written in the prophet, They shall all be
taught of God. Everyone that listeneth to
the Father, and learneth from him, cometh
40 unto me. Not that any man seeth the „ 46
Father, save he which is from God: he it is
41 that seeth the Father. Verily, verily, I say „ 47
unto you, He that believeth in me hath
42 eternal life. I am the bread of life. „ 48
43 Your fathers did eat the manna in the „ 49
44 wilderness, and they died. This is the „ 50
bread which cometh down out of heaven,
that a man may eat thereof and not die.
45 I am the bread of life which came down „ 51
out of heaven: and[1] if any man eat
of this bread, he shall live for ever: and

[1] This is made the commencement of John vi. 52 (as in the Vulgate), and the numbers of the remaining verses of John vi. are increased by one.

the bread which I will give, is my body,
which I will deliver up for the life of the
world.
19 46 The Jews therefore strove[1] one with Jn. 6 52
another, saying, How can he give us his
47 body to eat? Jesus said unto them, Verily, „ 53
verily, I say unto you, Except ye eat the body
of the Son of man, and drink his blood, ye
48 shall not have life in yourselves. He that „ 54
eateth of my body, and drinketh of my
blood, hath eternal life; and I will raise
49 him up in the last day. My body is food[2] „ 55
indeed, and my blood is drink[3] indeed.
50 He that eateth my body, and drinketh my „ 56
51 blood, abideth in me, and I in him. Even „ 57
as the living Father sent me, and I live
because of the Father, he that eateth me,
52 he also shall live because of me. This is „ 58
the bread which came down from heaven:
but not in that way wherein your fathers
did eat manna, and died: he that eateth of
53 this bread shall live for ever. This said „ 59
he in the synagogue, as he taught in
Capernaum.
54 And many of his disciples, when they „ 60
heard *this*, said, Surely this saying is hard;
20 1 who can hear it? But Jesus, knowing in „ 61
himself that his disciples murmured about
this, said unto them, Doth this cause you to
2 stumble? *What* then if ye see the Son of „ 62
man ascending to the place, where he was
3 before? It is the spirit that quickeneth; „ 63
but the body profiteth nothing: the saying
that I speak unto you is spirit and life.
4 But some of you do not believe. For Jesus „ 64
knew beforehand who they were that believeth not, and who would betray him.
5 And he saith unto them, For this cause „ 65

[1] Or, "questioned." [2] Lit. "what is eaten."
[3] Lit. "what is drunk."

have I said unto you, No man can come
unto me, except this be given unto him of
the Father.
20 6 And because of this word many of the Jn. 6 66
disciples turned back, and walked not with
7 him. Jesus said therefore unto the twelve, „ 67
8 Do ye also wish to go away? Simon Cephas „ 68
answered, and saith, Lord, to whom shall we
go? thou hast[1] the words of eternal life.
9 And we have believed, and know that thou „ 69
art the Christ, the Son of the living God.
10 Jesus said unto them, Did not I choose you, „ 70
11 the twelve, and one of you is a devil? He „ 71
said this because of Judas, the son of Simon
Iscariot, who, being one of the twelve, was
going to betray him.
12 And as he spake, a certain Pharisee came, Lu. 11 37
and asked him to eat with him: and he
13 went in and lay down *to meat*. And the „ 38
Pharisee, when he saw him, marvelled that
he had not first purified himself, before he
14 ate.[2] Jesus saith unto him, Now do ye „ 39
Pharisees cleanse the outside of the cup and
of the platter, and think that ye are clean;
but the inside of yourselves is full of un-
15 righteousness and wickedness. Ye foolish „ 40
ones, did not he that made that which is
outside, make that which is inside also?
16 Now give your substance as alms, and all „ 41
things are clean unto you.
17 And there came up to him Pharisees and Mk. 7 1
18 scribes from Jerusalem; and when they had „ 2
seen that some of his disciples ate their
bread without having washed their hands,
19 they found fault with them. For all the „ 3
Jews and Pharisees, unless they wash their
hands thoroughly, eat not, because they hold
20 to the tradition of the elders: and that „ 4
which is bought from the market, except

[1] Or, "with thee are." [2] Lit. "before his eating.'

they wash *it*, they eat not: and many other
things they keep of those which they have
received in the way of washings of cups, and
measures, and brazen vessels, and couches.

20 21 And the scribes and Pharisees asked him, Mk. 7 5
Why walk not thy disciples according to the
traditions of the elders, but eat bread with-
22 out having washed their hands? Jesus Mt. 15 3
answered, and said unto them, Why do ye
also transgress the commandment of God
23 because of your tradition? God said, „ 4[a]
Honour thy father and mother: and, Who- Mk. 7 10[b]
soever shall reproach his father or his
24 mother, let him die the death: but ye say, „ 11
If a man shall say to his father or to his
mother, Whatsoever thou receivest[1] from
25 me is a sacred gift, *then he is free.* And ye „ 12
do not allow him to do anything for his
26 father or his mother. And ye make vain „ 13
and reject the word of God because of the
tradition which ye have delivered. And
ye command about the washing of cups and
pots: and many such like things ye do.
27 For leaving the commandment of God, ye „ 8[a]
28 hold fast the tradition of men. Do ye „ 9
well, when ye transgress against the commandment of God, that ye may keep your
29 tradition? Ye hypocrites, well did Isaiah Mt. 15 7
the prophet prophesy of you, saying,
30 This people honoureth me with their lips; „ 8
But their heart is very far from me.
31 But in vain do they reverence me, „ 9
Teaching the commandments of men.
32 And Jesus called unto him the whole multi- Mk. 7 14
tude, and said unto them, Hear me all of
33 you, and understand: there is nothing out- „ 15
side the man that, going into him then, can
defile him: but that which proceedeth out

[1] The Arabic is corrupt: a change in the pointing only solves the difficulty. But cf. 4

20 34 of him, that is what defileth the man. If Mk. 7 16
any man hath ears to hear, let him hear.
35 Then his disciples came near, and said unto Mt. 15 12
him, Knowest thou that the Pharisees that
heard this saying, were filled with indigna-
36 tion? He answered, and said unto them, „ 13
Every planting which my Father, which is
in the heavens, planted not, shall be rooted
37 up. Let them alone: for they, whilst „ 14
they are blind, lead the blind. And if a
blind man guide a blind man, both fall into
a pit.
38 And when Jesus had entered into the Mk. 7 17[a]
house from the multitude, Simon Cephas Mt. 15 15
asked him, saying unto him, Lord, explain
39 unto us this parable. He saith unto them, Mk. 7 18
Do ye also so comprehend not? Under-
stand ye not that everything entering the
man from without cannot render him un-
40 clean; because it entereth not into his heart; „ 19
it goeth into his stomach only, and from
thence is cast out in purgation, which
41 maketh all meats clean? That which Mt. 15 18
proceedeth out of a man's mouth, cometh
forth out of the heart; and this is what
42 defileth the man. From within, out of the Mk. 7 21
heart of men, evil thoughts proceed,
43 adulteries, fornications, thefts, false wit- „ 22
ness, murders, injustice, wickedness, deceit,
folly, an evil glance, railing, pride, foolish-
44 ness: all these evil things proceed from „ 23
within out of the heart; and these are
45 what defile the man. But if any one eat Mt. 15 20[b]
without having washed *his* hands, he is
not defiled.
46 And Jesus went out thence, and came {Mt. 15 21[a] Mk. 7 24[b]}
into the borders of Tyre and Sidon. And
he entered into a house, and was unwilling
that any one should know about him:
47 and he could not be hid. For straight- „ 25

way a woman of Canaan heard of him,
whose daughter had an unclean spirit.
20 48 And the woman was a Gentile from Mk. 7 26[a]
49 Emesa[1] of Syria. And she came out, Mt. 15 22[b]
and cried after him, saying, Have mercy
on me, O Lord, thou son of David; my
daughter is very grievously vexed with a
50 devil. And he answered her not a word. „ 23
And his disciples came near, and besought
him, saying, Send her away, for she crieth
51 after us. He answered, and said unto them, „ 24
I was not sent but unto the sheep that
have wandered from the house of Israel.
52 But she came and worshipped him, saying, „ 25
53 Lord, help me, have mercy on me. Jesus „ 26
said unto her, It[2] is not good that the
children's bread should be taken, and cast
54 to the dogs. But she said, Yea, Lord: even „ 27
the dogs eat of the crumbs which fall from
55 their masters' table, and live. Then Jesus „ 28[a]
saith unto her, O woman, great is thy faith:
56 be it done unto thee even as thou wilt. Go, Mk. 7 29[b]
and for this saying the devil is gone out of
57 thy daughter. And her daughter was healed Mt. 15 28[b]
58 in that hour. And the woman went away Mk. 7 30
unto her house, and found her daughter laid
upon the bed, and that the devil was gone
out of her.
21 1 And again Jesus went out from the „ 31
borders of Tyre and Sidon, and came unto
the sea of Galilee, towards the borders of
2 Decapolis. And they brought unto him a „ 32
deaf and dumb *man;* and sought from him

[1] Lit. Ḥims, the chief city of Phoenicia, now called Homs. "Hims of Syria" may have come into the text from a corrupt reading of the Syriac for "Syro-Phoenician." The name Justa is given to this woman in the Clementine *Homilies;* and as the quotations from the gospel narrative in that work appear to have been taken from the *Diatessaron*, the name Justa may have been put there by Tatian.

[2] Omitting Mark vii. 27, "Let the children first be filled."

that he would lay his hand upon him, and
21 3 heal him. And leading him out from the Mk. 7 33
multitude, he went away by himself, and
spitting on his own fingers,[1] put them into
4 his ears, and touched his tongue; and look- „ 34
ing up into heaven, he sighed, and saith
5 unto him, Be opened. And in that hour „ 35
his ears were opened, and the bond of his
tongue was loosed, and he spake readily.
6 And Jesus charged them much, that they „ 36
should tell this to no man: and all things,
which he forbade them, they published the
7 more. And they were much astonished, „ 37
saying, He doeth all things well: he hath
made even the deaf to hear, and the dumb
to speak.
8 And as he was passing through the land Jn. 4 4
9 of Samaria,[2] he came to a city of the „ 5
Samaritans, that is called Sychar, near to
the parcel of ground that Jacob gave to his
10 son Joseph: and Jacob's spring of water „ 6
was there. And Jesus, being wearied with
the toil of his journey, sat by the spring.
11 The time was about the sixth hour. And „ 7
there came a woman of Samaria to draw
water: Jesus said unto her, Give me water,[3]
12 that I may drink. Now his disciples were „ 8
gone into the city to buy themselves food.
13 The Samaritan woman therefore said unto „ 9
him, How dost thou, since thou art a Jew,
ask of me, which am a Samaritan woman,
to give thee to drink? (For Jews have no

[1] MS. W[d] has a similar reading.

[2] Tatian seems to make this happen on the way from Galilee to Judaea, if we connect it with the opening of this chapter—this is the reverse of S. John's order (John iv. 3). Yet at the close of this visit (xxi. 47) Jesus departs from Sychar to Galilee, as in S. John's Gospel. Perhaps we should rather understand an interval between ver. 7 and 8, during which Jesus has gone to Judaea, so that he is now on his return journey.

[3] So Ephraem. Added by Tatian for explanation, not to support Encratite views.

21 14 dealings with Samaritans.) Jesus answered, Jn. 4 10
and said unto her, If thou knewest the gift
of God, and who it is that said to thee,
Give me to drink; thou wouldest have asked
of him, and he would have given thee
15 the water of life. The woman said unto „ 11
him, Sir, thou hast no bucket, and the well
is deep: from whence hast thou the water
16 of life? Art thou greater than our father „ 12
Jacob, who gave us this well, and drank
thereof himself, and his children, and his
17 cattle? Jesus answered, and said unto her, „ 13
Every one that drinketh of this water shall
18 thirst again: but whosoever drinketh of the „ 14
water, that I shall give him, shall never
thirst; but[1] the water that I shall give
him, shall become in him a spring of water
19 springing up unto eternal life. The woman „ 15
said unto him, Sir, give me of this water,
that I thirst not again, nor come to draw
20 from hence. Jesus said unto her, Go, and „ 16
21 call thy husband, and come hither. She „ 17
said unto him, I have no husband. Jesus
said unto her, Thou saidst well, I have no
22 husband: thou hast had five husbands; and „ 18
he whom thou now hast is not thy husband:
23 and in this thou spakest truly. The woman „ 19
said unto him, Sir, I see that thou art a prophet.
24 Our fathers worshipped in this mountain; „ 20
and ye say, that at Jerusalem is the place
25 where *men* ought to worship. Jesus said „ 21
unto her, O woman, believe me, the hour
cometh, when neither in this mountain, nor
in Jerusalem, shall ye worship the Father.
26 Ye worship that which ye know not: but „ 22
we worship that which we know: for salva-
27 tion is from the Jews. But the hour shall „ 23
come, and now is, when the true worshippers
shall worship the Father in spirit and truth:

[1] John iv. 14 is made to begin here as in the Vulgate.

for the Father also seeketh such worshippers.
21 28 For God is a Spirit: and they that worship Jn. 4 24
him, must worship him in spirit and truth.
29 The woman said unto him, I know that the „ 25
Messiah will come: when therefore he is
30 come, he will teach us all things. Jesus „ 26
said unto her, I that speak with thee,
31 am *he*. And meanwhile his disciples „ 27
came, and marvelled how he was speaking
with a woman: yet no one of them said
unto him, What seekest thou? or, Why
32 speakest thou with her? And the woman „ 28
left her waterpot, and went away into the
33 city, and said to the men, Come, and see a „ 29
man which told me all things that I have
34 done. Perhaps he is the Messiah? And „ 30
some went out of the city, and came to him.
35 In the meanwhile his disciples besought „ 31
36 him, saying unto him, Master, eat. But he „ 32
said unto them, I have food to eat, that ye
37 know not. The disciples therefore said one „ 33
to another, Hath any man brought him
38 what he could eat? Jesus said unto them, „ 34
My food is to do the will of him that sent
39 me, and to accomplish his work. Say not „ 35
ye, that there are yet four months, and the
harvest will come? behold, I say unto you,
lift up your eyes, and see the countries,
that they are white; for the harvest is come
40 before the time. And he that reapeth re- „ 36
ceiveth his hire, and gathereth the fruit of
life eternal; and he that soweth, and he
41 that reapeth, rejoice together. For herein „ 37
is the saying true,[1] There is one that soweth,
42 and there is another that reapeth. I sent „ 38
you to reap that whereon ye have not
laboured: others have laboured, and ye have
entered into their labours.
43 And from that city many of the Samari- „ 39

[1] Lit. "herein is the saying of truth found."

tans believed on him because of the word
of the woman, who bare witness and said,
He told me all things that I have done.
21 44 And when the Samaritans were come unto Jn. 4 40
him, they besought him to abide with them:
45 and he abode with them two days. And „ 41
many believed on him because of his speech;
46 and they said to the woman, Now we be- „ 42
lieve on him, not because of thy saying: for
we ourselves have heard, and know that this
is indeed the Messiah, the Saviour of the
world.
47 And after the two days Jesus went forth „ 43
from thence, and departed into Galilee.
48 And[1] Jesus testified that a prophet hath „ 44
49 no honour in his own country. When „ 45[a]
therefore he was come unto Galilee, the
Galilaeans received him.
22 1 And when Jesus was come to a certain Lu. 5 12
village, there came near unto him a man full
of leprosy:[2] and falling down at his feet,
he besought him, saying, If thou wilt, thou
2 canst make me clean. And Jesus had com- Mk. 1 41
passion on him, and stretched forth his hand,
and touched him, and said, I will that thou
3 be made clean. And straightway the leprosy „ 42
departed from him, and he was made clean.
4 And he strictly charged him, and sent him „ 43
5 out, and said unto him, See thou tell no „ 44
man: but go thy way, show thyself to the
priests, and offer for thy cleansing an offering, even as Moses commanded, for their
6 testimony. But he went out, and began to „ 45[a]
publish it much, and to spread abroad the

[1] Instead of "For."

[2] Professor Fuller, in his article on Tatian in Smith's *Dictionary of Christian Biography*, suggests that this miracle may have been put so late as a continuation of the subject of cleansing begun at xx. 13, and which he thinks has been going on in different forms ever since. The *Codex Fuldensis* has it earlier.

news, insomuch that Jesus could not openly
enter into any of the cities, because his fame
was spread abroad exceedingly, but he was
22 7 without in a desert place: and much people Lu. 5 15[b]
came to him from many places to hear his
word, and to be healed of their infirmities.
8 And he withdrew himself from them into „ 16
the desert, and prayed.
9 After that there was a feast of the Jews, Jn.[1] 5 1
and Jesus went up to Jerusalem.
10 Now there was at Jerusalem a place pre- „ 2
pared for bathing, which is called in Hebrew
11 House of Mercy,[2] having five porches. In „ 3
these lay a great multitude of *them that were*
sick, blind, lame, and withered, waiting for
12 the moving of the water. For the angel „ 4
went down at fixed seasons[3] into the place
of bathing, and moved the water. And the
first who should go down after the move-
ment of the water, all the infirmities that
13 were in him were cured. And a certain „ 5
man was there, that was already suffering
from a disease for thirty and eight years.
14 When Jesus saw him lying, and had learnt „ 6
that he had *it* a long time,[4] he said unto
him, Wishest thou to be made whole?
15 The sick man answered, and said, Yea, Lord, „ 7
I have no man, when the water is moved,
to put me into the bath: but while I am
coming, another passeth before me, and goeth
16 down. Jesus said unto him, Arise, take up „ 8
17 thy bed, and walk. And straightway the „ 9
man was made whole, and arose, and took
up his bed, and walked. Now that day was

[1] Repeated xxx. 31.

[2] "Bait ar Raḥma"—the Arabic equivalent of the Syriac Bethesda, which the translator should have left unchanged, especially after saying "in Hebrew."

[3] Or, "season after season;" lit. "in the season after the season."

[4] Lit. "had a long time."

22 18 the sabbath. And when the Jews saw him Jn. 5 10
that had been healed, they said unto him,
It is the sabbath day: thou hast no right
19 to take up thy bed. He answered, and said „ 11
unto them, He that made me whole,[1] the
same said unto me, Take up thy bed, and
20 walk. They asked him therefore, Who is „ 12
the man that said unto thee, Take up thy bed,
21 and walk? But he that had been made whole, „ 13
knew not who it was: for Jesus turned
aside from that place into another because
of the press of the multitude, which was
22 there. And after two days Jesus met him „ 14
in the temple, and said unto him, Behold,
thou art whole, sin no more, lest something
23 worse befall thee. And the man went away „ 15
and told the Jews, that it was Jesus, who
24 made him whole. For these things did the „ 16
Jews persecute[2] Jesus, and sought to kill
him, because he did these things on the
25 sabbath. But Jesus said unto them, My „ 17
Father worketh until now, and I also work.
26 And for this especially the Jews sought to „ 18
kill him, not only because he brake the
sabbath, but also because he said God was
his Father, and made himself equal with
27 God. Jesus answered, and said unto them, „ 19
Verily, verily, I say unto you, The Son can
do nothing of himself, but whatsoever he
seeth the Father doing: whatsoever the
Father doeth, this the Son also doeth in
28 like manner. The Father loveth his Son, „ 20
and sheweth him all things that himself
doeth: and greater works than these will
29 he shew him, that ye may marvel. For „ 21
even as the Father raiseth the dead, and
quickeneth them, so the Son also quickeneth
30 whom he will. For neither doth the Father „ 22
judge any man, but he hath given all judg-

[1] Lit. "exempt." [2] Or, "cast out."

22 31 ment unto the Son; that all may honour the Jn. 5 23
Son, even as they honour the Father. And
he that honoureth not the Son honoureth
32 not the Father which sent him. Verily, „ 24
verily, I say unto you, He that heareth my
word, and believeth him that sent me, hath
eternal life, and shall not come into judgment, but shall pass from death unto life.
33 Verily, verily, I say unto you, The hour „ 25
shall come, and now is, when the dead shall
hear the voice of the Son of God; and who-
34 soever hear shall live. For even as the „ 26
Father hath life in himself, so gave he to
35 the Son also to have life in himself: and „ 27
also authority to execute judgment, because
36 he is the Son of man. Marvel not at this: „ 28
namely the arrival of the hour, in which all
that are in the tombs shall hear his voice,
37 and shall come forth; they that have done „ 29
good, unto the resurrection of life; but they
that have done evil, unto the resurrection of
judgment.
38 I can of myself do nothing: but even „ 30
as I hear, I judge: and my judgment is
righteous. I seek not mine own will, but
39 the will of him that sent me. If I bear „ 31
witness of myself, my witness is not true.
40 It is another that beareth witness of me; „ 32
and I know that the witness which he
41 beareth of me is true. Ye have sent unto „ 33
John, and he hath borne witness unto the
42 truth. But I seek not witness from man: „ 34
howbeit I say this, that ye may be saved.
43 He was the lamp that burneth and shineth: „ 35
and for the while ye were willing to boast
44 in his light. But I have witness greater „ 36
than that of John: the works which the
Father hath given me to accomplish them,
the very works that I do, bear witness of
45 me, that the Father hath sent me. And „ 37

the Father which sent me, himself hath
borne witness of me. Ye have neither
heard his voice at any time, nor seen his
22 46 form. And his word is not confirmed in Jn. 5 38
you: for whom he sent, him ye believe not.
47 Seek ye the scriptures, in which ye boast „ 39
that ye have eternal life; and they are they
48 which bear witness of me; and ye are un- „ 40
willing to come to me, that ye may have
49 eternal life. I seek not glory from men. „ 41
50 But I know you, that the love of God is „ 42
51 not in you. I am come in my Father's „ 43
name, and ye received me not: but if another
come in his own name, him ye will receive.
52 How can ye believe, which[1] receive glory „ 44
one of another, and seek not glory from
53 the only God? Think ye that I am going „ 45
to accuse you to the Father? there is one
that accuseth you, *even* Moses, in whom ye
54 boast. If ye had believed Moses, ye would „ 46
have believed me also; of me Moses wrote.
55 But if ye believe not his writings, how „ 47
shall ye believe my words?
23 1 And Jesus departed thence, and came nigh Mt. 15 29
unto the sea of Galilee; and he went up
2 into the mountain, and sat there. And „ 30[a]
there came unto him great multitudes, having
with them the lame, blind, dumb, withered,
and many others, and they cast them down
3 at the feet of Jesus: for they had seen all Jn.[2] 4 45
the signs that he did at Jerusalem, when
they were assembled on the feast day: and Mt. 15 30[b]
4 he healed them all: and the multitudes „ 31
wondered, when they saw the dumb speaking, the withered healed, the lame walking,
and the blind seeing: and they magnified
the God of Israel.

[1] Or, "seeing that ye."
[2] A passing remark of the evangelist, which Tatian displaced to improve the order.

23 5 And Jesus called his disciples together, Mt. 15 32
and said unto them, I have compassion on
this multitude, because they are continuing
with me three days, and have nothing to eat:
and I am unwilling to send them away fasting, lest they faint in the way, for some of Mk. 8 3b
6 them are come from far. His disciples said Mt. 15 33
unto him, Whence should we have in the
desert the bread, wherewith we may fill all
7 this multitude? Jesus saith unto them, " 34
How many loaves have ye? They said unto
8 him, Seven, and a few small fishes. And " 35
he commanded the multitudes to lie down
9 on the ground; and he took the seven loaves " 36
and the fishes; and he blessed, and brake,
and gave to his disciples to set before them;
and the disciples set *them* before the multi-
10 tudes. And they did all eat, and were " 37
filled: and they took up seven baskets full,
which remained over of the broken pieces.
11 And they that did eat, were four thousand " 38
12 men, besides women and children. And " 39
when the multitudes were gone away, he
went up into the boat, and came into the
borders of Magheda.
13[1] And the Pharisees and Sadducees came " 16 1a
unto him, and began to question with him, Mk. 8 11b
seeking of him, that he would show them
14 a sign from heaven, tempting him. And " 12a
Jesus sighed in himself, and said, What
sign seeketh this evil and adulterous genera- Mt.[2] 16 4b
tion? it seeketh after a sign; and there
shall no sign be given unto it, but the sign
15 of Jonah the prophet. Verily I say unto Mk. 8 12b
you, There shall no sign be given unto this
16 generation. And he sent them away, and " 13
went up into the boat; and they departed
across the sea.

[1] With ver. 13–15 cf. xvi. 1–4; see also notes to xiv. 37 and 39.
[2] This is blended with Mark viii. 12.

23 17 And his disciples forgot to take bread; Mk. 8 14
for they had not even one loaf in the boat
18 with them. And Jesus charged them, say- „ 15
ing, Take heed, and beware of the leaven of
the Pharisees and Sadducees, and of the
19 leaven of Herod. But they reasoned among Mt. 16 7
themselves, because they had taken no bread
20 with them. And Jesus perceiving it said „ 8[a]
unto them, O ye of little faith, why reason
ye within yourselves, and are anxious because Mk. 8 17[b]
ye have no bread? do ye not yet perceive,
nor understand? is your heart still hard?
21 Having eyes, see ye not? and having ears, „ 18
hear ye not? and do ye not remember,
22 when I brake the five loaves unto the five „ 19
thousand, how many baskets [1] full of broken
pieces ye took up? They said, Twelve.
23 He said unto them, And again the seven „ 20
unto the four thousand: how many baskets [2]
full of broken pieces took ye up? They
24 said, Seven. He said unto them, How do ye { Mk. 8 21[a] Mt. 16 11
not perceive, that I spake not to you con-
cerning bread, but that ye should beware of
the leaven of the Pharisees and Sadducees?
25 Then understood they how that he said not, Mt. 16 12
that they should beware of the leaven of
bread, but of the teaching of the Pharisees
and Sadducees, which he called leaven.[3]
26 After these things he came unto Beth- Mk. 8 22
saida; and they brought to him a certain
blind man, and besought him to touch him.
27 And he took hold of the blind man's hand, „ 23
and brought him outside the village. And
when he had spit on his eyes, and applied
his own hand, he asked him, What seest
28 thou? And the blind man looked up,[4] and „ 24
said unto him, I see men as trees walking.

[1] Arabic, "ṣinn." [2] Arabic, "zumbîl," a basket of palm leaves.
[3] No MSS. support this reading, which is evidently due to Tatian.
[4] Or, "considered."

23 29	And again he laid his hand upon his eyes, and they were restored, and he saw all	Mk. 8	25
30	things clearly. And he sent him away to his home, saying, Do not either enter into the village, or tell anyone in the same.	„	26
31	And Jesus went forth and his disciples into the villages of Caesarea Philippi: and as he was walking in the way, himself and	„	27[a]
32	his disciples apart, he asked his disciples, saying, What[1] do men say concerning me,	Mt. 16	13[b]
33	that I, the Son of man, am? They said unto him, Some say John the Baptist; and some, Elijah; but others, Jeremiah,[2] or one	„	14
34	of the prophets. He said unto them, But	„	15
35	ye, who say ye that I am? Simon Cephas answered, and said, Thou art the Messiah,	„	16
36	the Son of the living God. Jesus answered, and said unto him, Blessed art thou Simon son of Jonah: flesh and blood hath not revealed it unto thee, but my Father which	„	17
37	is in the heavens. And I say unto thee, that thou art the rock, and upon this rock I will build my church; and the gates of the	„	18
38	lower world shall not subdue it. I will give unto thee the keys of the kingdom of the heavens, and whatsoever thou shalt bind on earth shall be bound in heaven: and whatsoever thou shalt loose on earth shall be	„	19
39	loosed in heaven. And he charged his disciples, and warned them, that they should tell no man concerning him, that he was the Messiah.	„	20
40	And from that time Jesus began to show unto his disciples, how that he must go unto	„	21[a]
41	Jerusalem, and suffer many things, and be	Mk. 8	31[b]

[1] S. Luke supposes this question put shortly after the return of the twelve, who may very naturally have heard opinions expressed during their journey. Tatian, however, preferred S. Matthew's order, which is supported by S. Mark.

[2] Cf. note to xviii. 3.

rejected by the elders, and by the chief
priests, and by the scribes, and be killed, and
23 42 on the third day rise again. And he spake Mk. 8 32[a]
clearly. And Simon Cephas, as if sympath- Mt. 16 22
ising[1] with him, said, Be this far from thee,
43 Lord: and he, turning about, and looking at Mk. 8 33[a]
44 his disciples, rebuked Simon, saying, Get Mt. 16 23[b]
thee behind me, Satan: thou art a stumbling
block unto me: for thou thinkest not those
things which belong to God, but those which
belong to men.

45 And he called unto him the multitudes Mk. 8 34[a]
with his disciples, and said unto them, He
that wisheth to come after me, let him deny
himself, and take up his cross daily, and Lu. 9 23[b]
46 follow me. And whosoever wisheth to save Mk. 8 35
his life shall lose it; but whosoever loseth
his life for my sake, and for the sake of my
47 gospel, shall save it. What doth a man Lu. 9 25
profit, if he gain the whole world, and lose
48 his own soul, or damage it? or what shall a Mk. 8 37
49 man give in exchange for his soul? Who- „ 38
soever shall deny me and my words in this
sinful adulterous generation, the Son of man
also shall deny him, when he cometh in the
glory of his Father with the holy angels.
50 For the Son of man is about to come in the Mt. 16 27
glory of his Father with his holy angels;
and then shall he render unto every man
according to his works.

24 1 And he said unto them, Verily I say unto Mk.[2] 9 1
you, there are indeed some standing here,
which shall not taste of death, till they
see the kingdom of God coming in
power, and the Son of man coming in his Mt. 16 28[b]
kingdom.

[1] Or, "vexed."

[2] Called viii. 39 as in the Vulgate, and all the verses from Mark ix. are numbered one less than in our Authorised Version; the numbers of the Authorised Version are given here.

24 2 And after six days Jesus took with him Mt. 17 1
Simon Cephas, and James, and John his
brother, and brought them unto a high
3 mountain, the three of them apart. And Lu. 9 29[a]
as they were praying,[1] Jesus was trans-
figured, and made into the form of another
4 person, and his face did shine as the sun, Mt. 17 2[b]
and his raiment became exceeding white Lu. 9 29[b]
as snow, and even as the brightness of
lightning, so that nothing on earth can Mk. 9 3[b]
5 become so white. And there appeared „ 4
unto him[2] Moses and Elijah talking with
6 Jesus. And they thought that his decease, Lu. 9 31[b]
destined to be accomplished at Jerusalem,
7 was already come. Now Simon and they „ 32
that were with him were oppressed with
the drowsiness of sleep, and they were
scarcely awakened,[3] and they saw his glory,
8 and the two men that stood with him. And „ 33[a]
when these had begun to depart from him,
Simon saith unto Jesus, Master, it is a good
9 thing that we are here: if thou wilt, let us Mt. 17 4[b]
make here three tabernacles; one for thee, Lu. 9 33[c]
and one for Moses, and one for Elijah, not
knowing what he said, because of the fear Mk. 9 6[b]
10 which had seized them. While he was yet Mt. 17 5[a]
saying this, thereupon a bright cloud over-
11 shadowed them: and when they had seen Lu. 9 34[b]
Moses and Elijah[4] entering into the cloud,
12 they feared again. And a voice was heard Mt. 17 5[b]
out of the cloud, saying, This is my beloved
Son, whom I have chosen;[5] hear ye him.

[1] The Ferrar group of MSS. has this reading in Mark ix. 3, showing that those MSS. are influenced by the *Diatessaron*. Tatian used considerable freedom of harmonisation throughout this passage.

[2] "Him" is apparently an error of the Arabic for "them;" there is no such reading in any other MS.

[3] Or, "by an effort they wakened themselves."

[4] The Peschito has "Moses and Elijah;" and the Curetonian Syriac implies that they were the ones that entered the cloud.

[5] Cf. Revised Version, Luke ix. 35, "my chosen."

24 13 And when this voice was heard, Jesus was Lu. 9 36a
14 found alone. And when the disciples heard Mt. 17 6
the voice, they fell on their face for the fear
15 which had seized them. And Jesus came, „ 7
and touched them, and said, Arise, be not
16 afraid. And lifting up their eyes they saw „ 8
Jesus even as he was.[1]
17 And as they were coming down from the „ 9
mountain, Jesus commanded them, and said
unto them, Tell no man what ye have seen,
until the Son of man riseth again from the
18 dead. And they kept the saying among Mk. 9 10a
themselves, and told no man in those days Lu. 9 36b
19 that which they had seen. And they Mk. 9 10b
reasoned among themselves, What is this
word which he said unto us: When I shall
20 have risen from the dead? And his disciples „[2] 11a
asked him, saying, What is it then that the Mt. 17 10b
scribes say, that Elijah must first come?
21 He saith unto them, Elijah will come first to Mk. 9 12
restore[3] all things; and how it was written
of the Son of man that he should suffer
22 many things and be rejected. But I say „ 13
unto you, Elijah is come, and they knew
him not, and did unto him whatsoever they
23 wished, even as it is written of him. Even Mt. 17 12b
so the Son of man is going to suffer from
24 them. Then understood the disciples, that „ 13
he had spoken unto them of John the
Baptist.
25 And on the day whereon they came Mk. 9 14
down from the mountain, there met him a
multitude of many men, standing with his
disciples; and the scribes were discussing
26 with them. And when the men saw Jesus, „ 15

[1] Perhaps an allusion to "as he is" (1 John iii. 2). As these words are evidently due to Tatian, this would imply that the first epistle of S. John was known to him.

[2] Or, Matt. xvii. 10a.

[3] Or, "put in order."

they were terrified, and in the midst of their
joy[1] saluted him.[2]
24 27 In that very day there came certain Lu. 13 31
of the Pharisees, saying to him, Get thee
out, and go hence: for Herod seeketh to
28 kill thee.[3] Jesus saith unto them, Go, and " 32
say to that fox, Behold, I cast out devils
and perform cures to-day and to-morrow,
and the third day I shall be perfected.
29 Howbeit I must be careful to-day and to- " 33
morrow, and depart the day following: for
a prophet cannot perish outside Jerusalem.
30 And after that a man from the multitude " 9 38a
came to him, and falling on his knees, said Mt. 17 14b
unto him, I beseech thee, O Lord, look upon Lu. 9 38b
31 my son; he is my only one: for a spirit " 39a
cometh unexpectedly upon him, and he be- Mt. 17 15b
32 cometh lunatic, and feeleth ill.[4] And where- Mk. 9 18
soever it falleth in with him, it dasheth him
down: and he foameth, and grindeth with
33 his teeth, and trembleth.[5] And oft-times it Mt. 17 15c[6]
casteth him into the water and into the fire
to destroy him: and it hardly departeth Lu. 9 39c
34 from him after it hath torn him. And I Mt. 17 16
brought him to thy disciples, and they could
35 not cure him. Jesus answered, and said, O " 17
faithless and perverse generation, how long
shall I be with you? and how long shall I
36 bear with you? bring thy son hither. And Mk. 9 20
he brought him unto him: and when he
saw him, straightway the spirit struck him;
and falling on the ground, he raged and
37 foamed. And Jesus asked his father, How " 21

[1] Possibly due to a misreading of the Greek.

[2] Omitting Mark ix. 16, "And he asked the scribes, What question ye with them?"

[3] No reason is apparent for the insertion of this incident between the Transfiguration and the cure of the demoniac boy.

[4] Lit. "meeteth evil." [5] Or, "crieth out."

[6] Parts of ver. 15 are called 14c and 14d in the Arabic.

long time is it during which he *hath been*
so? And he said, From youth even until
24 38 now: but wherein thou canst, Lord, help me, Mk. 9 22[b]
39 and have compassion on me. Jesus saith „ 23
unto him, If thou canst believe: then all
things are possible to him that believeth.
40 And straightway, weeping, the father of the „ 24
child cried out, saying, I believe, Lord; help
41 thou my lack of faith. And when Jesus „ 25
saw a running together of men, and their
assembling together at the cry, he rebuked
the unclean spirit, saying unto him, Thou
deaf spirit which speakest not, I command
thee, come out of him, and enter no more
42 into him. And the spirit the devil,[1] crying „ 26
out much, and rending him, went out: and
the child fell as dead; and many thought
43 that he was dead. But Jesus took him by „ 27[a]
the hand, and raised him up, and gave him Lu. 9 42[b]
44 to his father: and the boy was cured from Mt. 17 18[b]
that hour. And they were all astonished Lu. 9 43[a]
at the greatness of God.
45 And when Jesus had entered into the Mk. 9 28
house, his disciples came near,[2] and questioning him between themselves and him, they
said unto him, Why could not we cure him?
46 Jesus said unto them, Because of your lack Mt. 17 20
of faith: verily I say unto you, If ye have
faith as a grain of mustard seed, ye shall
say unto this mountain, Remove hence; and
it shall remove; and nothing shall with-
47 stand you: for this kind can be cast out by Mk. 9 29
nothing, save by fasting and prayer.
48 And when he had gone forth from thence, „ 30
they passed through Galilee; and he was
unwilling that any man should know about
49 him. And[3] he taught his disciples, and said „ 31[a]

[1] Lit. "the Satan." [2] Cf. Matt. xvii. 19.

[3] Omitting Luke ix. 43[b], "But while they wondered every one at all things that Jesus did."

unto them, Keep ye these sayings in your Lu. 9 44[a]
24 50 ears and hearts. For the Son of man shall Mk. 9 31[b]
be delivered up into the hands of men, and
they shall kill him; and when he is killed,
51 he shall rise again on the third day. But Lu. 9 45
they knew not the word, which he said unto
them, for it was hidden from them, that
they should not understand it: and they
were afraid to ask him about this matter.
52 And they were exceeding sorry. Mt. 17 23[b]
25 1 In that day this questioning arose among Lu. 9 46
the disciples, for they said, Who of them
2 was the greater? And when they were Mk. 9 33
come to Capernaum, and had entered into
the house, Jesus saith unto them, What
were ye reasoning among yourselves in the
3 way? But they held their peace, since „ 34[a]
they had reasoned about this.
4 And when Simon was gone outside, they Mt. 17 24[b]
that received the didrachma[1] of the tribute,
came to Cephas, and said unto him, Doth
5 not your master pay the didrachma?[1] He „ 25
saith unto them, Certainly. And when
Cephas had entered into the house, Jesus
anticipated him, saying unto him, What
thinkest thou, Simon? the kings of the
earth, from whom do they receive toll and
tribute? from their sons, or from strangers?
6 Simon said unto him, From strangers. Jesus „ 26
said unto him, Therefore the sons are free.
Simon saith unto him, Yea. Jesus said
unto him, Give thou also unto them as if a
7 stranger.[2] And lest it should distress them, „ 27
go thou to the sea, and cast a hook; and
when thou hast opened the mouth of the
fish that first cometh up, thou shalt find a
stater: that take, and give *it* for me and thee.
8 In that hour came the disciples unto „ 18 1
Jesus, and said unto him, Who, think you,

[1] Lit. "two dirhems." [2] Found in *Codex Algerinae Peckover*

is the greater in the kingdom of the
25 9 heavens? But Jesus, knowing the reason- Lu. 9 47[a]
ings of their heart, called a child, and set Mk. 9 36
him in the midst: and taking him into his
10 arms, he said unto them, Verily I say unto Mt. 18 3
you, Except ye turn, and become as little
children, ye shall not enter into the kingdom
11 of the heavens. Whosoever receiveth one Lu. 9 48[a]
like this child in my name, receiveth me:
and whosoever receiveth me, receiveth not Mk. 9 37[b]
12 me, but him that sent me: for he that is Lu. 9 48[c]
less among you all, the same is greater.
13 But whosoever causeth one of these little Mt. 18 6
ones which believe in me, to stumble, it were
better for him if a great millstone should be
hanged about his neck, and he should be
sunk into the depth of the sea.
14 John answered, and said, Teacher, we saw Lu. 9 49
some one casting out devils in thy name;
and we forbade him, because he followeth
15 thee not with us. Jesus saith unto them, Mk. 9 39
Forbid him not: for there is no man that
doeth mighty works in my name, and is able
16 quickly to speak evil of me. Everyone that Lu. 9 50[b]
17 is not against you is with you. Woe unto Mt. 18 7
the world because of strifes![1] but woe to
that man through whom the strife cometh!
18 If thy hand or thy foot causeth thee to " 8
stumble, cut it off, and cast it from thee:
for it is better for thee to enter into life
lame or maimed, than having two hands or
two feet to be cast into the fire kindled
19 for ever, where their worm dieth not, and Mk. 9 44
20 their fire is not quenched. And if thine eye Mt. 18 9[a]

[1] Omitting "for it must needs be that offences come." Aphraates here inserts before the missing part, "It must needs be that good come, and blessed be he by whom it cometh." It seems probable that some one struck out this latter, and in doing so erased too much. That it was originally in the *Diatessaron* is the more probable, as it occurs in the Clementine *Homilies*, xii. 29.

incite thee to strife, pluck it out, and cast it
25 21 from thee: for it is better for thee to enter Mk. 9 47[b]
into the kingdom of God with one eye, than
having two eyes to fall into the fire of
22 Gehenna, where their worm dieth not, and „ 48
23 their fire is not quenched. Everyone shall „ 49
be salted with fire; and every sacrifice shall
24 be salted with salt. How good is salt! „ 50[a]
but if even the salt have lost its savour, Lu. 14 34[b]
25 wherein shall it be salted? It is fit neither „ 35
for the land nor for the dung; but it is cast
out. He that hath ears to hear, let him
26 hear. Let there be salt in yourselves, and Mk. 9 50[c]
be ye at peace one with another.
27 And he arose[1] from thence, and came into „ 10 1
the borders of Judaea beyond Jordan: and
great multitudes came unto him thither, and
he healed them; and, as he had been wont,
28 he taught them again. And there came „ 2
unto him Pharisees, to tempt him, and say
unto him, Is it lawful for a man to put
29 away his wife?[2] He said, What did Moses „ 3
30 command you? They said, Moses gave us „ 4
permission that, if any man wished, he might
write a certificate of divorcement, and put
31 away his wife. Jesus answered, and said „ 5[a]
unto them, Have ye not read this, He which Mt. 19 4[b]
made *them* from the beginning, made them
32 male and female, and said, For this cause „ 5
shall a man leave his father and mother, and
shall cleave to his wife; and they both shall
33 be one body? So that now they are not „ 6
two, but one body. What therefore God
hath joined together, let not man put
34 asunder. The Pharisees said unto him, Why „ 7
did Moses consent that a certificate of

[1] S. Mark's order is here preferred to S. Matthew's. The journey referred to at xxviii. 9 is the same, according to the evangelists; yet between the two statements of it Jesus is represented as walking in Galilee (xxvii. 30).

[2] Omitting Matt. xix. 3, "for every cause."

divorcement should be given, and she should
25 35 be put away? Jesus saith unto them, Moses Mt. 19 8
for the hardness of your heart gave you
permission to put away your wives: but in
36 the beginning it was not so. I say unto „ 9[a]
you, Whosoever shall put away his wife
without fornication, and shall marry another,
37 exposeth her to adultery. And when he had Mk. 10 10
entered into the house, his disciples asked
38 him also about the same thing. And he „ 11
saith unto them, Whosoever shall put away
his wife, and marry another, exposeth her
39 to adultery: and if a woman shall put away „ 12
her husband, and marry another, she committeth adultery: and whosoever marrieth her Mt. 19 9[b]
when she is put away, committeth adultery.
40 His disciples said unto him, If between a „ 10
husband and a wife there is such blame, it
is not expedient for a man to marry a wife.
41 He said unto them, All men do not endure „ 11
this saying, but he to whom it was given.
42 There are eunuchs, which were so born „ 12
from their mother's womb: and there are
eunuchs, which were made *so* by men: and
there are eunuchs, which made themselves
eunuchs for the sake of the kingdom of the
heavens. He that is able to refrain, let him
refrain.
43 Then were there brought unto him little „ 13[a]
children, that he should lay his hand on
them, and pray: and the disciples rebuked Mk. 10 13[b]
44 those that were bringing them. When Jesus „ 14
saw it, it grieved him, and he saith unto
them, Suffer the little children to come unto
me, and forbid them not: for of such is the
45 kingdom of God. Verily I say unto you, „ 15
Whosoever shall not receive the kingdom of
God as this little child, he shall not enter
46 into it. And he took them up into his arms, „ 16
and blessed them, laying his hand upon them.

26 1 And the publicans and sinners drew near Lu.[1] 15 1
2 unto him, to hear his word. And the scribes ,, 2
and Pharisees murmured, saying, This man
receiveth sinners, and eateth with them.
3 And Jesus, when he had perceived their ,, 3
murmuring, said unto them this parable,
4 What man of you that hath a hundred sheep, ,, 4
if one of them wander, doth not leave the
ninety and nine in the wilderness, and go
and seek the straying *one*, until he find it?
5 Verily I say unto you, When he findeth it, Mt. 18 13[b]
he rejoiceth over it more than over the ninety
6 and nine which did not go astray. And he Lu. 15 5[b]
layeth it on his shoulders, and bringing it ,, 6
home, he calleth together his friends and
neighbours, saying unto them, Rejoice with
me, for I have found my straying sheep.
7 Even so your Father, which is in the heavens, Mt. 18 14
willeth not that one of these little ones
should perish, whom after erring he calleth
8 to repentance. I say unto you, that even so Lu. 15 7
there shall be joy in heaven over one sinner
that repenteth, more than over ninety and nine
righteous persons, which need no repentance.
9 And what woman having ten drachmas, ,, 8
and losing one of them, doth not light a
lamp, and sweep the house, and seek it dili-
10 gently until she find it? And when she ,, 9
findeth it, she calleth together her friends
and neighbours, saying unto them, Rejoice
with me, for I have found my drachma,
11 which was lost. I say unto you, that even ,, 10
so there shall be joy in the presence of the
angels of God over one sinner that repenteth,
more[2] than over ninety and nine righteous
persons, which need no repentance.

[1] Identified with Matt. xviii. 12–14, and put with it into a position due to the preference of S. Mark's order noticed at xxv. 27.

[2] This clause has evidently been copied from Luke xv. 7, where alone this allusion to ninety-nine is appropriate.

26 12 And again Jesus saith unto them another Lu. 15 11
13 parable, A certain man had two sons: and „ 12
the younger said unto him, Father, give me
my portion of thy property that falleth to me.
And he divided unto them his substance.
14 And after a few days the younger son „ 13
gathered all together that belonged to him,
and took his journey into a far country: and
there he squandered his substance in living
15 extravagantly. And when he had spent all, „ 14
there arose a mighty famine in that country,
16 and he was reduced to want, and went and „ 15
joined himself unto one of the citizens of
that country; and he sent him into a field
17 to feed swine. And he longed to fill his „ 16
belly with the pods that those swine were
18 eating: and no man gave unto him. But „ 17
when he came to himself, he said, How many
now of hired servants in my father's house
abound in bread, and I am perishing with
19 hunger! I will arise and go to my father's „ 18
house, and will say unto him, My father, I
have sinned against heaven, and in thy sight:
20 I am not worthy now to be called thy son: „ 19
21 make me as one of thy hired servants. And he „ 20
arose, and came to his father. But while he
was yet afar off, his father saw him, and had
compassion on him, and made haste, and fell
22 on his neck, and kissed him. And his son „ 21
said unto him, My father, I have sinned
against heaven, and in thy sight: and I am
23 not worthy to be called thy son. His father „ 22
said to his servants, Bring forth the best
robe, and put it on him; and put a ring on
his hand, and with shoes clothe his feet:
24 and bring the fatted calf, and kill it, that we „ 23
25 may eat, and make merry: for this my son „ 24
was dead, and is alive; he was lost, and is
26 found. And they began to feast. Now his „ 25
elder son was in the field: and as he came,

and drew nigh to the house, he heard the
26 27 sound of the singing of many. And he Lu. 15 26
called one of the lads, and asked him, What
28 is this? He said unto him, Thy brother „ 27
hath arrived; and thy father hath killed the
fatted calf, because he hath found him well.
29 And he was angry, and would not go in: „ 28
and his father came out, and intreated him
30 to enter. But he said to his father, So many „ 29
years do I serve thee as a slave; and I never
transgressed thy commandment: and *yet* thou
never gavest me a kid, that I might feast
31 with my friends: and after this thy son „ 30
came, having squandered thy substance with
harlots, thou killedst for him the fatted
32 calf. His father said unto him, My son, „ 31
thou art ever with me, and all mine is
33 thine. But it was meet to rejoice and to „ 32
feast, since this thy brother, *that* was dead,
is now alive: and *that* was lost, hath been
found.
34 And he spake a parable unto his disciples, „ 16 1
There was a certain rich man, and he had a
steward, and he was denounced unto him,
35 that he had wasted his substance. His lord „ 2
therefore called him, and saith unto him,
What is this that I hear of thee? give me
the account of thy stewardship; for now thou
36 wilt[1] not be able to be my steward. The „ 3
steward saith within himself, What shall I
do, seeing that my lord taketh away the
stewardship from me? I cannot dig; and
37 to beg I am ashamed. I know what I will „ 4
do, that when I am put out of the stewardship, they may receive me into their houses.
38 Therefore calling unto him each one of his „ 5
lord's debtors, he said unto the first, How
39 much owest thou unto my lord? He said „ 6
unto him, A hundred jars[2] of oil. He said

[1] Or, "canst not be my steward." [2] Or, "vessels."

unto him, Take thy bond,[1] sit down, and
26 40 write quickly fifty jars. And he said to the Lu. 16 7
next, but how much owest thou unto my
lord? He said unto him, A hundred cors[2]
of wheat. He said unto him, Take thy
account, sit down and write fourscore cors.
41 And his lord commended the steward of „ 8
unrighteousness, because he had done a wise
deed: for the sons of this world are in their
own generation wiser than the sons of the
42 light. And I say unto you, Make to your- „ 9
selves friends from the money of this unrighteousness; that, when it shall fail, they
may receive you into the eternal tabernacles.
43 He that is faithful over a little is faithful „ 10
also in much: and he that is unrighteous
over a little is unrighteous also in much.
44 If therefore ye have not been faithful in the „ 11
unrighteous money, who will commit to your
45 trust the true? If therefore ye have not „ 12
been found faithful in that which is not
your own,[3] who will give you what is your
own?[3]
27[4] 1 Therefore have I likened the kingdom Mt. 18 23
of the heavens unto a certain king, that
wished to make a reckoning with his servants.
2 And when he had begun to make *it*, one was „ 24
brought unto him, which owed him ten
3 talents.[5] But as he had not wherewith to „ 25
pay, his lord commanded him to be sold, and
his wife, and children, and all that he had,
4 and payment to be made. And the servant, „ 26
falling down and worshipping, said unto him,
Lord, have patience with me, and I will pay
5 thee all. And the lord of that servant had „ 27

[1] Or, "bill:" lit. "writing."

[2] A "cor" contained about 87 gallons.

[3] Or, "peculiar to you."

[4] In ver. 1–29 of this chapter Tatian has dealt very freely with the internal arrangement of passages relating to offences.

[5] Arabic "badra:" valued by some at 10,000 drachmas each.

mercy, and released him, and forgave him
27 6 his debt. But that servant went out and Mt. 18 28
found one of his fellowservants, which owed
him a hundred pence: and he laid hold on
him, and treated him with hardness, saying,
7 Give me what thou owest. And the fellow- „ 29
servant fell down at his feet, and besought
him, saying, Grant me delay, and I will
8 satisfy thee. And he would not: but went „ 30
and cast him into prison, till he should pay
9 the debt. And when the fellowservants of „ 31
both saw what had happened, they were very
displeased, and came and told unto their
10 lord all that had been done. Then his lord „ 32
called him unto him, and saith to him, Thou
wicked servant, I forgave thee all that debt
11 because thou besoughtest me: shouldest not „ 33
thou also have had mercy on thy fellow-
12 servant, even as I had mercy on thee? And „ 34
his lord was wroth, and delivered him to the
tormentors, till he should pay everything
13 that he owed. So shall also my Father „ 35
which is in heaven do unto you, if a man
forgive not his brother from his heart his
trespasses.
14 Take heed to yourselves: if thy brother Lu. 17 3
sin, rebuke him; and if he repent, forgive him.
15 And if he sin against thee seven times in the „ 4
day, and seven times in the day turn again to
16 thee, saying, I repent, forgive him. And if thy Mt. 18 15
brother sin against thee, go and reprove him
between thee and him alone: if he hear thee,
17 thou hast gained thy brother. But if he hear „ 16
thee not, take with thee one or two; for
in the mouth of two or three every word
18 standeth.[1] And if he hear not even them, „ 17
tell it unto the church: and if he hear not
the church also, let him be unto thee as a
19 publican and a heathen. Verily I say unto „ 18

[1] Or, "is confirmed."

you, What things soever ye shall bind on
earth shall be bound in heaven: and whatsoever ye loose on earth shall be loosed in
27 20 heaven. Again I say unto you, If two of Mt. 18 19
you shall agree on earth to ask anything, it
shall be done for them by my Father which
21 is in heaven. For where two or three are „ 20
gathered together in my name, there am I
22 in the midst of them. Then Cephas came „ 21
near, and said unto him, Lord, how often, if
my brother sin against me, shall I forgive
23 him? until seven times? Jesus said unto „ 22
him, I say not unto thee, Until seven times;
24 but, Until seventy times seven times.[1] For Lu. 12 47
the servant, which knew his Lord's will, and
prepared not for him according to his will,
25 shall be punished much; but he that knew „ 48
not, and did something worthy of punishment, shall be punished little. And every
one, to whom much is given, of him shall
much be required: and *every one*, to whom
much is committed, at his hand much will
be sought.
26 I came to cast fire upon the earth; and „ 49
I could wish that it were already kindled.
27 And I have a baptism to be baptized with; „ 50
and I am much straitened till it be accomplished.
28 See that ye despise not one of these Mt. 18 10
little ones, which believe in me; verily I say
unto you, Their angels[2] always see the face
29 of my father which is in heaven. The Son „ 11
of man came to save that which was lost.
30 And after these things Jesus walked in Jn. 7 1
Galilee: for he would not walk in Judaea,
because the Jews sought to kill him.

[1] Lit. "seventy times seven, seven." The Peschito adds "and seven times." Ephraem has "seventy times seven seven times."

[2] Addai alludes to this, saying, "Let your solicitude for the young lambs be great, for their angels behold the face of the invisible Father."

27 31 Now there came some which told him of Lu.[1] 13 1
the Galilaeans, whose blood Pilate mingled
32 with their sacrifices. Jesus answered, and „ 2
said unto them, Think ye that these Galilaeans
were sinners more than all the Galilaeans, so
33 that this happened unto them? Nay: verily „ 3
I say unto you, Except ye also all repent,
34 ye shall in like manner perish. Or those „ 4
eighteen, upon whom the tower in Siloam
fell, and killed *them*, think ye that they were
guilty more than all the men that dwell in
35 Jerusalem? Nay: verily I say unto you, „ 5
Except ye all repent, ye also shall perish
even as they.
36 And he spake this parable unto them, A „ 6
certain man had a fig-tree planted in his
vineyard; and he came seeking fruit thereon,
37 and found none. And he said unto the „ 7
husbandman, Behold, for three years I come
seeking fruit on this fig-tree, and find none:
cut it down; why doth it leave the ground
38 unoccupied? The husbandman said unto „ 8
him, Sir, let it alone this year also, that I
39 may dig about it, and dung it: and if indeed „ 9
it bear fruit, *well:* but if not, next year cut
it down.
40 And when Jesus was teaching on the „ 10
41 sabbath day in a certain synagogue, there was „ 11
a woman there, which had a spirit of infirmity
eighteen years; and she was bowed together,
42 and could not raise herself up. And when „ 12
Jesus saw her, he called her, and saith unto
her, O woman, be set free from thine in-
43 firmity. And he laid his hand upon her: and „ 13
immediately she was raised up, and glorified
44 God. The ruler of the synagogue, being „ 14
moved with indignation because Jesus had
healed on the sabbath, answered and said to

[1] This passage seems correctly put before leaving Galilee for the Feast of Tabernacles.

the multitudes, There are six days in which
men ought to work: in them therefore come
and be healed, and not on the day of the
27 45 sabbath. But Jesus answering saith unto Lu. 13 15
him, Ye hypocrites, doth not each one of
you on the sabbath day loose his ox or his
ass from the stall, and go away to give him
46 water? Ought not this woman, that is a „ 16
daughter of Abraham, and whom Satan hath
bound for eighteen years, to have been loosed
from this bond on the day of the sabbath?
47 And as he said this, all his adversaries „ 17
standing by were put to shame: and all the
people rejoiced in all the marvellous things
that were done by him.
28 1 At that time the Jews' feast of Taber- Jn. 7 2
2 nacles was at hand. And the brethren of „ 3
Jesus said unto him, Depart hence, and go
into Judaea, that thy disciples may see the
3 works which thou doest. Surely no man „ 4
doeth anything in secret, and wisheth to be
known openly. If thou doest this, manifest
4 thyself to the world. For until this time even „ 5
the brethren of Jesus did not believe in him.
5 Jesus said unto them, My time is not yet „ 6
6 come; but your time is always ready. The „ 7
world cannot hate you; but me it hateth,
because I bear witness of it, that its works
7 are evil. Go ye up unto this feast: but I „ 8
go not up now unto this feast, because my
8 time is not yet accomplished. He said this, „ 9
and remained in Galilee.
9 But when his brethren were gone up unto „ 10[a]
the feast, he removed from Galilee, and came Mt. 19 1[b]
into the borders of Judaea beyond Jordan;[1]
10 and great multitudes followed him; and he „ 2
11 healed them all there. And he departed, Jn. 7 10[b]
and went to the feast, not openly, but like
12 one who conceals himself. Now the Jews „ 11

[1] Cf. note to xxv. 27.

sought him at the feast, and said, Where is
28 13 he? And much murmuring took place there Jn. 7 12
concerning him in the great multitude, which
had come to the feast: for some said, He is
good; and others said, Nay, but he leadeth
14 the people astray. Howbeit no man spake „ 13
an open word concerning him for fear of
the Jews.
15 But when the days of the feast of Taber- „ 14
nacles were now dividing in half, Jesus went
16 up into the temple and taught. And the „ 15
Jews marvelled, saying, How knoweth this
man letters, since he hath not learned?
17 Jesus answered, and said, My teaching is not „ 16
18 mine, but his that sent me. Whosoever „ 17
desireth to do his will, he shall know my
teaching, whether it be of God, or *whether*
19 I speak from myself. He that speaketh „ 18
from himself, seeketh glory for himself: but
he that seeketh glory for him that sent him,
is true, and unrighteousness is not found in
20 his heart. Did not Moses give you the „ 19
law,[1] and no one of you keepeth the law?
21 Why do ye seek to kill me? The multitude „ 20
answered, and said unto him, Thou hast a
22 devil: who seeketh to kill thee? Jesus „ 21
answered, and said unto them, I did one
work, and ye all marvel because of this.
23 Moses hath given you circumcision (not „ 22
that it is of Moses but of the fathers); and
24 on the sabbath ye circumcise a man. And „ 23
if a man is circumcised on the day of the
sabbath, so that the law[2] of Moses may not
be broken; are ye wroth with me because I
made an entire man whole on the day of the
25 sabbath? Judge not according to appear- „ 24
ance, but give a righteous decision.
26 And some out of Jerusalem said, Is not „ 25

[1] Arabic, "sunna."
[2] Arabic, "nâmûs," *i.e.* νόμος.

28 27 this he whom they seek to kill? And lo, Jn. 7 26
he speaketh openly to them, and they say
nothing unto him. Think you, that our
elders know that this man is really the
28 Messiah? But this man is known whence „ 27
he is: now when the Messiah cometh, no
29 man will know whence he is. But Jesus „ 28
lifting up his voice, while he was teaching
in the temple, said, Ye both know me, and
know whence I am; and I am not come of
myself, but he that sent me is true, whom
30 ye know not. But I know him; because I „ 29
31 am from him, and he sent me. And they „ 30
sought to take him: and no man laid his
hand on him, because his hour was not
32 yet come. But of the multitude many „[1] 31
believed in him; and they said, Will the
Messiah when he cometh, do more signs
than those which this man doeth?
33 And a certain man[2] out of that multi- Lu. 12 13
tude said unto the Lord, Teacher, tell my
brother to divide the inheritance with me.
34 Jesus said unto him, Man, who appointed „ 14
35 me a judge and a divider over you? And „ 15
he said unto his disciples, Beware of every
evil: for life consisteth not in the abund-
36 ance of possessions. And he set this parable „ 16
before them, The ground of a certain rich
37 man brought forth abundant fruits: and he „ 17
reasoned within himself, saying, What shall
I do, because I have not a place where I can
38 collect my fruits? And he said, This will „ 18
I do: I will pull down the buildings of my
barns, and build again, and make greater
ones; and there will I collect all my corn
39 and my goods. And I will say to my soul, „ 19

[1] Repeated xxxiv. 48.

[2] This passage seems to have been asserted here on account of its similarity of subject with what follows at ver. 42, etc. It is thus made to appear as if the incident happened at the Feast of Tabernacles.

Soul, thou hast many goods laid up for many
years; take thine ease; eat, drink, enjoy
28 40 thyself. God said unto him, O destitute of Lu. 12 20
understanding, this night thy soul shall be
taken away from thee; and the things which
thou hast prepared, whose shall they be?
41 So is he that layeth up treasures for himself, " 21
and is not rich toward God.
42 And when Jesus had walked on his way, Mk.[1] 10 17
there came near [2] to him a young man of the
rulers, and fell upon his knees, and asked
him, saying, Good Teacher, what shall I do
43 that I may have eternal life? Jesus said " 18
unto him, Why callest thou me good?
whereas there is none good save one, *even*
44 God. Thou knowest the commandments: [3] " 19[a]
if thou desirest to enter into life, keep the Mt. 19 17[b]
45 commandments.[4] The young man said unto " 18[a]
him, Which commandments? [3] Jesus said
46 unto him, Do not commit adultery, Do not Mk. 10 19[b]
steal, Do not kill, Do not speak false witness, Do not defraud, Honour thy father and
thy mother, and, Love thy neighbour as Mt. 19 19[b]
47 thyself. The young man said unto him, All " 20
these things have I guarded from my youth:
48 what is *there* then that I lack? And Jesus Mk. 10 21[a]
looking upon him loved him, and said unto
49 him, If thou desirest to be perfect, one Mt. 19 21[b]
thing thou lackest, go away, sell all that
thou hast, and give to the poor, and thou
shalt have treasure in heaven: and take up
50 thy cross, and follow me. At this word " 22
the young man frowned, and he went away

[1] Tatian here resumes the thread of the common order of S. Matthew and S. Mark, which he dropped at the close of xxv., but whether Jesus has meanwhile returned to the place, where they represent this as happening, viz. "the borders of Judaea beyond Jordan," is not made clear.

[2] Omitting "running."

[3] Arabic, "awâmir."

[4] Arabic, "waṣ-âyâ," primarily meaning a commission from one dying, but used also of the "ten commandments."

28 51 sad; for he was very rich. And Jesus {Lu. 18 23[b] / „ 24[a]}
seeing his sadness, looked towards his dis- Mk. 10 23
ciples, and saith unto them, How difficult
it is for them that have riches to enter into
the kingdom of God!

29 1 Verily I say unto you, It is difficult for Mt. 19 23[b]
a rich man to enter into the kingdom of
2 heaven. And again I say unto you, It is „ 24
easier for a camel to press through the eye
of a needle, than for a rich man to enter
3 into the kingdom of God. And the dis- Mk. 10 24
ciples were amazed at these words. But
Jesus answered again, and said unto them,
My children, how difficult it is for them
that trust in their possessions to enter into
4 the kingdom of God. And they that heard „ 26
were the more astonished, saying among
themselves, being now afraid, Who, think
5 you, can be saved? And Jesus looking „ 27
upon them, said unto them, With men this
is not possible, but with God. God can do
6 all things. Simon Cephas saith unto him, Lu. 18 28
Lo, we have left all, and followed thee:
7 what then shall we have? Jesus saith {Mt. 19 27[b] / „ 28}
unto them, Verily I say unto you, Ye which
have followed me, in the new world when
the Son of man shall sit on the throne of
his glory, ye also shall sit upon twelve
thrones, and shall judge the twelve tribes
8 of Israel. Verily I say unto you, There is Mk. 10 29[b]
no man that leaveth houses, or brethren, or
sisters, or father, or mother, or wife, or
children, or kindred, or lands, for the kingdom of God's sake, or for my sake, and for
9 my gospel's sake, and that doth not receive Lu. 18 30
twice as many in this time and in the world
10 to come inherit eternal life: now in this Mk. 10 30[b]
time, houses, and brethren, and sisters, and
mothers, and children, and lands, with persecution; and in the world to come ever-

29 11 lasting life. Many *that are* first shall be Mk. 10 31
last; and the last first.
12 And when the Pharisees had heard all Lu.[1] 16 14
these things, because they loved riches, they
13 scoffed at him. But Jesus knowing what „ 15
was in their hearts, said unto them, Ye are
they that justify yourselves in the sight of
men; but God knoweth your hearts: for
that which is exalted among men, is small
in the sight of God.
14 And he began to say, A certain man was „ 19
rich, and was clothed in silk and purple, and
15 enjoyed himself surpassingly every day: and „ 20
there was a certain beggar named Lazarus,
who lay at the rich man's gate afflicted with
16 sores, and longed to fill his belly out of the „ 21
crumbs that fell from the rich man's table;[2]
so that the dogs came and licked his sores.
17 And it happened that the beggar died, and „ 22
the angels carried him into Abraham's
bosom: and the rich man also died, and was
18 buried. And while he was tormented in the „ 23
lower world, he lifted up his eyes from afar
off, and saw Abraham, and Lazarus in his
19 bosom. And he cried with a loud voice, „ 24
and said, Father Abraham, have mercy on
me, and send Lazarus, that he may wet the
tip of his finger with water, and moisten
my tongue; for behold, I am scorched in
20 this flame. Abraham said unto him, My „ 25
son, remember that thou receivedst good
things in thy lifetime, and Lazarus his
calamities: but now behold, he resteth here,
21 but thou art tormented. Add to all these „ 26
things, that between us and you a great

[1] This passage appears to have been removed to this position for the purpose of comparing its teaching about the use of riches with that of the passages which here precede and follow it. The words "all these things" are thus applied differently. Cf. pp. 32, 33.

[2] Aphraates adds "and no man gave unto him;" cf. Luke xv. 16.

abyss hath been placed,[1] so that they that
wish to cross from hence to you may not be
able, nor to cross over from thence to us.
29 22 He said unto him, I beseech thee therefore, Lu. 16 27
my father, to send him unto my father's
23 house: for I have five brethren; that he „ 28
may go, lest they also sin,[2] and come into
24 this place of torments. Abraham saith „ 29
unto him, They have Moses and the
25 prophets; let them hear them. He said „ 30
unto him, Nay, my father Abraham: but if
one of the dead go to them, they will re-
26 pent. Abraham saith unto him, If they „ 31
hear not Moses and the prophets, not even
if one of the dead rise again, will they
believe him.
27 The kingdom of heaven is like unto a man Mt. 20 1
that is a householder, which went out early
in the morning to hire labourers into his vine-
28 yard. And when he had made an agreement „ 2
with the labourers for a penny a day for
each labourer, he sent them into his vine-
29 yard. And he went out about the third „ 3
hour, and seeing others standing in the
30 marketplace idle, he said unto them, Go ye „ 4
also into my vineyard, and that which is fair
31 I will give you. And they went their way. „ 5
And again he went out at the sixth and
ninth hour, and did likewise, and sent them.
32 And about the eleventh hour he went out, „ 6
and finding others standing idle, he said unto
33 them, Why stand ye all the day idle? They „ 7
said unto him, Because no man hath hired
us. He said unto them, Go ye also into the
vineyard; and[3] that which is fair ye shall

[1] Or, "is placed."

[2] Mr. Rendel Harris accounts for this peculiar reading as arising from the confusing of two similar Greek words.

[3] "And . . . receive" is omitted in the Revised Version as deficient in MS. authority. It seems to have been added from the preceding verses to

29 34 receive. And when even was come, the lord Mt. 20 8
of the vineyard said unto his overseer, Call
the labourers, and pay them their hire:
begin indeed from the last, and continue
35 until the first. And the labourers of the „ 9
eleventh hour came and received every man
36 a penny. And when the first were come, „ 10
they supposed that they were going to receive
more; but they also received every man a
37 penny. And when they received it, they „ 11
38 murmured against the householder, saying, „ 12
These last have laboured one hour, and thou
hast made them equal unto us, which have
borne the scorching heat of the day and its
39 burden. He answered one of them, and said, „ 13
Friend, I do thee no wrong: didst not thou
40 agree with me for a penny? Take up that „ 14
which is thine, and go thy way; but it is my
will to give unto this last, even as I have
41 given unto thee. Either have I not a right „ 15
to do what I will about mine own business?
or perchance is thine eye evil, because I am
42 good? So the last shall be first, and the „ 16
first last: many are called, and few chosen.
43 And when Jesus entered into the house Lu. 14 1
of a certain ruler of the Pharisees on a
sabbath day to eat bread, they were watch-
44 ing him to see what he would do. And there „ 2
was before him a certain man which had
45 the dropsy. Jesus answered, and said unto „ 3
the lawyers and Pharisees, Is it lawful to
46 heal on the sabbath? But they held their „ 4
peace. However he took him, and healed
47 him, and let him go. And he said unto „ 5
them, Of which of you shall a son or an ox
fall into a well on a sabbath day, and he
will not straightway draw him up, and give

make the eleventh hour correspond to the others mentioned. But, in fact, the eleventh was an exceptional hour, not being one of the regular quarters of the day.

29 48 him to drink? And they could not answer Lu. 14 6
him a word unto these things.
30 1 And he set a parable before those which „ 7
were bidden there, because he saw them
2 choosing out the chief couches: When any „ 8
one bids thee to a feast, do not go to recline
in the chief place of the assembly; lest haply
a more honourable man than thou be there,
3 and he that bade you, come and say to thee, „ 9
Give this man place; and thou be put to
shame in the presence of them that stand
by, and another place shall receive thee.
4 But when thou art bidden, go and lie down „ 10
last; that when he that hath bidden thee
cometh, he may say to thee, Friend, go up
higher: and thou shalt have glory in the
presence of all them that are invited with
5 thee. For everyone that exalteth himself „[1] 11
shall be humbled, and every one that humbleth
himself shall be exalted.
6 And he said to him that had bidden him, „ 12
When thou makest a supper or a breakfast,
call not thy friends, nor thy brethren, nor
thy kinsmen, nor rich neighbours; lest haply
they also bid thee, and a recompense be
7 made thee. But when thou makest a feast, „ 13
bid the poor, the weak, the lame, and the
8 blind: and thou shalt be blessed; because „ 14
they have not from whence they may recompense thee: that thy recompense may be
made in the resurrection of the righteous.
9 When one of them that were bidden had „ 15
heard these things, he said unto him, Blessed
is he that shall eat bread in the kingdom of
God.
10 Jesus answering again in parables, said, Mt.[2] 22 1

[1] Cf. xxxii. 21 taken from Luke xviii. 14, and xl. 40 taken from Matt. xxiii. 12.

[2] Tatian is at variance with most modern harmonists in combining as one the two parables of S. Matthew and S. Luke. The position he assigns to the result is not at variance with S. Luke, but is earlier than S. Matthew places it.

30 11 The kingdom of the heavens is likened unto Mt. 22 2
a certain king, which made a feast for his
son, and prepared a great banquet, and Lu. 14 16b
12 invited many: and he sent forth his servants „ 17
at the time of the banquet to signify to them
that were bidden, Come; for all things are
ready for you: and they would not come. Mt. 22 3b
13 But they all began with one mouth[1] to Lu. 14 18
excuse themselves. The first saith unto
them, Tell him, I have bought a farm, and I
am obliged to go out to see it: I beseech
14 thee, let me go, for I am excused. And „ 19
another said, I have bought five yoke of
oxen, and I go to look at them: I beseech
15 thee to let me go, for I am excused. And „ 20
another said, I have married a wife, and
therefore I cannot come.
16 Again the king sent forth other servants, Mt. 22 4
saying, Tell them that are bidden, My feast
is prepared: my oxen and my fatlings are
killed, and all things are ready: come to
17 the banquet. But they disregarded it, and „ 5
went their ways, one to his farm, and an-
18 other to his merchandise: but the rest laid „ 6
hold on his servants, and entreated them
19 shamefully, and killed them. And one of Lu. 14 21a
the servants came, and told his lord that
20 which had happened. But the king, when Mt. 22 7
he heard *it*, was wroth; and he sent his
armies, and they destroyed those murderers,
21 and burned their cities. Then saith he to „ 8
his servants, The banquet is ready; and they
22 that were bidden were not worthy. Go out Lu. 14 21b
quickly into the streets and lanes of the city,
and bring in hither the poor and sick and
lame and blind. And the servants did as
23 the king had commanded them; and they „ 22
came, and said unto him, Lord, we have done
whatsoever thou didst command, and yet

[1] Or, "saying."

30 24 there is room here. And the lord said unto — Lu. 14 23[a]
his servants, Go out into the highways and
lanes and wider roads, and whomsoever ye — Mt. 22 9[b]
shall find, invite to the banquet, and con- — Lu. 14 23[b]
strain them to come in, that my house may
25 be filled. I say unto you, that no one of — „ 24
those men which were invited shall taste of
26 my breakfast. And the servants went out — Mt. 22 10
into the highways, and gathered together all
that they found, good and bad: and the
banqueting house was filled with those re-
27 clining. But when the king came in to see — „ 11
those reclining, he saw there a man not
28 clothed in a wedding-garment: and he saith — „ 12
unto him, Friend, how camest thou in hither
not having a wedding-garment? And he
29 was speechless. Then the king said to the — „ 13
attendants, Bind his hands and feet, and
cast him out into the outer darkness; there
shall be the weeping and gnashing of teeth.
30 Many are called, and few chosen. — „ 14
31 After these things was the Jews' feast of — Jn.[1] 5 1[a]
unleavened *bread;* and Jesus went forth to — Lu.[2] 17 11
32 go unto Jerusalem. And as he was making — „[3] 12
the journey[4] there met him ten leprous men,
33 which stood afar off: and they lifted up — „ 13
their cry, saying, Jesus, Master, have mercy
34 on us. And when he saw them, he said — „ 14
unto them, Go and shew yourselves unto the
priests. And when they went, they were
35 cleansed. And one of them, when he saw — „ 15
that he was cleansed, turned back, and with
36 a loud voice praised God; and he fell upon — „ 16
his face before the feet of Jesus, giving him
37 thanks: and he was a Samaritan. Jesus — „ 17
answered, and said, Were not they that were
cleansed ten? and the nine, where are they?

[1] Repeated from xxii. 9 with variation. [2] Part only, and varied.
[3] Varied: omitting "through the midst of Samaria and Galilee."
[4] Or, "going in the way."

30 38 Not even one of them hath turned aside to Lu. 17 18
come and give glory to God, save this one,
39 who is of an alien tribe. He saith unto „ 19
him, Arise, go thy way: thy faith hath
40 made thee whole. And as they were in the Mk.[1] 10 32
way, going up to Jerusalem, Jesus was going
before them: and they were amazed; and
they were following him afraid. And he
took his twelve disciples apart, and began
to make known to them, between himself
and them, the things that were going to
41 happen unto him. For he saith unto them, Lu. 18 31[b]
We are going up to Jerusalem, and all the
things that are written in the prophets concerning the Son of man shall be accomplished.
42 He shall be delivered unto the chief priests Mk. 10 33[b]
and the scribes; and they shall condemn
him to death, and shall deliver him unto
43 the Gentiles: and they shall mock him, and „ 34[a]
scourge him, and shall spit into his face:
44 they shall condemn him: they shall crucify Lu. 18 33
and kill him: and the third day he shall
45 rise again. And they understood none of „ 34
these things; but this saying was hid from
them, and they knew not these things that
were said.
46 Then came near to him the mother of Mt. 20 20
the sons of Zebedee, herself and both her
sons, and worshipped him, and asked something of him. He said unto her, What wilt „ 21[a]
47 thou? And there came near unto him Mk. 10 35
James and John, her sons, and said unto
him, Teacher, we wish that thou shouldest
48 do for us whatsoever we shall ask. He „ 36
saith unto them, What will ye that I should
49 do for you? They said unto him, Grant „ 37
unto us that one may sit on thy right, and
the other on thy left, in thy kingdom and
50 glory. But Jesus saith unto them, Ye „ 38

[1] Varied: resuming S. Mark's order from xxix. 11.

know not what ye ask. Are ye able to
drink the cup that I am going to drink?
and to be baptized with the baptism that I
30 51 am going to be baptized with? They said Mk. 10 39
unto him, We are able. Jesus saith unto
them, The cup that I am going to drink ye
shall drink; and with the baptism that I
am going to be baptized with shall ye be
52 baptized: but that ye should sit on my „ 40
right and on my left is not mine to give:
but *it is for them* for whom my Father hath
31 1 prepared *it*. And when the ten had heard „ 41
it, they were moved with indignation at
2 James and John. And Jesus called them, „ 42
and said unto them, Ye know that the
chiefs of the Gentiles are their lords, and
their rulers are those who have dominion
3 over them. It shall not be so among you: „ 43
but whosoever shall wish to become the
greater among you, let him be your minister:
4 and whosoever shall wish to be the first of „ 44
5 you, let him be the servant of all. Even as Mt. 20 28
the Son of man also came not to be ministered unto, but to minister, and to give his
life as a ransom for many.
6 He said these things, and went round Lu. 13 22
the villages and cities, and taught, and made
7 a journey unto Jerusalem. And a certain „ 23
man asked him, Are they few that shall be
saved? Jesus answered, and saith unto
8 them, Strive to enter in through the „ 24
narrow gate: for I say unto you, Many
shall seek to enter in, and shall not find *it*.
9 From the hour, when the master of the „ 25
house shall rise up, and shut the door, ye
shall be standing without, and shall knock
at the door, and shall begin to say, Lord,
open to us; and he shall answer and say,
I say unto you,[1] I know you not whence

[1] "I tell you" removed from ver. 11.

31 10 ye are; and ye shall begin to say, We did Lu 13 26
eat in thy presence, and drink, and thou
11 didst teach in our streets; and he shall say „ 27
unto you, I know you not whence ye are;
depart from me, ye servants of iniquity.[1]
12 There shall be the weeping and gnashing of „ 28
teeth, when ye shall see Abraham, and Isaac,
and Jacob, and all the prophets, in the
kingdom of God, but yourselves cast forth
13 without. And they shall come from the „ 29
east and west, and from the north and south,
and shall recline in the kingdom of God.
14 And then the last shall become first, and „ 30
the first shall become last.
15 And when Jesus had entered and walked „[2] 19 1
16 through Jericho, a certain man Zacchaeus by „ 2
name, a rich man, and the chief of the
17 publicans, wished to see Jesus, who he was; „ 3
and could not for the closeness of the crowd,
because Zacchaeus was little in stature.
18 And he made haste and went before Jesus, „ 4
and climbed up into a sycomore tree to see
Jesus: for so he was going to pass by.
19 And when Jesus was come to the place, he „ 5
saw him, and said unto him, Zacchaeus, make
haste, and come down; to-day I must be in
20 thy house. And he made haste, and came „ 6
21 down, and received him joyfully. And when „ 7
they had all seen it, they murmured, saying,
He hath gone in to a man that is a sinner,
22 and remained. But Zacchaeus stood *still*, „ 8
and said unto Jesus, Behold, the half of my
goods, Lord, I give to the poor; and what
I have taken in excess from each man I
23 restore fourfold. Jesus saith unto him, „ 9
To-day is salvation come to this house, for-
asmuch as he also is a son of Abraham.
24 For the Son of man came to seek and to „ 10
save that which was lost.

[1] Or, "lies. [2] On this displacement of S. Luke's order see note to xxxi. 25.

31 25 And when Jesus went out from Jericho, Lu.[1] 18 35[a]
himself and his disciples, a great multitude Mt. 20 29[b]
26 followed him, and a blind man was sitting Lu. 18 35[b]
by the wayside begging: and his name was Mk. 10 46[b]
27 Bartimaeus,[2] the son of Timaeus. And hear- Lu. 18 36
ing the sound of a multitude going by, he
28 inquired who it was. They said unto him, " 37
29 Jesus of Nazareth passeth by. And when Mk. 10 47[a]
he had heard that it was Jesus, he cried Lu. 18 38
with a loud voice, saying, Jesus, thou son of
30 David, have mercy on me. And they that " 39[a]
were going in front of Jesus rebuked him,
that he should hold his peace: but he cried Mk.[3] 10 48[b]
out the more, saying, Thou son of David,
31 have mercy on me. And Jesus stood *still*, " 49
and commanded him to be called. And they
called the blind man, saying unto him, Be
of good cheer: rise, for behold, he calleth
32 thee. And the blind man, casting away " 50
his garment, stood up, and came to Jesus.
33 Jesus said unto him, What wilt thou that " 51
I should do unto thee? And the blind
man said unto him, My lord and master,
that thou mayest open mine eyes, and I
34 may see thee.[4] And Jesus had mercy on Mt. 20 34[a]
him, and touched his eyes, and said unto
him, Receive thy sight: thy faith hath Lu. 18 42[c]
35 made thee whole. And immediately he " 43
received his sight, and followed him, praising God: and all the people that saw it,
gave praise unto God.

[1] Or Mark x. 46[a]. Placed after leaving Zacchaeus's house in accordance with S. Mark's account, from which the words "went out" are taken.

[2] Arabic, "Ibn-Ṭîmî."

[3] Or Luke xviii. 39[b].

[4] This reading is in the Curetonian Syriac of S. Matthew and S. Luke. Ephraem and Aphraates do not quote it, but Ephraem's comment is "that He might be visible and manifest unto him," etc. And at Moes. p. 248, he says, "who could open the eyes of the blind, *that they might see Him.*" We may conclude that this reading is due to Tatian.

31 36 And he employed a parable,[1] for the — Lu. 19 11b
reason that he was near Jerusalem, and
because they supposed that the kingdom of
God would be made known at that time.
37 He saith unto them, A certain man of a — " 12
noble family went into a far country, to
receive for himself a kingdom, and to return.
38 And when he had called his ten servants, — " 13
he gave them ten minas, and saith unto
them, Trade ye *herewith* until my arrival.
39 But his citizens hated him, and sent ambas- — " 14
sadors after him, saying, We do not wish
40 this man to reign over us. And when he — " 15
came back again, having received the kingdom, he commanded the servants, unto
whom he gave the money, to be called to
him, that he might know how much each
41 one had traded. And the first came, saying, — " 16
Lord, thy mina hath acquired ten minas
42 more. The king said unto him, O thou — " 17
good and faithful servant, who hast been
found faithful in a very little, be thou
43 holding authority over ten districts. And — " 18
another came, saying, Lord, thy mina hath
44 gained five minas. And to this man he — " 19
said, Thou also shalt be holding authority
45 over five districts. And another came, say- — " 20
ing, Lord, behold thy mina, which I kept
46 laid up in a napkin: I feared thee, because — " 21
thou art an austere man: thou takest up
that which thou layedst not down, thou
exactest that which thou gavest not, and
47 reapest that which thou sowedst not. His — " 22
lord said unto him, Out of thy mouth I
judge thee, thou wicked servant, negli-
gent[2] and unfaithful.[3] Thou knewest

[1] Tatian does not identify this parable with that of the talents (Matt. xxv. 14–30), which he inserts at xliii. 22–38.

[2] Cf. Matt. xxv. 26, "slothful."

[3] Curetonian Syriac, "that art not faithful."

that I am an austere man, taking up that
which I laid not down, and reaping that
31 48 which I sowed not; wherefore didst thou Lu. 19 23
not place my money at the bank, so that at
my coming I might have exacted it with
49 interest? And he said unto them that „ 24
stood by, Take away from him the mina,
and give it unto him that hath the ten
50 minas. They said unto him, Lord, he hath „ 25
51 ten minas. He saith unto them, I say unto „ 26
you, Unto every one that hath shall be
given; but from him that hath not, even
that which he hath shall be taken away
52 from him. Howbeit those mine enemies, „ 27
which did not wish me to reign over them,
bring hither, and slay them before me.
32 1[1] And when Jesus had entered Jerusalem, Mt. 21 12[a]
he went up into the temple of God; and he Jn. 2 14[a]
2 found there oxen, sheep, and doves. And Mt. 21 12[b]
when he saw them that sold and bought, Jn. 2 14[b]
and the money changers sitting, he made „ 15
for himself a scourge of cords, and cast all
of them out of the temple, the sheep also,
and the oxen, and the money changers,
whose money he poured out, and overthrew
the tables, and the seats of them that sold Mt. 21 12[c]
3 the doves; and he was teaching and saying „[2] 13
unto them, Is it not written, My house is a
house of prayer for all nations: but ye have
4 made it a den of robbers? And to them Jn. 2 16
that sold the doves he said, Take these
things hence; and make not my Father's
5 house a house of merchandise. And he Mk. 11 16
suffered not that any man should carry
6 vessels through the temple. And his dis- Jn. 2 17
ciples remembered the scripture, The zeal

[1] Most modern harmonists agree in recognising two Cleansings; but Tischendorf admits that it is a great question.

[2] Mk. xi. 17 seems to agree more closely with the text than the reference given in the Arabic.

9

32 7 of thine house hath eaten me up. The Jn. 2 18
Jews answered and said unto him, What
sign shewest thou unto us, that thou
8 shouldest do this? Jesus answered, and „ 19
said unto them, Destroy this temple, and in
9 three days I will raise it up. The Jews „ 20
said unto him, In forty and six years was
this temple built, and wilt thou raise it up
10 in three days? But[1] he spake unto them „ 21
of the temple of his body: that when they
destroyed it, he would raise it up in three
11 days. And when he rose again from the „ 22
dead, his disciples remembered that he had
said this; and they believed the scriptures,
12 and the saying that Jesus spake. And Mk. 12 41
Jesus sat down[2] over against the treasury,
and observed how the multitudes cast their
offerings into the treasury: and many that
13 were rich cast in much. And there came „ 42a
a poor widow, and she cast in two mites.[3]
14 And Jesus called his disciples, and said unto Lu.[4] 21 3
them, Verily I say unto you, This poor
widow cast in more than *they* all into the
15 treasury: for all these did cast in of the Mk. 12 44
superfluity of their substance into the ark[5]
of the offering of God; but she of her want
did cast all that she possessed.[6]
16 And he set before them this parable[7] Lu. 18 9
about certain which trusted in themselves
that they were righteous, and despised the
17 rest. Two men went up into the temple „ 10
to pray; the one a Pharisee, and the other

[1] Aphraates has, "And his disciples understood that he spake of his body, in that he would, after they had broken it, raise it up in three days."

[2] Placed a little earlier than the evangelists have it, but during the same visit to Jerusalem.

[3] Omitting Mark xii. 42b, "which make a farthing."

[4] Or Mark xii. 43 slightly varied.

[5] Lit. "house."

[6] Omitting "*even* all her living."

[7] S. Luke puts this parable before the arrival at Jericho. Tatian seems to have thought it likely from its nature to have been spoken in the temple.

32 18 a publican. The Pharisee stood and prayed Lu. 18 11
thus with himself, Lord, I thank thee, that I
am not as the rest of men, unjust, adulterers,
19 extortioners, or even as this publican. But „ 12
I fast twice in the week, and I give tithes
20 of all my substance. And the publican, „ 13
standing afar off, would not lift up even
his eyes unto heaven, but smote his breast,
saying, Lord, be propitious to me the
21 sinner. I say unto you, This man went „ 14
down to his house justified more than the
Pharisee: Every[1] one that exalteth himself
shall be humbled; and every one that
humbleth himself shall be exalted.
22 And when evening was come, he left { Mk.[2] 11 19a
them all, and went forth outside the city { Mt. 21 17
to Bethany, himself and the twelve, and was
23 there. And all the people, because they Lu.[3] 9 11
knew the place, came unto him; and he
received them; and he healed those that
24 had need of healing. And on the morning Mk. 11 12
after, when he returned from Bethany to
25 the city, he hungered. And he saw from „ 13
afar beside the road a fig-tree having leaves,
and he came to it, that he might find something on it: and when he was come, he
found nothing on it but leaves; for it was
26 not the season of figs. And he said unto it, „ 14
Henceforward and for ever no man shall eat
fruit from thee.[4] And his disciples heard it.
27 And they came to Jerusalem. Now { Mk. 11 15a
there was there a man of the Pharisees, { Jn. 3 1
named Nicodemus,[5] a ruler of the Jews:

[1] Cf xxx. 5 and xl. 40.

[2] Tatian may have meant this for Mark xi. 11b, especially as Mark xi. 12 follows in ver. 24. He gives Mark xi. 19 at xxxiii. 1.

[3] Repeated with variations from xviii. 26. Tatian exercised considerable freedom with general statements of this class.

[4] Omitting Matt. xxi. 19: "And presently the fig-tree withered away."

[5] The account of this interview is naturally moved along with S. John's

32 28 this man came to Jesus by night, and Jn. 3 2
said unto him, Teacher, we know that thou
wast sent from God as a teacher: for no
man can do these signs that thou doest,
29 except he with whom God is. Jesus answered, " 3
and said unto him, Verily, verily, I say unto
thee, except a man be born anew, he cannot
30 see the kingdom of God. Nicodemus said " 4
unto him, How can a man be born *when he*
is old? can he again enter a second time
into his mother's womb, and be born?
31 Jesus answered, and said unto him, Verily, " 5
verily, I say unto thee, Except a man be
born of water and the Spirit, he cannot
32 enter into the kingdom of God. That which " 6
is born of the flesh is flesh; and that which is
33 born of the Spirit is spirit. Marvel not that " 7
I said unto thee, Ye must be born anew.
34 The wind bloweth where it will, and thou " 8
hearest the voice thereof, but knowest not
whence it cometh, and whither it goeth:
so is every one that is born of the Spirit.
35 Nicodemus answered, and said unto him, " 9
36 How can this be? Jesus answered, and " 10
said unto him, Art thou a teacher of Israel,
37 and art ignorant of these things? Verily, " 11
verily, I say unto thee, We speak that which
we know, and testify that which we have
38 seen; and ye receive not our witness. If I " 12
told you earthly[1] things, and ye believe not,
how shall ye believe, if I tell you heavenly[2]
39 things? And no man hath ascended into " 13
heaven, but he that descended out of heaven,

version of the Cleansing of the Temple, since they clearly belong to the same visit to Jerusalem. From its nature such an interview would seem more likely, when Jesus was well known, and had come to stay at Jerusalem. Professor Fuller observes, "This position ignores John vii. 50; and has not been imitated." This is not accurate, since that allusion to Nicodemus does not occur in the *Diatessaron* until xxxv. 14.

[1] Lit. "what is in the earth." [2] Lit. "what is in heaven."

even the Son of man, which is in heaven.[1]
32 40 And as Moses lifted up the serpent in the Jn. 3 14
wilderness, even so is the Son of man about
41 to be lifted up: that everyone that believeth „ 15
on him may not perish, but have eternal life.
42 God so loved the world that he gave his „ 16
only Son, that everyone that believeth in
him should not perish, but have eternal life.
43 God sent not his Son into the world to „ 17
judge the world; but that the world should
44 be saved through him. He that believeth „ 18
in him is not judged: he that believeth not
is judged already, because he believeth not
45 in the name of the only Son of God. This „ 19
is the judgment: the light is come into the
world, and men loved the darkness rather
than the light; for their works were evil.
46 Everyone that worketh infamies hateth the „ 20
light, and cometh not to the light, that his
47 works may not be reproved. But he that „ 21
worketh truth cometh to the light, that his
works may be recognised, that they have
been wrought in God.[2]
33 1 And when the evening was come, Jesus Mk.[3] 11 19
went forth outside the city, himself and his
2 disciples. And as they passed by in the „ 20
morning, the disciples saw that fig-tree
3 withered away from the root. And as they Mt. 21 20b
went by, they said, How did the fig-tree
4 wither away already? And Simon, calling Mk. 11 21
to remembrance, said unto him, Teacher,[4]
behold, that fig-tree which thou cursedst, is
5 withered away. And Jesus answering saith „ 22

[1] Ephraem omits "which is in heaven;" this does not prove that he had not this clause; but that is probable, as it is wanting in some of the best Greek MSS.

[2] The *Codex Fuldensis* inserts here John viii. 1–11 (the Woman taken in Adultery), followed by the Cursing of the Fig-tree given above, ver. 24–26.

[3] Part of this verse occurred at xxxii. 22a. See note there.

[4] Or, "Master."

unto them, Let the faith of God be in you.
33 6 Verily I say unto you, If ye shall believe, Mk.[1] 11 23
and shall not be undecided in your hearts,
and shall hold it as certain, that whatsoever
ye shall say is coming to pass, whatsoever
ye shall say shall come to pass unto you.
7 Even if ye shall say unto this mountain, Mt. 21 21[b]
Remove, and fall into the sea, it shall be
8 done. And all things, whatsoever ye shall „ 22
ask of God in prayer, believing, he shall give
you.
9 And the apostles said unto the Lord, In- Lu.[2] 17 5
10 crease our faith. He said unto them, If „ 6
there be in you faith as a grain of mustard
seed, ye shall say unto this fig-tree, Be thou
rooted up, and be thou transplanted into the
11 sea, and it shall obey you. Who is there of „ 7
you, having a servant guiding[3] oxen or feeding sheep, to whom, when he cometh from the
field, he saith straightway, Go, and lie down
12 *to meat?* But he will say unto him, Make „ 8
ready for me wherewith I may sup, and gird
thy loins, and serve me, until I eat and
drink; and afterward thou also shalt eat
13 and drink? Will that servant who did the „ 9
thing that he had commanded him, receive
14 his thanks? I think not. Even so ye also, „ 10
when ye shall have done all the things that
are commanded you, say, We are unprofitable
servants; we have done that which it was
our duty to do.
15 Therefore I say unto you, All things, Mk. 11 24
whatsoever ye pray and ask for, believe
that ye shall receive them, and they
16 shall be unto you. And when ye stand „ 25
for praying, forgive that which ye have in

[1] With the first part of Matt. xxi. 21.

[2] S. Luke is not very definite as to when this occurred. Tatian has put it where it would illustrate the previous narrative.

[3] Perhaps equivalent to the Authorised Version, "plowing."

your heart against *any* man; and your
Father which is in the heavens shall forgive
33 17 you also your trespasses.[1] And if ye for- Mk. 11 26
give not men their trespasses,[1] neither
will your Father forgive you also your
trespasses.[1]
18 And he set forth also a parable[2] unto Lu. 18 1
them to the end that they should always
19 pray, and not be slothful. There was in „ 2
a city a judge, which feared not God, and
20 regarded not men: and there was a widow „ 3
in that city; and she came unto him,
saying, Avenge me of mine adversary.
21 And he would not for a long time: after- „ 4
wards he said within himself, Though I
22 fear not God, nor regard men, yet because „ 5
of the importunity of this widow, I will
avenge her, that she may not come per-
23 petually, and bring me weariness. And „ 6
our Lord said, Hear what the judge of un-
24 righteousness said. And shall not God per- „ 7
form still more the avenging of his elect,
which cry to him day and night, and be
25 longsuffering[3] in respect to them? I say „ 8
unto you, He will perform the avenging of
them speedily. When the Son of man
cometh, think you he will find faith on the
earth?
26, 27 And they came again to Jerusalem. And { Mk.[4] 11 15[a]; Lu. 20 1 }
it came to pass, on one of the days, as
Jesus was walking, and teaching the people
in the temple, and announcing the good
tidings, there stood near him the chief
priests and the scribes with the elders;
28 and they said unto him, Tell us: By what Lu. 20 2[a]
authority doest thou this? and who gave Mk. 11 28[b]

[1] Or, "follies."

[2] Placed here because it relates to the subject of prayer now being referred to.

[3] Or, "tarry."

[4] A mistake for 27[a]. Cf. xxxii. 27[a].

33 29 thee this authority to do this? And Jesus { Mk. 11 29[a] / Mt. 21 24[b] }
saith unto them, I also will ask you one
word; and if ye tell me, I also will tell
30 ye by what authority I do this. The bap- Mt. 21 25[a]
tism of John, whence was it? from heaven
31 or from men? tell me. But they reasoned { Mk. 11 30[b] / Mt. 21 25[b] }
among themselves, saying, If[1] we shall say
unto him, From heaven, he will say unto
32 us, Why did ye not believe him? But if Mt. 21 26[a]
we shall say, From men, we fear that all Lu. 20 6[b]
33 the people may stone us: for all held, that Mk. 11 32[b]
34 John was a true prophet. They answered, " 33
and said unto him, We know not. Jesus
saith unto them, Neither tell I you by
what authority I do *these things.*

35 What think ye? A certain man had two Mt. 21 28
sons; and he came to the first, and said unto
him, My son, go to-day, and work[2] in the
36 vineyard. He answereth, and saith, I will " 29
not: but at last he repented himself, and
37 went. And he came to the other, and said " 30
unto him likewise. And he answered and
38 said, Yea, sir: and went not. Which of " 31
these two did the will of his father? They
said unto him, The first. Jesus saith unto
them, Verily I say unto you, The publicans
and the harlots go before you into the king-
39 dom of God. John came unto you in the " 32
way of righteousness, and ye believed him
not: but the publicans and the harlots believed him: but ye, not even after ye had
seen it, did ye at last repent, that ye might
believe him.

40 Hear another parable: There was a man, " 33[a]
a householder, which planted a vineyard, and
set a hedge about it, and digged a winepress
41 in it, and built a tower in it, and granted it Lu. 20 9[b]
to husbandmen, and was abroad for a long
42 time. And when the season of the fruits Mt. 21 34

[1] Ver. 26 begins here as in the Vulgate. [2] Or. "till."

had come near, he sent his servant[1] to the
husbandmen, that they might send him of
33 43 the fruits of his vineyard. But these hus- Mk. 12 3
bandmen beat him, and sent him away empty.
44 And again he sent unto them another ser- „ 4
vant; and they stoned and wounded him,
45 and sent him away shamefully handled. And „ 5[a]
again he sent another; and him they killed:
and many other servants sent he unto them.
46[2]And the husbandmen took his servants, Mt. 21 35
and beat one, and stoned another, and killed
47 another. Again, he sent other servants „ 36
more than the former: and they did unto
48 them in like manner. And the lord of the Lu. 20 13
vineyard said, What shall I do? I will
send my beloved son: for perchance they
49 will see him, and reverence him. At last he Mk. 12 6[a]
50 sent unto them his beloved son.[3] But the Mt. 21 38[a]
husbandmen, when they saw the son, said
51 among themselves, This is the heir; and Lu. 20 14[b]
they said, Let us kill him, and the inherit-
52 ance will be ours. And they took him, and Mt. 21 39
brought him forth outside the vineyard, and
53 killed him. When therefore the lord of the „ 40
vineyard cometh, what will he do unto those
54 husbandmen? They said unto him, He will „ 41
miserably destroy the miserable men, and
will let out the vineyard unto other husbandmen, who will render him the fruits in
55 their seasons.[4] Jesus said unto them, Did „ 42[a]
ye never read in the scripture,

The stone which the builders rejected,
The same was made into the head of the Lu.[5] 20 17[b]
corner:

[1] Arabic, "servants," but see "him" in ver. 43.

[2] Ver. 46, 47 appear to repeat from S. Matthew the substance of ver. 42-45.

[3] Lit. "his beloved son which was his."

[4] Omitting Luke xx. 16[b]: "And when they heard it, they said, God forbid."

[5] Or continuation of Matt. xxi. 42.

33 56 This was done by God; Mt. 21 42c
And it is marvellous in our eyes?
57 Therefore I say unto you, The kingdom „ 43
of God shall be taken away from you, and
shall be given to a nation bringing forth
58 fruits. And whosoever falleth on this „ 44
stone, shall be broken to pieces: but on
whomsoever it shall fall, it will grind him
59 to powder. And when the chief priests and „ 45
the Pharisees had heard his parables, they
60 perceived that he spake of them. And[1] „ 46
they sought to lay hold on him; and they
feared the multitudes, because they regarded
him as a prophet.

34 1 Then the Pharisees went away, and took „ 22 15
counsel how they might catch him in *his*
talk, and deliver him up to the authority Lu. 20 20b
of the court, and to the authority of the
2 governor. And they sent to him their Mt. 22 16
disciples with the Herodians,[2] saying unto
him, Teacher, we know that thou art true,
and teachest the way of God in truth, and
carest not for anyone: for thou regardest
3 not man. Tell us therefore, What thinkest „ 17
thou? Is it lawful to give tribute unto
Caesar, or not? Shall we give, or shall Mk.[3] 12 15a
4 we not give? But Jesus, knowing their
craftiness, saith unto them, Why tempt ye Mt. 22 18b
5 me, ye hypocrites? Show me the tribute „ 19
penny. And they brought unto him a
6 penny. Jesus saith unto them, Whose is „ 20
7 this image and inscription? They said unto „ 21
him, Caesar's. He said unto them, Render
unto Caesar the things that are Caesar's;
and unto God the things that are God's.
8 And they could not bring[4] it to pass that Lu. 20 26

[1] Omitting Luke xx. 19, "the same hour."
[2] Omitting Luke xx. 20, "spies, which should feign themselves just men."
[3] Part of this is called 14b, as in the Vulgate.
[4] "Bring . . . fall," or "succeed in making him slip."

he should fall in his speech before the people:
and they marvelled at his saying, and restrained themselves.[1]
34 9 On that day there came Sadducees, and — Mt. 22 23
said unto him, The dead have no life: and
10 they asked him, saying unto him, Master, — „ 24
Moses said unto us, If a man die, having no
children, let his brother marry his wife, and
11 raise up seed unto his brother. Now there — „ 25[a]
were with us seven brethren: and the first — Lu. 20 29[b]
took a wife, and died without children;[2]
12 and the next took his wife, and died without — „ 30
13 children; and the third also took her; and — „ 31
likewise all the seven, and they died without
14 leaving a child. And at the last of all of — Mt. 22 27
15 them the woman also died. In the resur- — „ 28
rection therefore[3] whose wife shall she be
of these seven? for they all took her.
16 Jesus answered, and saith unto them, Do ye — {Mt. 22 29; Mk. 12 24[b]}
not therefore err, because ye know not the
17 scriptures, nor the power of God? The sons — Lu. 20 34[b]
of this age marry wives; and the women are
18 delivered up to husbands: but they that — „ 35
shall be accounted worthy of that age, and
the resurrection from the dead, shall not
marry wives; nor shall the women be for
19 husbands: nor shall they be able to die any — „ 36
more: but they shall be even as the angels[4]
and the sons of God, because they have been
20 made sons of the resurrection. Moreover, — Mt. 22 31[a]
concerning the resurrection of the dead,
have ye not read in the book of Moses, how — Mk. 12 26[b]
God said unto him out of the bramble bush,
I am the God of Abraham, and the God of
21 Isaac, and the God of Jacob? Now he is — Lu. 20 38
not the God of the dead, but of the living:

[1] Omitting Matt. xxii. 22, "and left him, and went their way."
[2] Omitting Matt. xxii. 25, "left his wife unto his brother."
[3] Omitting Mark xii. 23, "when they shall rise."
[4] Omitting Mark xii. 25, "which are in heaven."

for all live with him. Ye therefore do Mk. 12 27[b]
greatly err.
34 22 And when the multitudes heard it, they Mt. 22 33
23 were astonished at his teaching. And cer- Lu. 20 39
tain of the scribes answering said unto him,
24 Teacher, thou hast well said. But all the Mt. 22 34
Pharisees, when they had seen that he had
put the Sadducees to silence in this way,
assembled themselves together against him,
25 to strive with him. And one of the scribes, " 35[a]
a doctor of the law, when he had seen the Mk. 12 28[b]
appropriateness of his answer to them,
26 wished to tempt him, saying, What shall I Lu.[1] 10 25[b]
do to inherit eternal life? and which is the Mk.[1] 12 28[c]
greater and first commandment in the law?
27 Jesus said unto him, The first command- " 29
ment of all is, Hear, O Israel; The Lord our
28 God, the Lord is one: and: Thou shalt love " 30[a]
the Lord thy God from all thy heart, and
from all thy soul, and from all thy mind, Mt. 22 37[b]
29 and from all thy strength. This is the " 38
30 greatest and first commandment. But *there* Mk. 12 31
is a second, which is like unto it, Thou shalt
love thy neighbour as thyself. There is no
other commandment greater than these.
31 From these two commandments hangeth the Mt. 22 40
32 law, and the prophets. The scribe saith Mk. 12 32
unto him, An excellent opinion, Master!
with truth thou hast said that *God* is one,
33 and there is none other but he: and that a " 33
man should love him from all his heart, and
from all his mind, and from all his soul, and
from all his strength, and that he should love
his neighbour as himself, is a better thing
than all the burnt offerings and sacrifices.
34 And when Jesus saw that he had answered " 34[a]
discreetly, he answered, and said unto him,

[1] Modern harmonisers do not combine these passages, but assign to S. Luke's incident an earlier place in the narrative, and thus avoid combining the two questions. Tatian puts the result in the order of the two first evangelists.

Thou art not far from the kingdom of God.
34 35 Thou hast said the right word: this do, and Lu. 10 28[b]
36 thou shalt live. But he, desiring to justify „ 29
himself, said unto him, And who is my
37 neighbour? Jesus said unto him, A certain „ 30
man was going down from Jerusalem to
Jericho; and robbers fell upon him, which
plundered him, and having beaten him
38 departed, leaving him half dead.[1] And it „ 31
happened that a certain priest was going
down the same way: and when he saw him,
39 he passed by. In like manner came a „ 32
Levite also, and when he reached the place,
40 and saw him, he passed on. But a certain „ 33
Samaritan, as he journeyed, when he came
to the place where he was, and saw him,
41 had compassion on him, and came near, and „ 34
bound up his wounds, pouring on *them* wine
and oil; and he set him on an ass, and
brought him to an inn, and took care of
42 him. And on the next day he took out „ 35
two pence, and gave them to the host, and
saith unto him, Take care of him; and
whatsoever thou spendest more, I, when I
43 come back again, will repay thee. Which „ 36
of these three seems to thee to have been
more a neighbour unto him that fell among
44 the robbers? He said unto him, He that „ 37
had compassion on him. Jesus saith unto
45 him, Go, and do thou likewise. And no man Mk. 12 34[b]
ventured to ask him anything after that.
46 And he was teaching daily in the temple. Lu. 19 47
But the chief priests and the scribes and the
elders of the people sought to destroy him:
47 and they could not do anything to him; for „ 48
all the people were in suspense to hear him.
48 Now of the multitude many believed on Jn.[2] 7 31

[1] Lit. "with only his soul left in him."
[2] Repeated from xxviii. 32.

him, and said, Will the Messiah, when he
cometh, do more signs than those which this
34 49 man doeth? And the Pharisees heard the Jn. 7 32
multitudes saying these things concerning
him; and the chief priests sent soldiers to
50 take him. And Jesus said unto them, Yet „ 33
a little while am I with you, and I shall go
51 unto him that sent me. And ye shall seek „ 34
me, and shall not find me: and where I am,
52 ye cannot come. The Jews said among „ 35
themselves, Whither is this man about to
go, so that we shall not be able to go? Do
you think, that he is about to go unto the
countries of the Gentiles, and teach the
53 heathen? What is this word that he said, „ 36
Ye shall seek me, and shall not find me:
and where I am, ye cannot come?
35 1 Now on the great day, the last of the „ 37
festival, Jesus stood, crying and saying, If
any man is thirsty, let him come unto me,
2 and drink. Everyone that believeth on me, „ 38
even as the scriptures say, out of his belly
3 shall flow rivers of sweet water. This spake „ 39
he signifying the Spirit, which they that
believed on him were about to receive: for
the Spirit had not yet been given, because
4 Jesus had not yet been glorified. And many „ 40
of the multitude that heard his words,
said, This is of a truth the prophet. And
5 some said, This is the Messiah. But others „ 41
said, Shall the Messiah come from Galilee?
6 Doth not the scripture say that the Messiah „ 42
shall come of the offspring of David, and
7 from Bethlehem the village of David? So „ 43
there arose a disagreement in the multitude
8 because of him. And some of them wished „ 44
to take him; and no man laid hand on him.
9 And the soldiers came to the chief priests „ 45
and Pharisees; and the priests said unto
10 them, Why did ye not bring him? The „ 46

soldiers said, Never man so spake, as this
35 11 man speaketh. The Pharisees said unto Jn. 7 47
12 them, Are ye also led astray? Hath anyone „ 48
of the rulers or of the Pharisees believed in
13 him? except this multitude which knoweth „ 49
14 not the law, who are accursed? Nicodemus, „ 50
one of themselves, who came to Jesus by
15 night, said unto them, Doth our law judge a „ 51
man, except it shall before have heard from
16 himself, and known what he doeth? They „ 52
answered, and said unto him, Art thou also
of Galilee? Search, and see, for from
Galilee ariseth no prophet.
17 Now when the Pharisees were gathered Mt. 22 41
18 together, Jesus asked them a question, saying, „ 42
What say ye of the Messiah? whose son is
he? They said unto him, The son of David.
19 He saith unto them, How then doth David „ 43
in the Holy Spirit call him Lord, for he
saith,
20 The Lord said unto my Lord, „ 44
Sit thou on my right hand,
That I may put thine enemies underneath
thy feet.
21 If David then calleth him Lord, how is he „ 45
22 his son? And no one was able to answer „ 46
him; neither did any man venture from that
day forth to ask him about any matter.
23 And again Jesus spake unto them, saying, Jn. 8 12
I am the light of the world: he therefore
that followeth me, doth not walk in the
darkness, but shall find the light of life.
24 The Pharisees said unto him, Thou bearest „ 13
witness of thyself; thy witness is not genuine.
25 Jesus answered, and said unto them, If I bear „ 14
witness of myself, my witness is genuine;
for I know whence I came, and whither I
go; but ye know not whence I came, nor
26 whither I go. For ye judge a material „ 15
27 judgment; but I judge no man. And if I „ 16

judge, my judgment is genuine; for I am
not alone, but I and my Father that sent
35 28 me. And in your law it is written, that the Jn. 8 17
29 witness of two men is genuine. I am he „ 18
that beareth witness of myself; and my
Father that sent me beareth witness of me.
30 They said unto him, Where is thy Father? „ 19
Jesus answered, and saith unto them, Ye
know me not, nor my Father: for if ye
knew me, ye would know my Father.
31 These words spake he in the treasury, as „ 20
he taught in the temple: and no man took
him, because his hour was not yet come.
32 Jesus said again unto them, I go away „ 21
indeed; and ye shall seek me, and shall not
find me, and shall die in your sins: and
33 whither I go ye cannot come. The Jews „ 22
said, Will he kill himself, that he may say,
34 Whither I go ye cannot come? He saith „ 23
unto them, Ye are from beneath; but I am
from above: ye are of this world; and I
35 am not of this world. I said unto you, Ye „ 24
shall die in your sins: if ye believe not that
36 I am *he*,[1] ye shall die in your sins. The „ 25
Jews said, And who art thou? Jesus said
37 unto them, If I begin to speak unto you, I „ 26
have many things to speak concerning you,
and to judge: but he that sent me is true;
and the things which I heard from him,
38 these speak I in the world. And they „ 27
understood not that he referred to the
39 Father in this. Jesus said again unto „ 28
them, When ye have lifted up the Son of
man, then shall ye perceive that I am *he*,[1]
and *that* I do nothing of myself, but as the
40 Father taught me, so I speak. And he that „ 29
sent me is with me; for my Father hath
not left me alone; for I do always the
41 things that are pleasing to him. As he „ 30

[1] Lit. "I am I."

spake these things many believed on him.
35 42 And Jesus said to those Jews which Jn. 8 31
believed on him, If ye abide in my word,
43 ye shall be truly my disciples; and ye shall „ 32
know the truth; and the truth shall make
44 you free. They said unto him, We are the „ 33
offspring of Abraham, and have never served
any man as bondsmen: how then sayest
45 thou, Ye shall be free children? Jesus „ 34
said unto them, Verily, verily, I say unto
you, Everyone that committeth sin is the
46 bondservant of sin. And the bondservant „ 35
abideth not in the house for ever: but the
47 son abideth for ever. If therefore the Son „ 36
shall make you free, ye shall be free chil-
48 dren indeed. I know that ye are the off- „ 37
spring of Abraham; yet ye seek to kill me,
49 because ye are unequal to[1] my word. For „ 38
I speak that which I have seen with my
Father: and ye do that which ye have seen
50 with your father. They answered, and said „ 39
unto him, Our father is Abraham. Jesus
said unto them, If ye were Abraham's children, ye would do the works of Abraham.
51 Now, behold, ye seek to kill me, a man that „ 40
speaketh the truth with you, which I have
heard from God: this did not Abraham.
52 But ye do the works of your father. They „ 41
said unto him, We are not of fornication;
53 we have one father, which is God. Jesus „ 42
said unto them, If God were your Father,
ye would certainly have loved me. I came
forth from God, and came down; nor have
54 I come of myself, but he sent me. For why „ 43
do ye not perceive my word? *Even* because
55 ye cannot hear my word. Ye are of *your* „ 44
father the devil, and the desire of your
father ye wish to do, who is a murderer
from the beginning, and abideth[2] not in the

[1] Or, "too weak for." [2] Or, "standeth."

truth, because there is no truth in him:
and when he speaketh a lie, he speaketh of
his own: for he is a liar, and the father of
35 56 lies. And I, that speak in the truth, ye Jn. 8 45
57 believe me not. Which of you rebuketh „ 46
me of sin? And if I say the truth, ye do
58 not believe me. He that is of God heareth „ 47
the words of God: for this cause ye hear
59 *them* not, because ye are not of God. The „ 48
Jews answered, and said unto him, Said we
not well that thou art a Samaritan, and
60 hast a devil? Jesus saith unto them, I „ 49
certainly have not a devil; but I honour
61 my Father, and ye dishonour me. I seek „ 50
not mine own glory: here is one who
36 1 seeketh and judgeth. Verily, verily, I say „ 51
unto you, Whosoever keepeth my saying
2 shall never see death. The Jews said unto „ 52
him, Now we know that thou hast a devil.
Abraham is dead, and the prophets; and
thou sayest, Whosoever keepeth my saying
3 shall never taste death. Art thou greater „ 53
than our father Abraham, which is dead?
and the prophets, which are dead? whom
4 makest thou thyself? Jesus saith unto „ 54
them, If I glorify myself, my glory is
nothing: it is my Father that glorifieth
5 me, of whom ye say, He is our God; and „ 55
ye know him not: but I know him; and if
I say, I know him not, I shall be a liar like
unto you: but I know him, and keep his
6 saying. Your father Abraham longed with „ 56
burning eagerness[1] to see my day; and he
7 saw it, and was glad. The Jews said unto „ 57
him, Thou art not yet fifty years old, and
8 hast thou seen Abraham? Jesus said unto „ 58
them, Verily, verily, I say unto you, Before
9 Abraham was, I am. And they took stones „ 59
to stone him: but Jesus hid himself, and

[1] Or, "earnestly longed."

went out of the temple, and[1] passing among
them went away.
36 10 And as he passed by, he saw a man blind Jn. 9 1
11 from his mother's womb. And his disciples " 2
asked him, Master, who did sin, this man or
12 his parents, that he was born blind? Jesus " 3
saith unto them, Neither did this man sin,
nor his parents: but that the works of God
13 may be made manifest in him. I must work " 4
the works of him that sent me, while the
day lasts: the night will come, and no man
14 will be able to work at will. As long as I " 5
am in the world, I am the light of the world.
15 When he had said these things, he spat on " 6
the ground, and made clay of the spittle, and
rubbed it upon the eyes of the blind man,
16 and said unto him, Go, wash in the bath " 7
of Siloam. He went away therefore, and
17 washed, and came seeing. And his neigh- " 8
bours which had seen him beg aforetime,
said, Is not this he that sat begging? Some
18 said, It is he: and others said, Not at all, " 9
but he is exactly like him. He said, I am
19 he. They said unto him, How then were " 10
20 thine eyes opened? He answered, and saith " 11
unto them, A man whose name is Jesus
made clay, and rubbed it upon mine eyes,
and said unto me, Go, and wash in the water
of Siloam; so I went away, and washed, and
21 received sight. They said unto him, Where " 12
is he? He saith, I know not.
22 And they brought to the Pharisees him " 13
23 that had before been blind. Now the day " 14
on which Jesus made the clay, and opened
24 his eyes, was the day of the sabbath. And " 15
again the Pharisees asked him: How didst
thou receive thy sight? He said unto them,
He put clay upon mine eyes; and I washed,
25 and received sight. Some of the Pharisees " 16

[1] The rest of this verse is called 60, and is absent from the Vulgate.

said, This man is not from God, because he
keepeth not the sabbath. But others said,
How can a man that is a sinner do these
signs? And a division took place among
36 26 them. And again they said unto the blind Jn. 9 17
man, What sayest thou of him that opened
thine eyes for thee? He said unto them, I
27 say, that he is a prophet. And the Jews „ 18
did not believe concerning him, that he had
been blind, and had received his sight, until
they called the parents of him that had
28 received his sight; and they asked them: Is „ 19
this your son, of whom ye say, that he was
born blind? how then doth he now see?
29 His parents answered, and said, We know „ 20
that this is our son, and that he was born
30 blind: but how he now seeth, or who opened „ 21
his eyes, we know not: ask him; he is
already arrived at the age of manhood, and
31 he may speak for himself. These things „ 22
said his parents, because they feared the
Jews: for the Jews had decided already, that
if any man should confess him to be the
Messiah, they would expel him from the
32 synagogue. Therefore said his parents, He „ 23
is arrived at the age of manhood; ask him.
33 And they called a second time him that had „ 24
been blind, and said unto him, Give glory to
God: we know that this man is a sinner.
34 He answered, and saith unto them, Whether „ 25
he be a sinner I know not: one thing I
know, that, whereas I was blind, now I see.
35 They said again unto him, What did he to „ 26
thee? how opened he thine eyes for thee?
36 He saith unto them, I told you, and ye did „ 27
not hear: wherefore do ye wish to hear it
again? do ye also wish to become his dis-
37 ciples? And they despised him, and said „ 28
unto him, Thou art his disciple; but we are
38 disciples of Moses. For we know that God „ 29

hath spoken unto Moses: but as for this
36 39 man, we know not whence he is. The man Jn. 9 30
answered, and said unto them, Therefore
indeed is the marvel, that ye know not
whence he is, and *yet* he opened mine eyes.
40 And we know that God heareth not the „ 31
voice of sinners: but he that feareth him,
41 and doeth his will, him he heareth. From „ 32
eternity it was never heard that anyone
opened the eyes of a blind man, born in
42 blindness. Therefore if this man were not „ 33
43 from God, he could not do this. They „ 34
answered, and said unto him, Thou wast
altogether born in sins, and dost thou teach
us? And they cast him out.
44 And Jesus heard of his casting out; and „ 35
finding him, he said unto him, Dost thou
45 believe on the Son of God? He that had „ 36
been made whole, answered, and said, Who
is he, Lord, that I may believe on him?
46 Jesus said unto him, Thou hast seen him, „ 37
47 and he it is that speaketh with thee. He „ 38
saith, Lord, I believe. And he fell down
37 1 worshipping him. And Jesus said, For „ 39
judging the world am I come, that they
which see not may see; and that they which
2 see may become blind. And some of the „ 40
Pharisees which were with him, heard this,
3 and said unto him, Are we blind? Jesus „ 41
said unto them, If ye were blind, surely ye
would have no sin: but now ye say, We see:
and for this cause your sin remaineth.
4 Verily, verily, I say unto you, He that „ 10 1
entereth not by the door into the fold of the
sheep, but climbeth up some other way, the
5 same is a thief and a robber. But he that „ 2
entereth in by the door is the shepherd of
6 the sheep. And to him the porter openeth „ 3
the door; and the sheep hear his voice: and
he calleth his own rams by name, and they

37 7 go out unto him. And when he hath sent Jn. 10 4
forth his own sheep, he goeth before them,
and his rams follow him: for they know his
8 voice. And a stranger the sheep do not „ 5
follow, but flee from him: for they hear not
9 the voice of a stranger. This proverb spake „ 6
Jesus unto them: but they understood not
what he spake unto them.
10 Jesus said unto them again, Verily, verily, „ 7
I say unto you, I am the door of the sheep.
11 For all, as many as came, are thieves and „ 8
robbers: but the sheep did not hear them.
12 I am the door: and if any man enter in „ 9
through me, he shall live, and shall go in
13 and out, and shall find pasture. Now the „ 10
thief cometh not, but that he may steal,
and kill, and destroy; I assuredly came that
they may have life, and may have what is
14 more excellent. I am the good shepherd: „ 11
now the good shepherd giveth his life for
15 his sheep. But the hireling, who is not „ 12
a shepherd, and whose the rams are not,
when he seeth the wolf coming, leaveth the
sheep, and fleeth; and the wolf cometh, and
16 snatcheth, and scattereth the sheep. Now „ 13
the hireling fleeth, because he is a hireling,
17 and hath no care for the sheep. I am the „ 14
good shepherd; and I know mine own; and
18 mine own know me. Even as my Father „ 15
knoweth me, I also know my Father; and I
19 lay down my life for my sheep. And other „ 16
sheep also I have, which are not of this
fold: them also must I call, and they shall
hear my voice; and there shall become one
20 flock and one shepherd. Therefore doth the „ 17
Father love me, because I lay down my life,
21 that I may take it again. No one shall „ 18
take it away from me; but I lay it down of
my own accord; and I have a right to lay
it down, and I have a right to take it.

This commandment received I from my
Father.
37 22 And there arose a disagreement among the Jn. 10 19
23 Jews because of these sayings. And many „ 20
of them said, He hath a devil, and suffereth
from epilepsy; why are ye silent in his
24 presence? And others said, These are not „ 21
the words of them that have a devil. Can
a devil open the eyes of the blind?
25 And the feast of the dedication in Jeru- „ 22
26 salem arrived: and it was winter; and Jesus „ 23
was walking in the temple in Solomon's porch.
27 And the Jews came round about him, and „ 24
said unto him, How long wilt thou torment
our hearts? If thou art the Messiah, tell us
28 plainly. He answered, and said unto them, „ 25
I told you, and ye believe not: and the works
that I do in my Father's name, themselves
29 bear witness of me. But ye believe not, „ 26
30 because ye are not of my rams. Even as I „ 27
told you,[1] My rams hear my voice, and I
31 know them, and they follow me: and I give „ 28
unto them eternal life; and they shall never
perish; and no one shall snatch them out of
32 my hand. For the Father, which hath given „ 29
them unto me, is greater than all; and no
one is able to take *them* away out of my
33 Father's hand. I and my Father are one. „ 30
34 And the Jews took up stones to stone „ 31
35 him. Jesus saith unto them, Many good „ 32
works have I showed you from my Father;
for which of those works do ye stone me?
36 The Jews said unto him, Not for good works „ 33
do we stone thee, but because thou blas-
phemest, and, being a man, makest thyself
37 God. Jesus said unto them, Is it not written „ 34

[1] The preceding words, "Even . . . you," which in the Greek and the Authorised Version are part of John x. 26, and belong to that sentence, are here removed to the next verse, and made to commence the new sentence. They are absent from the Revised Version.

37 38 thus in your law, I said, Ye are gods. And Jn. 10 35
if he called them gods, because the word of
God came unto them (and nothing can be
39 broken in the scripture), tell ye him, whom „ 36
the Father sanctified and sent into the world,
that he blasphemeth; because I said unto
40 you, I am the Son of God? For if I do „ 37
not the works of my Father, believe me not.
41 But if I do *them*, even though ye believe not „ 38
me, believe the works: that ye may know
and believe that my Father is in me, and I
42 in my Father. And they sought again to „ 39
take him: and he went forth out of their
hands.
43 And he went away beyond Jordan into „ 40
the place where John was before baptizing;
44 and there he abode. And many men came „ 41
unto him; and they said, John did not even
45 one sign: but all things whatsoever John
spake of this man are true. And many „ 42
believed on him.
46 Now a certain man was sick, Lazarus by „ 11 1
name, of the village of Bethany, the brother
47 of Mary and Martha. Now Mary is she „ 2
who anointed the feet of Jesus with ointment, and wiped them with her hair, whose
48 brother was Lazarus the sick man. His „ 3
sisters therefore sent unto Jesus, saying,
Lord, behold, he whom thou lovest is sick.
49 But Jesus said, This sickness is not unto „ 4
death, but for the glory of God, that the
50 Son of God may be glorified thereby. Now „ 5
Jesus loved Martha, and Mary, and Lazarus.
51 When therefore he heard that he was sick, „ 6
he abode two days in the place where he
52 was. And after these things he said to his „ 7
53 disciples, Come, let us go into Judaea. His „ 8
disciples said unto him, Master, the Jews
now wish to stone thee; and goest thou
54 thither again? Jesus said unto them, Are „ 9

37 55 there not twelve hours in the day? If any
man walk in the day, he stumbleth not, because he seeth the light of the world. But Jn. 11 10
if a man walk in the night, he stumbleth,
56 because the brightness is not in him. These „ 11
things said Jesus: and afterwards he said
unto them, Our friend Lazarus sleepeth;[1]
but I go that I may awake him out of
57 sleep. His disciples said unto him, Lord, if „ 12
58 he is sleeping,[2] he will get well. Jesus „ 13
had spoken this of his death: but they
thought that he spake of taking rest in
59 sleep. Then Jesus said unto them plainly, „ 14
60 Lazarus is dead. And I am glad for your „ 15
sakes that I was not there, in order that ye
may believe; nevertheless let us go thither.
61 Thauma,[3] who is called Thoma,[4] said unto „ 16
his fellow-disciples, Let us also go, that we
may die with him.

38 1 Jesus therefore came to Bethany, and found „ 17
that he had been in the tomb four days.
2 Now Bethany was nigh unto Jerusalem, and „ 18
3 was distant from it fifteen furlongs; and „ 19
many of the Jews came to Mary and
Martha, to console their heart concerning
4 their brother. Martha therefore, when she „ 20
heard that Jesus was coming, went out to
meet him: but Mary was sitting at home.
5 Martha therefore said unto Jesus, Lord, if „ 21
thou hadst been here, my brother would not
6 have died. But now I know that, whatso- „ 22
ever thou shalt ask of God, he will give thee.
7 Jesus said unto her, Thy brother shall rise. „ 23
8 Martha said unto him, I know that he shall „ 24
rise again in the resurrection at the last
9 day. Jesus said unto her, I am the resur- „ 25
rection, and the life; he that believeth in

[1] Or, "resteth;" cf. ver. 58, "taking rest."
[2] Or, "resting;" cf. ver. 58.
[3] Arabic, Thâwamâ.
[4] Arabic, Thâmâ; cf. liv. 17.

38 10 me, even though he die, shall live: and Jn. 11 26
everyone that liveth and believeth in me
11 shall never die. Believest thou this? She „ 27
said unto him, Yea, Lord: I believe that thou
art the Messiah, the Son of God, who art come
12 into the world. And when she had said „ 28
this, she went away, and called Mary her
sister secretly, and said unto her, The Master
13 is come, and calleth thee. And Mary, when „ 29
she heard it, arose quickly, and came unto
14 him. For Jesus was not yet come into the „ 30
village, but was in that place where Martha
15 had met him. The Jews also which were „ 31
with her in the house to console her, when
they saw Mary rising up quickly and going
out, followed her, supposing that she was
16 about to go unto the tomb to weep. Mary „ 32
therefore, when she was come where Jesus
was, and had seen him, fell down at his feet,
and said unto him, Lord, if thou hadst been
17 here, my brother would not have died. And „ 33
Jesus came, and when he saw her weeping,
and the Jews which were with her, weeping
18 *also*, he was distressed in his soul, and sighed, „ 34
and said, Where have ye laid him? They
19 said unto him, Lord, come and see. And the „ 35
20 tears of Jesus were shed. The Jews there- „ 36
21 fore said, See how much he loved him! And „ 37
some of them said, Could not this man,
which opened the eyes of that blind man,
also have caused that this man should not die?
22 Jesus therefore, being distressed in his soul, „ 38
cometh to the tomb. Now the tomb was a
cave, and a stone was laid at the mouth of
23 it. Jesus saith, Take ye away this stone. „ 39
Martha, the sister of him that was dead,
said unto him, Lord, by this time he
stinketh: for he hath been *dead* four days.
24 Jesus said unto her, Said I not unto thee, If „ 40
thou believest, thou shalt see the glory of

38 25 God? So they moved away the stone. Jn. 11 41
And Jesus lifted up his eyes, and said, My
Father, I thank thee that thou heardest me.
26 I indeed know that thou hearest me always: „ 42
but because of this multitude which standeth
by I say this to thee, that they may believe
27 that thou didst send me. When he had „ 43
said these things, he cried with a loud voice,
28 Lazarus, come forth. And the dead man „ 44
came forth, bound hand and foot with
bandages; and his face was wrapped up in
a napkin. Jesus said unto them, Loose
him, and let him go.
29 And many of the Jews, which were „ 45
come to Mary, when they saw what was
30 done by Jesus, believed in him. But some „ 46
of them went away to the Pharisees, and told
them all the things which Jesus had done.
31 And the chief priests and the Pharisees „ 47
gathered together, and they said, What do
we? for, behold, this man doeth many signs.
32 For if we let him thus alone, all men will „ 48
believe in him: and the Romans will come
and take away our country and nation.
33 But one of them, Caiaphas by name, who „ 49
was the high priest of that year, said unto
34 them, Ye know nothing at all, nor do ye „ 50
take into account that it is expedient for us
that one man should die for the people, and
35 that the whole nation perish not. Now this „ 51
he said not of himself: but as he was the
high priest of that year, he prophesied that
36 Jesus was going to die for the people; and „ 52
not only for the people, but that he might
also gather together at one time the children
37 of God that had been scattered abroad. So „ 53
from that day forth they took counsel to put
him to death.
38 Jesus therefore walked not openly among „ 54
the Jews, but departed thence into a place

near to the wilderness, into a hermitage[1]
which is called Ephraem; and there he was
38 39 going about with his disciples. Now the Jn. 11 55
passover of the Jews was near: and many
went up to Jerusalem out of the villages before
40 the feast, to purify themselves. And they „ 56
sought for Jesus, and said one to another in
the temple, What think ye of his lateness[2]
41 for the feast? Now the chief priests and „[3] 57
the Pharisees had given commandment, that,
if any man knew where he was, he should
disclose it unto them, that they might take
him.
42 And when the days of his going up[4] were Lu. 9 51
fulfilled, he prepared himself to go to Jeru-
43 salem, and sent messengers before him: and „ 52
they went, and entered into a village of
44 Samaria, to make ready for him. And they „ 53
did not receive him, because he was prepared
45 to go to Jerusalem. And when his disciples „ 54
James and John saw *this*, they said unto
him, Lord, wilt thou that we bid fire to come
down from heaven, and uproot them, even as
46 Elijah did? And Jesus turned, and rebuked „ 55
them, saying, Ye know not what *manner of*
47 spirit ye are of. Surely the Son of man „ 56
came not to destroy lives, but to save them.
And they went to another village.
39 1 Jesus therefore six days before the pass- Jn. 12 1
over came to Bethany,[5] where Lazarus was,

[1] Arabic, "kirḥ." [2] Or, "absence from."

[3] Included in ver. 56, as in Vulgate.

[4] Referred by Tatian to the last visit, six days before the crucifixion, perhaps because of the first part of this verse.

[5] Tatian here follows S. John, who fixes the exact time of the Anointing by Mary, and puts it before the Triumphal Entry. In *internal* harmonisation, however, he displaces John xii. 9–11 for the sake of neatness in the combined account. Ephraem follows the same peculiarities of order (Moes. p. 205). The mention of Simon's house is followed by the plot to kill Lazarus before the Anointing. The *Codex Fuldensis* identifies this anointing with that in Luke vii. 36, etc.

39 2	whom Jesus raised from the dead. And a	Jn.	12	2
	breakfast was made for him there: and			
	Martha served; but Lazarus was one of them			
3	that reclined *at meat* with him. And while	Mk.	14	3a
	Jesus was at Bethany, in the house of Simon			
4	the leper, a great multitude of the Jews	Jn.	12	9
	heard that Jesus was there: and they came,			
	not for Jesus' sake only, but that they might			
	see Lazarus also, whom he raised from the			
5	dead. But the chief priests took counsel	"		10
	that they might put Lazarus also to death,			
6	because by reason of him many of the Jews	"		11
	went away, and believed on Jesus.			
7	Now Mary took a case of ointment of the	"		3a
	best nard, very costly, and opened it, and	Mk.	14	3c
	poured it upon the head of Jesus, as he			
8	reclined *at meat;* and anointed his feet,	Jn.	12	3b
	and wiped them with her hair: and the			
	house was filled with the odour of the			
9	ointment. But one of the disciples, Judas	"		4
	Iscariot, who was going to betray him, said,			
10	Why was not this ointment sold for three	"		5
11	hundred pence, and given to the poor? He	"		6
	said this, not because of his care for the			
	poor; but because he was a thief, and hav-			
	ing the bag himself carried the things that			
12	were put therein. The rest of the disciples	Mk.	14	4
	also were vexed at this among themselves,			
	and said, To what purpose is this ointment			
13	wasted? For it might have been sold for	Mt.	26	9
	much, and given to the poor. And they	Mk.	14	5b
14	murmured at Mary. But Jesus perceiving	Mt.	26	10a
	it, saith unto them, Let her alone; why	Mk.	14	6b
	trouble ye her? she hath performed a good			
	work on me. She hath kept it for the day	Jn.	12	7b
15	of my burying. For the poor are always	"		8a
	with you; and when ye will ye can do	Mk.	14	7b
	them good: but I am not always with you.			
16	On that account, when pouring this ointment	Mt.	26	12
	upon my body, she did it as it were for my			

burial, and came beforehand to anoint my Mk.[1] 14 8b
39 17 body. Verily I say unto you, Wheresoever „ 9
this my gospel shall be preached in the whole
world, that which this woman hath done
shall be related for a memorial of her.
18 And when he had said these things,[2] Jesus Lu. 19 28
went forth slowly to proceed to Jerusalem.
19 And when he was arrived at Bethphage and „ 29a
Bethany, near the mount that is called the
20 mount of Olives, Jesus sent two of his Mt. 21 1b
disciples, saying unto them, Go into the „ 2a
21 village that is over against you, and when Mk. 11 2b
ye are entered into it, ye shall find an ass Mt. 21 2b
tied, and a colt with her, whereon no man Lu. 19 30b
ever yet sat:[3] loose it, and bring *them* unto Mt. 21 2c
22 me. And if anyone say unto you, Why do Lu. 19 31a
ye loose them? say thus unto him, We seek Mt. 21 3b
them for the Lord; and straightway send[4]
23 them both hither. All this is come to pass, „ 4
that it might be fulfilled which was spoken
through the prophet, saying,
24 Tell ye the daughter of Sion, „ 5
Behold, thy King cometh unto thee,
Meek, and sitting upon an ass,
And upon a colt the foal of an ass.
25 This understood not his disciples at that time: Jn.[5] 12 16
but after Jesus was glorified, his disciples remembered that these things had been written
of him, and that they did these things unto him.
26 And the disciples went, and found even {Mt. 21 6a / Lu. 19 32b}
as he had said unto them,[6] and they did as Mt. 21 6b

[1] Omitting 8a: "She hath done what she could."

[2] S. John's order continued.

[3] Or, "rode."

[4] So in the Arabic. The dual form is used, "send *ye both* them *both.*" Ciasca has taken the alternative rendering, "they *both* sent them *both,*" which, however, is contrary to the meaning here.

[5] This verse being a comment of the evangelist, and not a part of the history, is put earlier by Tatian in connection with the prophecy which in a different form S. John puts after the bringing of the ass.

[6] Omitting Mark xi. 4: "and found the colt tied by the door without, in a place where two ways met."

39 27 Jesus had commanded them. And when Lu. 19 33
they had loosed them, the owners thereof
28 said unto them, Why loose ye them? They „ 34
said unto them, We seek them for our Lord;
and they let them go. Mk. 11 6[b]
29 And they brought the ass and the colt, Mt. 21 7
and put their garments upon the colt; and
30 Jesus rode thereon. And the most part of „ 8
the multitude spread their garments before
him on the ground; and others cut branches
from the trees, and spread them in the way.
31 And when he drew near his descent of the Lu. 19 37
mount of Olives, all the disciples began to
rejoice and praise God with a loud voice for
all the mighty works which they had seen;
32 saying, Glory in the highest: glory to the Mt. 21 9[b]
son of David: blessed is he that cometh in the
33 name of the Lord: and blessed is the kingdom Mk. 11 10[a]
which cometh, *even* our father David's: peace Lu. 19 38[b]
in heaven, and glory in the highest.
34 And a great multitude that had come to Jn. 12 12
the feast, when they had heard that Jesus
35 was coming to Jerusalem, took the branches „ 13
of the palm trees, and went forth to meet
him, and cried out, saying, Praise: blessed
is he that cometh in the name of the Lord,
36 even the King of Israel. And some of the Lu. 19 39
Pharisees from the multitudes said unto him,
37 Master, rebuke thy disciples. He saith unto „ 40
them, Verily I say unto you, If these held
their peace, the stones would cry out.
38 And when he drew nigh, and had seen „ 41
39 the city, he wept over it, saying, Would that „ 42
thou hadst known the things which are for
thy peace in this thy day! this now is
40 hidden from thine eyes. The days shall „[1] 43
come unto thee, when thine enemies shall
compass thee round, and keep thee in on
41 every side, and shall take possession of thee, „ 44

[1] Cf. note to xli. 30.

and of thy children that are within thee;
and they shall not leave in thee one stone
upon another; because thou knewest not the
time of thy visitation.
39 42 And when Jesus had entered into Jeru- Mt 21 10
salem, all the city was stirred, saying, Who
43 is this? And the multitudes said, This is „ 11
Jesus, the prophet from Nazareth of Galilee.
44 And the multitude that was with him bare Jn. 12 17
witness, that he had called Lazarus out of
the tomb, and raised him from the dead.
45 For this cause many multitudes went out to „ 18
meet him, for they heard the sign that he
had done.
40 1 And when Jesus had gone into the temple, Mt. 21 14
they brought unto him the blind and the
2 lame; and he healed them. But when the „ 15
chief priests and the Pharisees saw the
wonderful things that he did, and the children that were crying in the temple, and
saying, Praise to the son of David; they
3 were annoyed, and said, Hearest thou what „ 16
these are saying? Jesus said unto them,
Yea: did ye never read, Out of the mouth
of children and babes thou hast selected my
4 praise? The Pharisees therefore said among Jn. 12 19
themselves, Lo, see you not, that we get no
advantage? for, lo, the whole world followeth
him.
5 Now there were also among them certain „ 20
Gentiles, that had come up to worship at
6 the feast: these therefore came to Philip, „ 21
which was of Bethsaida of Galilee, and asked
him, saying unto him, Sir, we wish to see
7 Jesus. Philip came and told Andrew: and „ 22
8 Andrew and Philip told Jesus. And Jesus „ 23
answered, and said unto them, The hour is
near in which the Son of man shall be glori-
9 fied. Verily, verily, I say unto you, Except „ 24
a grain of wheat fall and die in the earth,

it[1] abideth by itself alone; but if it die, it
40 10 beareth much fruit. He that loveth his Jn. 12 25
life shall lose it; and he that hateth his life
in this world shall keep it unto life eternal.
11 If any man serveth me, let him follow me; „ 26
and where I am, there shall also my servant
be: and whosoever serveth me, him will the
12 Father honour. Now is my soul troubled; „ 27
and what shall I say? My Father, save[2]
me from this hour. But for this cause came
13 I unto this hour. My Father, glorify thy „ 28
name. And a voice was heard out of heaven,
saying, I have glorified it, and will glorify
14 it. The multitude therefore, that stood by, „ 29
heard it, and said, This is thunder. Others
15 said, An angel speaketh to him. Jesus „ 30
answered, and said unto them, This voice
hath not come for my sake, but for your
16 sakes. Now is the judgment of this world: „ 31
and the prince of this world shall now be
17 cast out. And I, when I am lifted up from „ 32
the earth, will draw all men unto myself.
18 This he said to signify by what manner of „ 33
19 death he was going to die. The multitudes „ 34
said unto him, We have heard from the law
that the Messiah abideth for ever: how then
sayest thou, that the Son of man is going to
20 be lifted up? who is this Son of man? Jesus „ 35
said unto them, Yet a little while will the
light be with you. Walk while ye have the
light, that darkness overtake[3] you not: for
he that walketh in the darkness knoweth not
21 whither he goeth. While ye have the light, be- „ 36[a]
lieve on the light, that ye may be sons of light.
22 And when some of the Pharisees had Lu. 17 20
asked Jesus, When will the kingdom of God
come? he answered, and said unto them,

[1] The Arabic begins ver. 25 here as the Vulgate does. [2] Or, "deliver."
[3] The Syriac word implied in the Arabic has also the meaning, "lay hold of;" cf. i. 5.

The kingdom of God will not come with
40 23 expectation: neither shall they say, Lo, Lu. 17 21
here it is! and, Lo, there! For the king-
dom of God is within you.
24 And by day he was teaching in the „ 21 37
temple; but at night he went out, and
passed the night on the mount that is called
25 the mount of Olives. And all the people „ 38
arrived before him in the temple to hear
his word.
26 Then spake Jesus to the multitudes and Mt. 23 1
27 to his disciples, saying unto them, The scribes „ 2
and the Pharisees have sat down on Moses'
28 seat: all things therefore whatsoever they „ 3
shall bid you to observe, *these* keep and do:
but do not ye according to their works; for
29 they say, and do not. For they bind heavy „ 4
burdens,[1] and lay them on men's shoulders;
but are unwilling to move one of their
30 fingers towards them. And all their works „ 5[a]
31 they do to be seen of men. And all the Mk. 17 37[b]
multitude heard these things with gladness.
32 And in his teaching he said unto them, „ 38
Beware ye of the scribes, which desire to
walk in long robes, and love to be saluted in
33 the streets, and to sit on chief seats in the „ 39
34 synagogues, and chief couches at feasts: for Mt. 23 5[b]
they make broad their phylacteries, and
lengthen the fringes of their garments, and „ 7[b]
35 *love* to be called of men, Master. But they Mk. 12 40
devour widows' houses, under the pretence
of making their prayers long; these truly
36 shall receive greater condemnation. But Mt. 23 8
be not ye called masters: for one is your
37 master, and all ye are brethren. And call „ 9
no man father on the earth: for one is your
38 Father, which is in the heavens. Neither „ 10
be ye called directors:[2] for one is your

[1] Omitting "and grievous to be borne;" cf. Revised Version, marginal note.
[2] Or, "arrangers;" the Peschito has "guides."

40 39 director, *even* the Messiah. But he that is Mt. 23 11
greater among you shall be your minister.
40 He[1] that exalteth himself shall be humbled; „ 12
and he that humbleth himself shall be
exalted.
41 Woe unto you Pharisees! for ye love the Lu. 11 43
front seats in the synagogues, and the salutation in the streets.
42 Woe[2] unto you, scribes and Pharisees, Mt. 23 14
hypocrites, for ye devour widows' houses by
reason of your long prayers: and therefore
ye shall receive greater condemnation.
43 Woe unto you, scribes and Pharisees, „ 13[a]
hypocrites! because ye shut the kingdom of
44 God against men. Woe unto you, lawyers! Lu. 11 52[a]
for ye have hidden the keys of knowledge:
ye enter not in yourselves, neither suffer ye Mt. 23 13[b]
them that are entering in to enter.
45 Woe unto you, scribes and Pharisees, „ 15
hypocrites! for ye compass sea and land to
draw away one proselyte; and when he is
become *so*, ye make him twofold more a son
of Gehenna than yourselves.
46 Woe unto you, ye blind guides, which „ 16
say, Whosoever shall swear by the temple,
it is nothing; but whosoever shall swear
by the gold, that is in the temple, he is
47 accountable. Ye blind ignorant ones: for „ 17
whether is greater, the gold, or the temple
48 that sanctifieth the gold? And, Whosoever „ 18
shall swear by the altar, it is nothing; but
whosoever shall swear by the offering that
49 is upon it, he is accountable. Ye blind „ 19
ignorant ones: whether is greater, the offering, or the altar that sanctifieth the offering?
50 He therefore that sweareth by the altar, „ 20

[1] Cf. xxx. 5 and xxxii. 21.

[2] Some of the statements regarding the scribes and Pharisees already made in this chapter are now repeated as "woes." Matt. xxiii. 14 is omitted in the Revised Version.

sweareth by it, and by all things that are
40 51 thereon. And he that sweareth by the Mt. 23 21
temple, sweareth by it, and by him that
52 dwelleth therein. And he that sweareth by „ 22
the heaven, sweareth by the throne of God,
and by him that sitteth thereon.
53 Woe unto you, scribes and Pharisees, „ 23
hypocrites! that tithe mint and rue, anise
and cummin, and all herbs, and leave undone
the weightier matters of the law, judgment,
and mercy, and faith, and the love of God:
these ye ought to do, and not to leave those
54 undone. Ye blind guides, which strain out „ 24
the gnat, and adorn [1] the camel.
55 Woe unto you, scribes and Pharisees, „ 25
hypocrites! for ye cleanse the outside of
the cup and of the platter, but within they
are full of iniquity and unrighteousness.
56 Ye blind Pharisees, cleanse first the inside „ 26
of the cup and of the platter, and the outside of them will be clean.
57 Woe unto you, scribes and Pharisees, „ 27
hypocrites! for ye are like unto whited
sepulchres, which outwardly appear beautiful,
but within are full of dead men's bones and
58 of all uncleanness. Even so ye also out- „ 28
wardly appear unto men as if righteous, but
within ye are full of iniquity and hypocrisy.
59 One of the scribes, answering, said unto Lu. 11 45
him, Teacher, in this thy speech thou makest
60 a reproach against us. He said, Woe unto „ 46
you also, ye scribes! for ye lade men with
heavy burdens, and ye yourselves touch not
those burdens even with one of your fingers.
61 Woe unto you, scribes and Pharisees, Mt. 23 29[a]
hypocrites! in that ye build the sepulchres
of the prophets, whom your fathers killed, Lu. 11 47[b]
and adorn the tombs of the righteous, Mt. 23 29[b]

[1] Mr. Rendel Harris attributes this peculiar reading to the transposition of two letters of the Arabic word for "swallow."

40 62 and say, If we had been in the days of Mt. 23 30
our fathers, we should not have been par-
takers with them in the blood of the
63 prophets. See therefore! ye bear witness „ 31
against yourselves, that ye are sons of them
64 that slew the prophets; and ye are finishing „ 32
65 the path of your fathers. Ye serpents, ye „ 33
offspring of vipers, whither shall ye flee
41 1 from the judgment of Gehenna? There- „[1] 34
fore, behold, I, the wisdom of God, send
unto you prophets, and apostles, and wise
men, and scribes: and some of them shall
ye kill and crucify; and some of them
shall ye scourge in your synagogues, and
2 cast out from city to city: that upon you „ 35
may come all the blood of righteous men
that hath been shed on the earth, from the
blood of Abel the innocent unto the blood
of Zacharias son of Barachias, whom ye
slew between the sanctuary and the altar.
3 Verily I say unto you, All these things „ 36
shall come upon this generation.
4 O Jerusalem, Jerusalem, the slayer of „ 37
the prophets, and the stoner of them that
were sent unto her! how often have I
wished to gather thy children together, even
as a hen gathereth her chickens under her
5 wings, and ye would not! Your house[2] „ 38
6 shall be left unto you deserted. Verily I „ 39
say unto you, Ye shall not see me henceforth, till ye say,[3] Blessed *is* he that cometh
in the name of the Lord.
7 And of the rulers also many believed on Jn.[4] 12 42
him; but because of the Pharisees they did

[1] Or omit "shall" throughout this verse; cf. Luke xi. 49. This remarkable change of reading seems connected with Gnostic ideas.

[2] The Doctrine of Addai has "Behold, your house is left desolate."

[3] It is remarkable that this statement should come after the account of the use of these very words by the multitudes; cf. xxxix. 32.

[4] John xii. 42–50 is here inserted before John xii. 36^b–41; cf. xli. 21–26.

not confess *it*, lest they should become outside
41 8 the synagogue: for they loved the glory of men more than to glory of God. Jn. 12 43
9 And Jesus cried, and said, He that believeth on me, believeth not on me, but „ 44
10 on him that sent me. And he that seeth „ 45
11 me, seeth him that sent me. I am come a light[1] into the world, every man therefore that believeth on me, abideth not in the „ 46
12 darkness. And whosoever heareth my sayings, and keepeth them not, I judge him not: for I came not to judge the world, but „ 47
13 to give life to the world. He that rejecteth me, and receiveth not my sayings, there is *one* that judgeth him: the saying that I spake, the same shall judge him in the last „ 48
14 day. I speak not from myself; but the Father which sent me, he hath given me a commandment, what I should say, and what „ 49
15 I should speak. And I know that his commandment is life eternal: the things therefore which I speak now, even as the Father hath said unto me, so I speak. „ 50
16 And when he said these things unto them, the scribes and the Pharisees began to be angry in their malice, and to find fault with his words, and to vex him in many things; Lu. 11 53
17 seeking to catch something out of his mouth, that they might be able to accuse him. „ 54
18 Now when many multitudes were gathering together, so that they almost trode one upon another, Jesus began to say unto his disciples, Beware ye of the leaven of the „ 12 1
19 Pharisees, which is hypocrisy. But there is nothing covered up, except that it will be „ 2

Of these verses 42, 43 are a comment of the evangelist, which might be placed at any point in the account of this visit. Ver. 44–50 naturally follow them, and with the verses from S. Luke following them, they explain in a very natural way why Jesus went and hid himself, John xii. 36[b].

[1] Or, "I, a light, am come."

revealed: nor hidden, except that it will be
41 20 known. All things that ye have said in the darkness, shall be heard in the light: and that which ye have whispered in the ears in the chambers, shall be proclaimed upon the housetops. — Lu.[1] 12 3
21 These things spake Jesus, and he departed, — Jn. 12 36b
22 and hid himself from them. And though he had done all these signs before them, — " 37
23 they believed not on him: that the saying of Isaiah the prophet might be fulfilled, which he spake, — " 38

Lord, who hath believed, that he may hear us?
And the arm of the Lord, to whom hath it been revealed?

24 For this cause they could not believe, for Isaiah said again, — " 39
25 Blind ye their eyes, and bring darkness to their heart; — " 40

Lest they should see with their eyes, and understand with their heart,
And should turn,
And I should heal them.

26 These things said Isaiah, when he saw his glory, and spake of him. — " 41
27 And Jesus went out from the temple; and some of his disciples came to him, and showed him the buildings of the temple, and its — Mt. 24 1
28 beauty and magnificence, and the strength of the stones used in it, and the elegance of its — Mk. 13 1b
construction, and how it was adorned with — Lu. 21 5b
29 costly stones and beautiful colours. Jesus answered, and said unto them, See ye these great buildings? Verily I say unto you, — Mt. 24 2a
30[2] the days will surely come, and there shall not be left here in them one stone upon another, that is not thrown down. — Lu. 19 43a; " 44b

[1] See note to xiii. 12b.
[2] No doubt Tatian meant this for Luke xxi. 6b; cf. xxxix. 40, 41

41 31 And two days before the passover of the Mk.[1] 14 1
unleavened *bread* the chief priests and the
scribes sought how they might take him with
32 subtilty, and kill him: but they said, Not „ 2
during the feast, lest haply the people make
33 a disturbance. And as Jesus sat on the „ 13 3
mount of Olives over against the temple,
Simon Cephas and James and John and
Andrew came unto him, and said unto him
34 between themselves and him, Teacher, tell {Lu.[2] 21 7[b] Mt. 24 3[b]}
us, when shall these things be? and what
shall be the sign of thy coming, and of the
35 end of the world? Jesus answered, and said Mt. 24 4[a]
unto them, The days will come, when ye Lu. 17 22[b]
shall desire to see one day of the days of
the Son of man, and ye shall not see it.
36 Take heed that no man lead you astray. Mt. 24 4[b]
37 Many shall come in my name, saying, I am „ 5[a]
38 the Messiah; and they shall say, The time Lu. 21 8[b]
is at hand; and shall lead many astray: Mk. 13 6[b]
39 go ye not therefore after them. When {Lu. 21 8[c] Mk. 13 7[a]}
therefore ye shall hear of wars and rumours
of insurrections, see that ye be not troubled: Mt. 24 6[b]
these things must come to pass first; but Lu. 21 9[b]
40 the end hath not yet come. Nation[3] shall Mt.[4] 24 7[a]
rise against nation, and kingdom against
41 kingdom: and there shall be great earth- Lu. 21 11
quakes in divers places, and famines, and
pestilences, and commotions: terrors and

[1] No more convenient place could be found for these two verses, in view of the fact that the prolonged discourse which follows immediately is at once followed by a reference made by Jesus to this date; cf. xliv. 1 and 2. The placing Mark xiv. 1, 2 before Mark xiii. 3 does not involve a chronological error, since xliv. 1 shows that the same day is still present.

[2] Besides taking Luke xxi. as the parallel to Matt. xxiv. and Mark xiii., Tatian inserts passages from other parts of S. Luke which deal with the same subject, though their position in the third Gospel implies that they were spoken earlier. In this way he is enabled to present to his readers a more complete account of our Lord's teaching upon this important subject.

[3] Omitting Luke xxi. 10[a]: "Then said he unto them."

[4] Or Luke xxi. 10[b].

tremblings shall there be, and great signs
shall appear from heaven; and great storms
41 42 shall there be. All these things are the Mt. 24 8
43 beginning of troubles. And[1] before all Lu. 21 12
these things, they shall lay hands on you,
and shall persecute *you*, and deliver you up
to the synagogues and prisons, and shall drag
you before kings and governors for my name's
44 sake. And this shall be unto you for a " 13
45 testimony. And my gospel must first be Mk. 13 10
46 preached unto all the nations. And when Lu. 12 11
they bring you into the synagogues before
the rulers, and the authorities, be not anxious
beforehand how to plead, or what ye shall
47 say: for it is not ye that speak, but the Mk. 13 11[b]
48 Holy Spirit. Put it therefore in your heart, Lu. 21 14
49 not to meditate beforehand what to say: for " 15
I will give you understanding and wisdom,
which all your adversaries shall not be able
to withstand.

50 For then shall they deliver you up unto Mt. 24 9
tribulation, and shall kill you: and ye shall
be hated of all the nations for my name's
51 sake. And then shall many be caused to " 10
stumble, and shall hate one another, and
52 shall deliver up one another to death. And Lu. 21 16
your parents, and brethren, and kinsfolk, and
friends shall deliver you up: and *some* of
53 you shall they put to death. And a lock "[2] 18
of the hair of your head shall not perish.
54 In your patience ye shall possess your " 19
souls.

55 And many false prophets shall arise, and Mt. 24 11
56 shall lead many astray. And because of " 12
the abundance of iniquity, the love of many
57 shall grow weak. But whosoever endureth " 13
58 to the end, the same shall be saved. And " 14
this gospel of the kingdom shall be preached

[1] Omitting Mark xiii. 9: "But take heed to yourselves."
[2] For the substance of ver. 17 see above in xli. 50

in the whole world for a testimony unto all
the nations; and then shall come the end
of all.

42 1 But when ye see Jerusalem compassed Lu. 21 20
with armies, then know that her desolation
2 is at hand. At that time let them that are „ 21
in Judaea flee unto the mountain; and let
them that are in the midst of her flee; and
let not them that are in the districts enter
3 therein. For these days are the days of „ 22
vengeance, that all things which are written
may be fulfilled.

4 When therefore ye see the abominable[1] Mt. 24 15
desolation, which was spoken of in Daniel
the prophet, standing in the holy place (let
5 him that readeth understand), then let them „ 16
that are in Judaea flee unto the mountain:
6 and let him that *is* on the housetop not go Mk. 13 15
down, nor enter in, to take anything out of
7 his house: and let him that shall be in the „ 16
field not return back to take his cloke.
8 Woe unto them that are with child, and to Lu. 21 23
them that give suck in those days! there
shall be great distress in the land, and wrath
9 upon this people. And they shall fall on „ 24
the edge of the sword, and shall be led
captive into every country: and Jerusalem
shall be trodden down of the Gentiles, until
10[2] the times of the Gentiles be fulfilled. Then Mk. 13 21
if any man shall say unto you, The Messiah
is here; or, Lo, he is there; believe *it* not.
11 Then shall arise false Christs, and false Mt. 24 24
prophets, and shall do signs and portents;
so as to lead into error, if they could, even
12 the elect. Therefore take ye heed: for I Mk. 13 23
have already told you all things beforehand.
13 If therefore they shall say unto you, Behold, Mt. 24 26
he is in the wilderness; go not forth, that

[1] Or, "unclean."

[2] Cf. xli. 36, 37. There is a little displacement of internal order here.

ye may not be seized: and if they shall say
unto you, Behold he is in the chamber; be-
42 14 lieve *it* not. For as the lightning appeareth Mt. 24 27
in the east, and is visible even unto the
west; so shall be the coming down of the
15 Son of man. But first must he suffer Lu. 17 25
many things, and be rejected of this genera-
16 tion. And pray ye that your flight may not Mt. 24 20
take place in the winter, nor on a sabbath
17 day: then shall be great tribulation, of which „ 21
there hath not been the like from the beginning of the world until now, nor shall
18 take place. And except the Lord had Mk. 13 20
shortened those days, no flesh would have
been saved: but for the elect's sake, whom
19 he chose, he shortened those days. And Lu. 21 25
there shall be signs in sun and moon and
stars; and upon the earth distress of nations,
and wringing[1] of hands for the roaring of
the noise of the sea and of the earthquake.
20 Men's souls shall depart for the fear, which „ 26[a]
21 shall come upon the earth. But in those Mk. 13 24[a]
days, immediately after the tribulation of those Mt. 24 29
days, the sun shall be darkened, and the moon
shall not give her light, and the stars shall fall
from heaven, and the powers of the heavens
22 shall be shaken: and then shall appear the „ 30
sign of the Son of man in heaven: and then
shall all the tribes of the earth mourn, and
they shall look at the Son of man coming
on the clouds of heaven with power and
23 great majesty. And he shall send forth his „ 31
angels with a great trumpet, and they shall
gather together his elect from the four winds,
from the end of heaven even to the end
24 thereof. But when these things begin to come Lu. 21 28
to pass, be of good cheer, and lift up your
heads; because your deliverance draweth
nigh.

[1] This passage is considerably altered from S. Luke.

42 25 From the fig-tree learn the parable: for Mt. 24 32
when its branches are tender, and it putteth
forth leaves, ye know that the summer is nigh;
26 even so ye also, when ye see these things „ 33
begin to take place, know ye that the kingdom
27 of God hath arrived at the door. Verily „ 34
I say unto you, This generation shall not
pass away, till all these things take place.
28 Heaven and earth shall pass away, but my „ 35
words shall not pass away.
29 Take heed to yourselves, lest haply your Lu. 21 34
hearts be at any time overcharged with
iniquity and drunkenness, and cares of the
age, and that day come on you suddenly:
30 for just as a blow shall it strike all them „ 35
that dwell on the face of all the earth.
31 Watch ye at every season, and pray, that ye „ 36
may be counted worthy to escape all these
things that are going to take place, and to
32 stand before the Son of man. Of that day Mk. 13 32
and of that hour knoweth no one, not even
the angels of heaven, nor the Son, but the
33 Father. Take ye heed, watch and pray: for „ 33
34 ye know not when that time is. Even as a „ 34
man, who went abroad, and left his house,
and gave his authority to his servants, and
left each one at his own work, and com-
35 manded the porter to be watchful. Watch „ 35
therefore: for ye know not when the lord of
the house shall come, whether at even, or
at midnight, or at cockcrowing, or in the
36 morning; lest coming suddenly he find you „ 36
37 sleeping. What I say unto you, I say unto „ 37
you all, Be watchful.
38 For even as it happened in the days of Mt. 24 37
Noah, so shall be the coming of the Son of
39 man. Even as before the flood they were „ 38
eating and drinking, marrying and delivering
up to marriage, until the day that Noah
40 entered into the ark, and they knew not „ 39

until the flood came, and took them all away;
so shall be the coming of the Son of man.
42 41 And likewise even as it came to pass in the Lu. 17 28
days of Lot; they ate and they drank, they
sold and they bought, they planted and they
42 builded; *but* in the same day wherein Lot „ 29
went out from Sodom, the Lord rained both
fire and brimstone from heaven, and destroyed
43 them all: so shall it be in the day wherein „ 30
44 the Son of man shall appear. And in that „ 31
day, he which shall be on the housetop, and
his garments in the house, let him not go
down to take them away: and he which
shall be in the field, let him not return
45 46 back. Remember Lot's wife. He that shall Lu. 17 32 „ 33
wish to save his life shall lose it: but he
47 that shall lose his life shall save it. Verily Lu. 17 34
I say unto you, In that night there shall
be two *men* in one bed; the one shall be
48 taken, and the other shall be left. And „ 35
there shall be two *women* grinding in one
mill; the one shall be taken, and the other
49 shall be left. And there shall be two *men* „ 36
in the same field; the one shall be taken,
50 and the other shall be left. They answered, „ 37
and said unto him, Where, Lord? He[1]
said unto them, Wherever the body is,
thither will the eagles[2] be gathered together.
51 Watch therefore; for ye know not in what Mt. 24 42
52 hour your Lord will come. This know, „ 43
If the master of the house had known
in what watch the thief would come, he
would certainly have watched, and his house
53 could not have been digged through. There- „ 44
fore be ye also ready: for in an hour
that ye think not the Son of man will
come.

[1] In the Arabic ver. 37 begins here, as in the Vulgate, and ver. 36, as marked 37 in the present text.

[2] Or, "vultures."

43 1 Simon Cephas saith unto him, Lord, Lu.[1] 12 41
speakest thou this parable unto us, or even
2 unto all men? Jesus said unto him, „ 42[a]
Who, think you, is the faithful and wise Mt. 24 45
overseer[2] of the house, whom his lord hath
set over his household, to give them food in
3 its season? Blessed is that servant, whom „ 46
when his lord is come, he shall find so doing.
4 Verily I say unto you, that he will set him {Lu.[3] 12 44[a] / Mt. 24 47[b]}
5 over all that he hath. But if that evil Mt. 24 48
servant shall say in his heart, My lord will
6 delay his coming; and shall begin to beat Lu. 12 45[b]
his menservants and the maidservants of his
lord, and shall begin to eat and drink with Mt. 24 49[b]
7 the drunken; the lord of that servant shall „ 50
come in a day wherein he thinketh not, and
8 in an hour which he knoweth not, and shall „ 51[a]
judge him, and appoint his portion with the
hypocrites, and with the unfaithful: there {Lu. 12 46[b] / Mt. 24 51[b]}
shall be the weeping and gnashing of teeth.
9 Then shall the kingdom of heaven be like Mt. 25 1
unto ten virgins, which took their lamps,
and went forth to meet the bridegroom and
10 the bride. Five of them were wise, and „ 2
11 five were foolish. Now these foolish *ones*, „ 3
when they took their lamps,[4] took no oil
12 with them: but the wise took oil in vessels „ 4
13 with the lamps. Now while the bridegroom „ 5
14 tarried, they all slumbered and slept. But „ 6
at midnight a cry was made, Behold, the
bridegroom cometh! Go ye forth to meet
15 him. Then all those virgins arose, and „ 7
16 trimmed their lamps. The foolish said unto „ 8
the wise, Give us of your oil; for our lamps

[1] The preceding parable is very like that in Luke xii. 39, 40, hence the sequence now; the order is that of S. Matthew.

[2] Cf. Luke xii. 42[b].

[3] Or Matt. xxiv. 47[a].

[4] Lit. "burning-lamps," a different word from that translated "lamps" in ver. 9 and 12, but used in ver. 39.

43 17 are gone[1] out. The wise answered, saying, Mt. 25 9
Peradventure there may not be enough for
us and you: go ye to them that sell, and
18 buy for yourselves. And when they had „ 10
gone to buy, the bridegroom came; and
they that were ready went in with him
to the marriage feast: and the door was
19 shut. But at last came also the other „ 11
20 virgins, saying, Lord, Lord, open to us. He „ 12
answered, and saith unto them, Verily I say
21 unto you, I know you not. Watch there- „ 13
fore; for ye know not that day nor that hour.
22 Even as a man, going abroad, called his „ 14
own servants, and delivered unto them his
23 goods. And unto one he gave five talents, „ 15
and to another two, but to another one; to
each according to his particular ability; and
24 he went on his journey immediately. Now „ 16
he that had received the five talents went
and traded with them, and gained five others.
25 In like manner he also that had received „ 17
26 the two gained two others. But he that „ 18
had received the one went away and digged
into the earth, and hid his lord's money.
27 But after a long time the lord of those „ 19
servants came, and made a reckoning with
28 them. And he that had received the five „ 20
talents came and paid five others, saying,
Lord, thou deliveredst unto me five talents:
lo, I have gained five others beside them.
29 His lord saith unto him, Well done, good „ 21
and faithful servant: thou hast been faithful
over a few things, I will set thee over many
things: enter thou into the joy of thy lord.
30 And he that had received the two talents „ 22
came, and saith, Lord, thou deliveredst unto
me two talents: lo, I have gained two others
31 beside them. His lord saith unto him, Well „ 23

[1] Not "going out," as the Revised Version and the margin of the Authorised Version.

done, good and faithful servant; thou hast
been faithful over a few things, I will set
thee over many things: enter thou into the
43 32 joy of thy lord. And he also that had Mt. 25 24
received the one talent came, and said, Lord,
I know that thou art a hard man, thou
reapest where thou dost not sow, and gatherest
33 where thou dost not scatter: and I was „ 25
afraid, and went away, and hid thy talent in
34 the earth: lo, thou hast what is thine. His „ 26
lord answered, and said unto him, Thou
wicked and slothful servant, thou knowest
me, that I reap where I did not sow, and
35 gather where I did not scatter; thou oughtest „ 27
to have put my money at the bank,[1] and at
my coming I should have exacted it with
36 interest. Take ye away therefore the talent „ 28
from him, and give it unto him that hath
37 the ten talents. Unto him that hath shall „ 29
be given, and he shall have abundance: but
from him that hath not, even that which he
38 hath shall be taken away from him. And „ 30
cast ye out the unprofitable servant into the
outer darkness: there shall be the weeping
and gnashing of teeth.
39 Let your loins be girded about, and your Lu. 12 35
40 lamps[2] burning; and be ye yourselves like „ 36
unto men looking for their lord, when he
returns from the feast; that, when he
cometh and knocketh, they may straightway
41 open unto him. Blessed are those servants, „ 37
whom their lord when he cometh shall find
watching: verily I say unto you, that he
shall gird his loins, and make them lie down
to meat, and shall pass by and serve them.
42 And if he shall come in the second watch, „ 38

[1] Mr. Rendel Harris thinks the saying, "Be approved money-changers," was in the *Diatessaron* near here.

[2] See note on ver. 11. These verses from Luke xii. serve as a kind of summary of the preceding lessons.

or in the third, and find them so, blessed are
those servants.
43 43 But when the Son of man shall come in Mt. 25 31
his glory, and all his holy angels with him,
then shall he sit on the throne of his
44 majesty: and before him he shall gather all „ 32
the nations: and he shall separate them one
from another, as the shepherd separateth
45 the rams from the kids: and he shall set „ 33
the rams on his right, but the kids on the
46 left. Then shall the King say unto them „ 34
that shall be on his right, Come, ye blessed
of my Father, inherit the kingdom prepared
for you from the foundation of the world:
47 I was hungry, and ye gave me to eat: I was „ 35
thirsty, and ye gave me to drink: I was a
48 stranger, and ye took me in: I was naked, „ 36
and ye clothed me: I was sick, and ye
visited me: I was in prison, and ye took
49 care of me. Then shall the righteous „ 37
say unto him, Lord, when saw we thee
hungering, and fed thee? or thirsting, and
50 gave thee a drink? And when saw we thee „ 38
a stranger, and took thee in? or naked, and
51 clothed thee? And when saw we thee sick, „ 39
52 or in prison, and took care of thee? The „ 40
King shall answer, and say[1] unto them,
Verily I say unto you, Whatsoever ye did
unto one of the least of these my brethren,
53 ye did unto me. Then shall he say also „ 41
unto them that shall be on his left, Depart
from me, ye cursed, into the eternal fire
which is prepared for the devil and his
54 armies: I was hungry, and ye gave me „ 42
not to eat: I was thirsty, and ye gave me
55 no drink: I was a stranger, and ye took me „ 43
not in: I was naked, and ye clothed me not:
I was sick, and in prison, and ye visited me
56 not. Then shall they also answer, saying, „ 44

[1] In the Arabic idiom, "answered and said."

Lord, when saw we thee hungering, or thirsting, or naked,[1] or a stranger, or sick, or in
prison, and did not minister unto thee?
43 57 Then shall he answer, and say unto them, Mt. 25 45
Verily I say unto you, When ye did it not
unto one of these lesser *ones*, ye did it not
58 even unto me also. And these shall go into „ 46
eternal punishment: but the righteous into
eternal life.

44 1 And when Jesus had finished all these „ 26 1
2 sayings, he said unto his disciples, Ye know „ 2
that after two days [2] the passover will take
place, and the Son of man will be delivered
3 up to be crucified. Then were gathered „ 3
together the chief priests and scribes, and
the elders of the people, unto the court of
4 the high priest, who is called Caiaphas; and „ 4
they took counsel concerning Jesus that they
might take him by subtilty, and kill him.
5 But they said, Not during the feast, lest „ 5
peradventure a tumult arise among the
people; for they feared the people. Lu. 22 2[b]
6 And Satan entered into Judas surnamed „ 3
Iscariot, who was of the number of the
7 twelve. And he went away, and had a „ 4[a]
conversation in the temple with the chief
priests and scribes and rulers, saying unto
them, What are ye willing to give me, and Mt. 26 15[b]
8 I will deliver him unto you? And they, Mk. 14 11[a]
when they heard it, were glad, and they Mt. 26 15[c]
appointed unto him thirty silver drachmas.[3]
9 And he promised them: and from that time Lu. 22 6
he sought opportunity to deliver Jesus unto
them without the multitudes.
10 And on the first day of *the feast of* un- Mk.[4] 14 12
leavened *bread*, the disciples came to Jesus,

[1] The order of "naked" and "stranger" is here reversed from ver. 47, 50, and 55.

[2] Cf. xli. 31.

[3] Arabic, "dirhems of money."

[4] This verse seems superfluous here; cf. ver. 36.

and said unto him, Where wilt thou that we
go and make ready for thee that thou mayest
eat the passover?
44 11 Now before the feast of the passover Jn. 13 1
Jesus knew that the hour was come that
he should depart out of this world unto his
Father, and he loved his own in this world,
12 and he loved them unto the end. And at „ 2
supper[1] time, Satan having put into the
heart of Judas, the son of Simon Iscariot, to
13 betray him, and Jesus, knowing that the „ 3
Father had delivered all things into his
hands, and that he came forth from the
Father, and was going unto the Father,
14 rose from supper, and laid aside his garments; „ 4
and he took a towel, and girded his loins.
15 And he poured water into the bason, and „ 5
began to wash his disciples' feet, and to wipe
them with the towel wherewith he had
16 girded his loins. And when he was come „ 6
to Simon Cephas, Simon said unto him,
17 Lord, dost thou wash my feet? Jesus „ 7
answered, and said unto him, What I do
now thou knowest not; but thou shalt know
18 hereafter. Simon said unto him, Thou shalt „ 8
never wash my feet. Jesus saith unto him,
If I wash thee not, thou shalt have no part
19 with me. Simon Cephas said unto him, „ 9
Then, Lord, wash not my feet only, but also
20 my hands and my head. Jesus said unto „ 10
him, He that is bathed needeth not save to
wash his feet; then he is entirely clean: and
21 ye are clean, but not all. For Jesus knew „ 11
who was his betrayer; therefore said he, Ye
are not all clean.
22 So after he had washed their feet, he took „ 12

[1] Tatian divides ver. 1–20 of this chapter of S. John from the remainder, and makes the meal here referred to take place before the hiring of the guest-chamber (xliv. 36, etc.), and consequently also before the meal, which preceded the institution of the Lord's Supper (xliv. 41).

his garments, and, sitting down, he said unto
them, Know ye what I have done to you?
44 23 Ye call me, Master, and, Lord: and ye say Jn. 13 13
24 well; so I am. If I then, your Lord and „ 14
Master, have washed your feet, how much
more fit is it, that ye should wash one
25 another's feet? For I have given you this „ 15
example, that ye also may so do, as I have
26 done to you. Verily, verily, I say unto you, A „ 16
servant is not greater than his lord; neither
is an apostle greater than he that sent him.
27 If ye know these things, happy shall ye be „ 17
28 if ye do them. This my saying is not for „ 18
you all: for I know whom I have chosen:
but that the scripture may be fulfilled, He
that eateth bread with me hath lifted up his
29 heel against me. From henceforth I tell „ 19
you before it come to pass, that when it is
come to pass, ye may believe that I am *he*.
30 Verily, verily, I say unto you, He that „ 20
receiveth whomsoever I send receiveth me;
and he that receiveth me receiveth him that
31 sent me. Which is greater, he that reclineth Lu. 22 27
at meat, or he that serveth? is not he that
reclineth *at meat?* I am in the midst of you
32 as he that serveth. But ye are they which „ 28
33 have continued with me in my sorrows, and „ 29
I promise unto you, even as my Father
promised unto me, a kingdom, that ye may „ 30[a]
eat and drink upon the table of my kingdom.[1]
34 And the first day of the feast of un- „ 7
leavened *bread* came, on which the Jews are
35 wont to kill the passover. And Jesus sent „ 8
two of his disciples, Cephas and John, saying
unto them, Go and make ready for us the
36 passover, that we may eat. And they said „ 9
unto him, Where[2] wilt thou that we make
37 ready for thee? He said unto them, Go, { Lu. 22 10[a] / Mk. 14 13[b] }

[1] Omitting "and sit on thrones judging the Twelve Tribes of Israel." But cf. xxix. 7.

[2] Cf. ver. 10.

enter into the city; and as ye are entering in, Lu. 22 10b
there shall meet you a man bearing a pitcher
of water; follow him; and where he entereth
44 38 in, say to the householder, Our Master saith, {Lu. 22 11a / Mt. 26 18b}
My time is come; and I keep the passover
with thee. Where is then the lodging, Lu. 22 11b
where I may eat *it* with my disciples?
39 And he will show you a large upper room " 12a
furnished and prepared: and there make Mk. 14 15b
40 ready for us. And his two disciples went " 16
forth, and came into the city, and found
even as he had said unto them: and they
made ready the passover, as he had commanded them.
41[1] And when the evening was come, and it Lu. 22 14
was the hour, Jesus came and lay down *to*
meat, and the twelve apostles with him.
42 And he saith unto them, With desire I have " 15
desired to eat this passover with you before
43 I suffer: I say unto you, henceforth I will " 16
not eat it, until it be fulfilled in the kingdom
of God.
44 Saying this, Jesus was troubled in the Jn. 13 21a
spirit, and testified, and said, Verily, verily,
I say unto you, One of you that eateth with Mk. 14 18b
45 me, he shall betray me. And they were " 19
very sorrowful, and began to say unto him
46 one by one, Is it I, Lord? He answereth, " 20
and saith unto them, One of the twelve, that
dippeth his hand with me in the dish, he
47 shall betray me. And behold, the hand of Lu. 22 21
him that betrayeth me *is* on the table.
48 And the Son of man shall go, even as it is Mk. 14 21
written of him: but woe unto that man
through whom the Son of man shall be
betrayed! better were it for that man if he
49 had not been born. And the disciples Jn. 13 22
observed one another, not knowing whom
50 he signified. And they began to question Lu. 22 23

[1] See note to ver. 12.

among themselves, which of them it was
that was going to do this thing.

45 1 Now there was reclining in his bosom one Jn. 13 23
2 of his disciples, whom Jesus loved. Simon „ 24
Cephas beckoned to him, that he should ask
3 him who this was of whom he spake. That „ 25
disciple therefore leaned back on Jesus'
breast, and said unto him, Lord, Who is he?
4 Jesus answered, and saith, He it is to whom „ 26
I shall give the bread *when it is* dipped. And
Jesus dipped the bread, and gave it to Judas,
5 the son of Simon Iscariot. And after the „ 27
bread Satan entered into him. And Jesus
said unto him, What thou wishest to do,
6 make haste to do. Now no one of those „ 28
reclining understood this, for what *intent* he
7 spake unto him. And some thought, because „ 29
Judas had the bag, that he commanded him
to buy what was needed for the feast; or
that he should give something to the poor.
8 Judas the betrayer answered, and said, Is Mt. 26 25
it I, Master? Jesus saith unto him, Thou
9 hast said. And Judas straightway received Jn. 13 30
the bread, and went out: and it was night.
10 And Jesus said, Now[1] shall the Son of „ 31
man be glorified, and God shall be glorified
11 in him; and if God shall be glorified in „ 32
him,[2] God shall also glorify him in himself,
12 and straightway shall he glorify him. And Mk. 14 22[a]
as they were eating, Jesus took bread, and Mt. 26 26[b]
blessed, and brake, and gave *it* to his disciples, and said unto them, Take, and eat;
13 this is my body. And when he had taken Mk. 14 23[a]
a cup, he gave thanks, and blessed it, and
gave *it* to them: and said, Take, and drink Mt. 26 27[b]
14 ye all of this; and they all drank of it. Mk. 14 23[b]

[1] The Doctrine of Addai has "Behold now is the Son of man glorified, and God glorifies Himself in Him by miracles and by wonders, and by honour of being at the right hand."

[2] Retaining the clause omitted in the Revised Version.

45 15 And he said unto them, This is my blood, Mk. 14 24[a]; Mt. 26 28
the new testament, shed for many unto
16 remission of sins. I say unto you, I will Mt. 26 29
not drink henceforth of this juice of the
vine, until the day when I shall drink
it new with you in the kingdom of
God; and so do for my remembrance.[1] Lu. 22 19[b]
17 And Jesus saith unto Simon, Simon, be- " 31
hold, Satan desires that he may sift you
18 as wheat: but I make supplication for thee, " 32
that thou lose not thy faith: and do thou
also, when once thou hast turned again,
stablish thy brethren.
19 My children, yet a little while I am with Jn. 13 33
you; and ye shall seek me: and as I said
unto the Jews, Whither I go, ye cannot
20 come; I say now unto you also. A new " 34
commandment I give unto you, that ye love
one another; and even as I have loved you,
21 love ye also each other. By this shall all " 35
men know that ye are my disciples, if ye
22 have love one to another. Simon Cephas " 36
said unto him, Lord, whither goest thou?
Jesus answered, and said unto him, Whither
I go, thou canst not follow me now; but
thou shalt come afterwards.
23 Then said Jesus unto them, All ye shall Mt.[2] 26 31
forsake me this night: it is written, I will
smite the shepherd, and the sheep of the
24 flock shall be scattered abroad. But after " 32
my resurrection I will go before you into
25 Galilee. Simon Cephas answered, and saith " 33
unto him, Lord, if all forsake thee, I will

[1] Aphraates adds here "as often as ye come together," showing clearly that Tatian borrowed from the account in 1 Cor. xi. in compiling the *Diatessaron.* The insertion of the Lord's Supper after the departure of Judas involved a displacement of the subject of Luke xxii. 17–20 from that evangelist's order. The preference was therefore given to other Gospels, only the last clause of Luke xxii. 19 being retained.

[2] S. Matthew and S. Mark put this after the arrival at Gethsemane.

45 26 never withdraw from thee: with[1] thee I Lu. 22 33b
am ready for prison and for death, and I Jn. 13 37b
27 will lay down my life for thee. Jesus said „ 38a
unto him, Wilt thou lay down thy life for
me? Verily, verily, I say unto thee, that Mk.[2] 14 30b
thou to-day, *even* this night, before the cock
crow twice, shalt thrice deny that thou Lu. 22 34b
28 knowest me. But Cephas kept speaking Mk. 14 31
further, Even if I come to death with
thee, I will not deny thee, Lord. And
in like manner also said all the disciples.
29 Then saith Jesus unto them, Let not your Jn. 14 1
hearts be troubled: believe in God, and
30 believe in me. In my Father's house are „ 2
many mansions; if it were not so, I would
have told you; for I go to prepare[3] a place
31 for you. And if I go away to prepare a „ 3
place for you, I will return again, and
receive you unto myself; and where I am,
32 there shall ye also be. And the place „ 4
whither I go, ye know, and the way ye
33 know. Thauma said unto him, Lord, we „ 5
know not whither thou goest; and how
shall we have a way to perceive this?
34 Jesus said unto him, I am the way, and „ 6
the truth, and the life: and no one cometh
35 unto my Father, but by me. And if ye had „ 7
known me, ye would have known my Father:
and from henceforth ye have known him,
36 and have seen him. Philip said unto him, „ 8
Lord, shew us the Father, and it sufficeth
37 us. Jesus said unto him, All this time am „ 9
I with you, and have ye not yet known me?
Philip, he that seeth me hath seen the
Father; how sayest thou then, Shew us the
38 Father? Believest thou not that I am in „ 10

[1] Omitting John xiii. 37: "why cannot I follow Thee now?"

[2] Cf. xlix 17.

[3] Addai alludes to this, saying, "He is gone to prepare for his worshippers blessed mansions, in which they may dwell."

my Father, and my Father is in me? for
the words that I speak I speak not from
myself: but my Father, who abideth in me,
45 39 he doeth these works. Believe that I am Jn. 14 11
in my Father, and my Father is in me:
40 or else believe for the works' sake. Verily, „ 12
verily, I say unto you, He that believeth on
me, the works that I do shall he do also;
and greater *works* than these shall he do.
41 I go unto the Father: and whatsoever ye „ 13
shall ask in my name, I will do with you,
that the Father may be glorified in his Son.
42 If therefore ye ask in my name, I will do „ 14
43 *it.* If ye love me, keep my commandments. „ 15
44 And I will pray my Father, and he shall „ 16
send you another Paraclete,[1] that he may be
45 with you for ever, *even* the Spirit of truth, „ 17
whom the world cannot receive; for it hath
not seen him, neither known him: but ye
know him; for he abideth with you, and is
46 in you. I will not leave you orphans: I „ 18
47 will come unto you. Yet a little while, and „ 19
the world shall not see me; but ye shall see
48 me: because I live, ye shall live also. And „ 20
in that day ye shall know that I am in my
46 1 Father, and ye in me, and I in you. He „ 21
that hath my commandments, and keepeth
them, he it is that loveth me: and he that
loveth me shall be loved of my Father, and
I will love him, and will manifest myself
2 unto him. Judas (not the Iscariot) said „ 22
unto him, Lord, what is the meaning of thy
resolution to manifest thyself unto us, and
3 not unto the world? Jesus answered, and „ 23
said unto him, He that loveth me will surely
keep my saying: and my Father will love
him, and we will come unto him, and make
4 our abode with him. But he that loveth „ 24
me not keepeth not my saying: and this

[1] This Greek form is retained in the Arabic: it is equivalent to "Comforter."

saying which ye hear is not my saying, but
the Father's who sent me.
46 5 These things have I spoken unto you, Jn. 14 25
6 while *yet* abiding with you. But the Para- „ 26
clete, *even* the Holy Spirit, whom my Father
will send in my name, he shall teach you
all things, and bring to your remembrance
7 all whatsoever I say unto you. Peace I „ 27
leave with you; my peace I give unto you:
but not as this world giveth, give I unto
you. Let not your heart be seized with
8 forebodings, neither let it be fearful. Ye „ 28
heard how I said to you, I go away, and I
will come unto you. If ye had loved me, would
ye not surely have rejoiced, because I go unto
my Father? for my Father is greater than I.
9 And now I tell you before it come to pass, „ 29
that, when it is come to pass, ye may believe
10 on me. I will not now speak much with „ 30
you, the prince of the world shall come, and
11 shall have nothing in me; but that the „ 31[a]
world may know that I love my Father,
and as my Father gave me commandment,
12 so I do. And he saith unto them, When Lu. 22 35
I sent you forth without purses,[1] and wallets,[1]
13 and shoes, lacked ye anything? They said „ 36
unto him, Nothing. He said unto them,
Henceforth he that hath a purse, let him
take it, and likewise a wallet also: and he
that hath no sword, let him sell his coat,
14 and buy himself a sword. I say unto you, „ 37
that this which is written must yet be
fulfilled in me, for I shall be reckoned with
transgressors: for all things that were said
15 concerning me are fulfilled in me. His dis- „ 38
ciples said unto him, Lord, behold, here are
two swords. He said unto them, They are
enough. Arise, let us go hence. Jn. 14 31[b]
16 And they rose up, and when they had Lu. 22 39

[1] Plural; so also in the Doctrine of Addai.

given thanks, they went out, and went,
according to their custom, unto the mount
of Olives, he and his disciples.
46 17 And he saith unto them, I am the true Jn. 15 1
vine, and my Father is the husbandman.
18 Every branch in me that beareth not fruit, „ 2
he will take it away: and that which beareth
fruit, he will cleanse, that it may bear much
19 fruit. Already ye are clean because of the „ 3
saying which I have spoken unto you.
20 Abide in me, and I in you. For even as „ 4
the branch of the vine cannot bear fruit of
itself, except it abide in the vine; so neither
21 *can* ye, except ye abide in me. I am the „ 5
vine, and ye *are* the branches: He that
abideth in me, and I in him, the same
beareth much fruit: for without me ye can
22 do nothing. But if any man abide not in „ 6
me, he shall be cast forth as a withered
branch, which is gathered, and cast into the
23 fire to burn. If ye abide in me, and my „ 7
word abide in you, whatsoever ye shall wish
24 to ask shall be done unto you. And herein „ 8
shall the Father be glorified, that ye bear
25 much fruit, and be my disciples. And even „ 9
as the Father hath loved me, I also have
26 loved you: abide ye in my love. If ye „ 10
keep my commandments, ye shall abide in
my love; even as I have kept my Father's
27 commandments, and abode in his love. These „ 11
things have I spoken unto you, that my joy
may be in you, and *that* your joy may be
28 fulfilled. This is my commandment, that „ 12
ye love one another, even as I have loved
29 you. And there is no greater love than this, „ 13
30 that a man give his life for his friends. Ye „ 14
are my friends, if ye do all things which I
31 have commanded you. I will not now call „ 15
you servants; for the servant knoweth not
what his lord doeth: but I have called you

friends; for all things whatsoever I heard
from my Father I have made known unto
46 32 you. Ye did not choose me, but I selected Jn. 15 16
you, and appointed you, that ye also should
go and bring fruit, and *that* your fruit should
abide: and whatsoever ye shall ask of the
Father in my name, he will give it you.
33 This I command you, that ye love one „ 17
34 another. And if the world hateth you, „ 18
know that it hath hated me before *it hated*
35 you. For if ye had been of the world, the „ 19
world would love what is its own: but ye
are not of the world. I chose you out of
the world, therefore the world hateth you.
36 Remember the saying that I spake unto you, „ 20
A servant is not greater than his lord. If
therefore they cast me out, they will cast
you out also; and if they kept my word,
37 they will keep your words also. But all „ 21
these things will they do unto you for my
name's sake, because they know not him
38 that sent me. For if I had not come and „ 22
spoken unto them, they would not have had
sin: but now they have no excuse for their
39 sins. He that hateth me hateth my Father „ 23
40 also. And if I had not done before them „ 24
the works which none other did, they would
not have had sin: but now have they seen
41 and hated both me and my Father, that the „ 25
saying may be fulfilled that is written in
their law, They hated me without a cause.
42 But when the Paraclete is come, whom I „ 26
will send unto you from my Father, *even*
the Spirit of truth, which proceedeth from
my Father, he shall bear witness of me:
43 and ye shall bear witness, because ye are „ 27
with me from the beginning.
44 These things have I spoken unto you, that „ 16 1
45 ye should not be disquieted. For they shall „ 2
put you out of their synagogues: and the

hour will come, that every one that shall
kill you will think that he presenteth an
46 46 offering unto God. And these things will Jn. 16 3
they do unto you, because they know not
47 me, nor my Father. These things have I „ 4
spoken unto you, that when the hour is
come, ye may remember them, how that I
48 told you. And these things I said not unto „ 5
you before, because I was with you. And
now I go unto him that sent me; and none
49 of you asketh me, whither I go. Now I „ 6
have spoken these things unto you, and
sorrow hath come, and seized your hearts.
50 Nevertheless I tell you the truth: It is „ 7
expedient for you that I go away: for if I
go not away, the Paraclete will not come
unto you; but if I go, I will send him unto
51 you. And when he cometh, he will convict „ 8
the world in respect of sin, and of righteous-
52 ness, and of judgment: of sin, because they „ 9
53 believed not on me; but of righteousness, „ 10
54 because I go to my Father; and of judg- „ 11
ment, because the prince of this world is
55 judged. And I have yet many things to „ 12
say unto you, but ye cannot bear them now.
56 And when the Spirit of truth is come, he „ 13
shall bring all the truth to your remembrance:[1] he shall not speak anything from
himself; but what things soever he shall
hear, *these* shall he speak: and he shall
teach you those things that are about to
57 come. And he shall glorify me: for he shall „ 14
take from me, and shall show *it* unto you.
58 All things that my Father hath are mine: „ 15
therefore said I unto you, that he shall
take of mine, and shall show *it* unto you.
47 1 A little *while*, and ye shall not see me; and „ 16
again a little *while*, and ye shall see me,
2 because I go to the Father. His disciples „ 17

[1] Cf. John xiv. 26.

therefore said one to another, What is this
that he said unto us, A little *while*, and ye
shall not see me; and again a little *while*,
and ye shall see me: and, I go to the
47 3 Father? And they said, What is this little Jn. 16 18
while which he said? We know not what
4 he saith. And Jesus perceived that they „ 19
were desirous to ask him, and said unto
them, Do ye inquire of one another, because
I said unto you, A little *while*, and ye shall
not see me; and again a little *while*, and ye
5 shall see me? Verily, verily, I say unto you, „ 20
that ye shall lament and be sad, but the
world shall rejoice: and ye shall be sorrowful,
but your grief shall be turned into joy.
6 For a woman, when the time of bearing „ 21
draweth near unto her, the coming of the
day of her delivery oppresseth her: but
when she hath brought forth the child, she
remembereth not the anguish, for the joy
7 that a man is born into the world. Even „ 22
ye therefore are sad now: but I will surely
see you, and your heart shall rejoice, and
your joy no one shall take away from you.
8 And in that day ye shall ask me nothing. „ 23
Verily, verily, I say unto you, Whatsoever
ye shall ask of my Father in my name, he
9 will give it you. Hitherto have ye asked „ 24
nothing in my name: ask, and ye shall receive, that your joy may be full.
10 Now have I spoken unto you in proverbs: „ 25
but an hour and a time shall come, when I
shall not speak unto you in proverbs, but
shall reveal to you the Father by an open
11 revelation. In that day ye shall ask in my „ 26
name: and I say not unto you, that I will
12 pray the Father for you; for the Father „ 27
loveth you, because ye have loved me, and
have believed that I came out from my
13 Father. I came out from my Father, and „ 28

am come into the world: and I leave the
47 14 world, and go unto my Father. His dis- Jn. 16 29
ciples said unto him, Lo, now thy words are
clear, and thou hast spoken nothing in a
15 proverb. Lo, now know we that thou „ 30
knowest all things, and neediest not that
any man should ask thee: and by this we
believe that thou camest out from God.
16} 17} Jesus said unto them, Believe that an hour {Jn. 16 31 „ 32
shall come, and is already come, and ye shall
be scattered, every man to his own place,
and shall leave me alone: and *yet* I am not
18 alone, because the Father is with me. These Jn. 16 33
things have I spoken unto you, that in me
ye may have peace. For in the world distress shall overtake you: but be of good
cheer, for I have overcome the world.
19 This spake Jesus; and lifting up his eyes „ 17 1
to heaven, he said, My Father, the hour is
come; glorify thy Son, that thy Son may
20 glorify thee: even as thou gavest him „ 2
authority over all flesh, that everything, that
thou hast given him, to it he should give
21 eternal life. And this is life eternal, that „ 3
they may know that thou art the only true
God, and that he, whom thou didst send, *is*
22 Jesus the Messiah. I have glorified thee „ 4
on the earth, and I have accomplished the
23 work which thou gavest me to do. Now „ 5
therefore, thou Father, glorify me with thine
own self with the glory which I had with thee
24 before the world was. I taught thy name „ 6
unto the men whom thou gavest me out of
the world: thine they were, and thou gavest
them to me; and they have kept thy say-
25 ing. Now they know that all things which „ 7
26 thou hast given me are from thee: and the „ 8
words which thou gavest me I have pre-
sented unto them; and they received *them*,
and knew of a truth that I came out from

thee, and they believed that thou didst
47 27 send me. And I pray for them: and my Jn. 17 9
petition is not for the world, but for these
whom thou hast given me; for they are
28 thine: and all my things are thine, and all „ 10
thine are mine: and I am glorified in them.
29 And now I am not in the world, and these „ 11
are in the world, and I come to thee. Holy
Father, keep them in thy name, whom thou
hast given me, that they may be one, even
30 as we *are*. When I was with them in the „ 12
world I kept them in thy name. For *those*,
whom thou hast given me, have I guarded,
and not one of them perished, but the son
of perdition;[1] that the scripture might be
31 fulfilled. Now I turn to thee; and this I „ 13
speak in the world, that they may have my joy
32 fulfilled in themselves. I have given them „ 14
thy saying; and the world hated them, because they are not of the world, even as I
33 am not of the world. For I seek not this, „ 15
that thou shouldest take them from the
world, but that thou shouldest keep them from
34 the evil *one*. They are not of the world, even „ 16
35 as I am not of the world. Father, sanctify „ 17
them in the truth: for thy saying is truth.
36 And even as thou didst send me into the „ 18
world, I also send them into the world.
37 And for their sakes I sanctify myself, that „ 19
they themselves also may be sanctified in
38 the truth. And not for them only do I „ 20
pray, but for them that are about to believe
39 on me through their word; that they may „ 21
all be one; even as thou *art* in me, and I in
thee, that they also may be one in us: that
the world may believe that thou didst send
40 me. And the glory which thou hast given „ 22
me I have given unto them; that they may
41 be one, even as we are one; I in them, and „ 23

[1] Lit. "perishing."

thou in me, that they may be perfected into
one; and that the world may know that
thou hast sent me, and that I have loved
47 42 them, even as thou hast loved me. Father, Jn. 17 24
those whom thou hast given me, I will that,
where I am, they also may be with me; that
they may see my glory, which thou hast
given me: for thou lovedst me before the
43 foundation of the world. O my righteous „ 25
Father, the world knew thee not, but I know
thee; and these knew that thou didst send
44 me; and I made known unto them thy „ 26
name, and will make it known; that the
love wherewith thou lovedst me may be in
them, and I may be in them.
48 1 This spake Jesus, and went forth with his „ 18 1
disciples to the place which is called Gethsemane, over the brook Cedron, to the
mountain, the place wherein was a garden,
into which he entered, himself and his
2 disciples. Now Judas the betrayer knew „ 2
that place: for Jesus ofttimes resorted
3 thither with his disciples. And when Jesus Lu. 22 40[a]
had arrived at the place, he said unto his
disciples, Sit ye here, that I may go and pray. Mt. 26 36[b]
4 Pray that ye enter not into temptation. Lu. 22 40[b]
5 And he took with him Cephas, and at the Mt. 26 37
same time the two sons of Zebedee, James
and John, and began to be sorrowful and
6 anxious. And he saith unto them, My soul „ 38
is in anguish, even unto death: abide ye
7 here, and watch with me. And he was Lu. 22 41
parted from them a little way, as far as a
stone's cast is; and he kneeled down and
8 fell forward on his face, and prayed that, Mk. 14 35[b]
if it could be done, that hour might pass
9 away from him. And he said, Father, thou „ 36[a]
canst *do* all things; if thou be willing, Lu. 22 42[b]
remove this cup from me: nevertheless not
10 my will, but thy will, be done. And he Mt. 26 40[a]

came unto his disciples, and found them
48 11 sleeping, and said unto Cephas, Simon, Mk. 14 37[b]
sleepest thou? So, could ye not watch Mt. 26 40[b]
12 with me one hour? Watch and pray, that „ 41[a]
ye enter not into temptation: the spirit is Mk.[1] 14 38[b]
eager and ready, but the body is weak.
13 Again a second time he went away, and Mt. 26 42
prayed, saying, O my Father, if this cup
cannot pass away, except I drink it, thy
14 will be done. And again he returned, and Mk. 14 40
found his disciples sleeping, for their eyes
were weighed down for sorrow and anxiety;
and they knew not what to answer him.
15 And he left them, and went away again, Mt. 26 44
and prayed a third time, saying the same
16 speech. And there appeared unto him an Lu. 22 43
17 angel from heaven, strengthening him. And „ 44
while he was afraid [2] he prayed with unin-
terrupted prayer: and his sweat became as
it were a stream of blood, and fell down
18 upon the ground. Then he rose up from „ 45[a]
the prayer, and came unto his disciples,
19 and found them sleeping, and said unto „ 46[a]
them, Sleep on now, and take your rest: Mt. 26 45[b]
20 the end is at hand; and the hour is come; Mk. 14 41[b]
and, behold, the Son of man shall be betrayed
21 into the hands of sinners. Arise, let us be „ 42[a]
going: he is at hand that shall betray me. Mt. 26 46[b]
22 While he yet spake, came Judas the „ 47
betrayer, one of the twelve, and with him a
great multitude carrying lanterns and torches,
and swords and staves, having been sent by
the chief priests and scribes and elders of
the people: and with him a man of the
23 Romans.[3] Now Judas the betrayer gave „ 48
them a sign, saying, He whom I shall kiss,

[1] Or continuation of Matt. xxvi. 41.

[2] Cf. Heb. v. 7, "in that he feared."

[3] Probably added to account for the Jews venturing to use armed violence. In Syriac "Romans" is equivalent to "soldiers."

is he: take him boldly,[1] and lead him Mk. 14 44[b]
away.
48 24 And Jesus, knowing all the things that Jn. 18 4[a]
were about to come upon him, went out unto
25 them: and straightway the traitor Judas Mt. 26 49
came to Jesus, and said, Hail, Master; and
26 kissed him. And Jesus said unto him, „ 50[a]
Judas, betrayest thou the Son of man Lu. 22 48[b]
with a kiss? Friend, art thou come for Mt. 26 50[b]
27 this? And Jesus said unto them which Lu.[2] 22 52[a]
were come unto him, Whom seek ye? Jn. 18 4[b]
28 They said unto him, Jesus of Nazareth. „ 5
Jesus said unto them, I am *he*. And Judas
also, the betrayer, was standing with them.
29 And when Jesus said unto them, I am *he*, „ 6
they went backward, and fell upon the
30 ground. And again Jesus asked them, „ 7
Whom seek ye? They answered, Jesus of
31 Nazareth. Jesus said unto them, I told „ 8
you that I am *he*: if therefore ye seek me,
32 let these go their way: that the saying „ 9
might be fulfilled which he spake, Of those
whom thou hast give me I have not lost
33 one. Then they that were with Judas, came Mt. 26 50[c]
and laid hands on Jesus, and took him.
34 And when his disciples saw what happened, Lu. 22 49
they said, Lord, shall we smite them with
35 the swords? Simon Cephas therefore hav- Jn. 18 10
ing a sword drew it, and struck the high
priest's servant, and cut off his right ear.
And that servant's name was Malchus.
36 Jesus said unto Cephas, The cup which my „ 11
Father hath given me, shall I not drink it?
37 Put up the sword into its sheath,[3] for all Mt. 26 52[b]
they that shall attack with the sword, shall
38 perish with the sword. Or thinkest thou „ 53

[1] Lit. "carefully."

[2] Tatian has made a convenience of this clause, its true place is at ver. 41 of this chapter.

[3] "Put . . . sheath" was omitted from the previous verse.

that I cannot beseech my Father, and he
shall even now furnish unto me more than
48 39 twelve legions of angels? How then shall Mt. 26 54
the scriptures be fulfilled, which say, that
40 thus it must come to pass? After this he Lu. 22 51[b]
gently touched the ear which he had struck,
41 and healed it. And in that hour said Jesus Mt. 26 55
to the multitudes, Are ye come out against
me, as an attack is made on a robber, with
swords and staves to seize me? I sat daily
with you in the temple teaching, and ye
42 took me not: but this is your hour, and the Lu. 22 53[b]
43 power of darkness. And this came to pass, Mt. 26 56
that the scriptures of the prophets might be
fulfilled. Then all the disciples left him,
and fled.

44 So the band and the captains and the Jn.[1] 18 12
soldiers of the Jews took Jesus, and went
45 their way. And a certain young man was Mk. 14 51
following him, naked, wrapped in a linen
46 cloth; and they laid hold on him; but he " 52
let go the linen cloth, and fled away naked.
47 Then they seized Jesus, and bound him, Jn. 18 12
and led him to Annas first; for he was " 13
father-in-law to Caiaphas, which was high
48 priest that year. Now it was Caiaphas " 14
which had given counsel to the Jews, It is
expedient that one man should die for the
people.

49 And Simon Cephas followed Jesus,[2] and *so* " 15
did another disciple. Now that disciple was
known unto the high priest, and entered in
50 with Jesus into the court; but Simon was " 16
standing at the door without. And that
other disciple, which was known unto the
high priest, went out and spake unto the

[1] See three verses lower.

[2] Omitting "afar off." As the trial of Jesus was going on simultaneously with the denials of S. Peter, evangelists differ in the order in which they relate the various occurrences. Tatian follows S. John's order.

48 51 portress, and she brought Simon in. And — Jn. 18 17
when the maid, the portress, saw Simon, she
looked at him, and saith unto him, Art not
thou also one of the disciples of this man,
52 that is to say, of Jesus of Nazareth? And — Lu. 22 57
he denied, saying, Woman, I know him not:
nor do I even understand what thou sayest. — Mk. 14 68[b]
53 Now the servants and the soldiers rose up, — Jn. 18 18[a]
and kindled a fire in the midst of the court
54 to warm themselves; for it was cold. And — Lu. 22 55[a]
when they had kindled the fire, they sat
55 down around *it:* and Simon also came, and — Jn. 18 18[b]
sat down with them, to warm himself, that — Mt. 26 58[b]
he might see the end of what would happen.
49 1 The high priest therefore asked Jesus of — Jn. 18 19
2 his disciples, and of his teaching. And — „ 20
Jesus said unto him, I was speaking openly
to the people; for I ever taught in the
synagogue, and in the temple, where all the
Jews come together; and in secret spake I
3 nothing. Why askest thou me? ask them — „ 21
that have heard, what I was speaking unto
them: for these know all things which I
4 said. And when he had said these *words,* — „ 22
one of the soldiers standing by struck the
cheek of Jesus, saying unto him, Answerest
5 thou the high priest so? Jesus answered, — „ 23
and saith unto him, If I have spoken evil,
bear witness of the evil: but if well, why
6 smitest thou me? And Annas sent Jesus — „ 24
bound unto Caiaphas the high priest.
7 And when Jesus went out, Simon Cephas — „ 25[a]
was standing in the outer court, warming
8 himself. And the maid saw him again, and — Mk. 14 69[a]
began to say to them that stood by, This — Mt. 26 71[b]
man also was there with Jesus of Nazareth.
9 And they that stood by came and said to — „ 73[a]
Cephas, Of a truth thou art one of his
10 disciples. And again he denied with an — „ 72
11 oath, I know not the man. And after a — Lu. 22 58[a]

little while one of the servants of the high Jn. 18 26^a
priest, a kinsman of him whose ear Simon
49 12 cut off, saw him, and disputing, said, Of a Lu.[1] 22 59^b
truth this man was with him; he also is a
13 Galilaean, for his speech is similar. And he {Mt. 26 73^b; Jn. 18 26^b}
said unto Simon, Did not I see thee in the
14 garden with him? Then Simon began to Mk. 14 71
curse and to swear, I know not this man,
15 whom ye mention. And immediately, while Lu. 22 60^b
16 he yet spake, the cock crew twice. And in „ 61^a
that hour Jesus, who was outside, turned,
and looked upon Cephas. And Simon remembered the word of our Lord, which he
17 had said unto him, Before the cock crow Mk.[2] 14 30^b
18 twice, thou wilt deny me thrice. And Lu. 22 62
Simon went out, and wept with a bitter
weeping.

19 And when the morning drew near, there „ 66^a
came together all the guards of the temple,
the chief priests and scribes, and elders of
the people, and all the multitude, and framed
20 devices; and they took counsel against Jesus Mt. 27 1^b
21 to put him to death. And they sought „ 26 59^b
false witnesses, who should bear witness
against Jesus, that they might put him to
22 death; and they found *them* not, and many „ 60^a
23 false witnesses came; and their witness was Mk.[3] 14 59
24 not in agreement. But at last came two Mt. 26 60^b
25 false witnesses, and said, We heard him say, {Mk. 14 57^b; „ 58}
I will destroy this temple of God, made
with hands, and after three days I will build
26 another made without hands. And not even Mk. 14 59
27 so was their witness in agreement. But Jesus Mt. 26 63^a
held his peace. And the high priest rose Mk. 14 60^a
up into the midst, and asked Jesus, saying,

[1] Tatian omits 59^a, which places this occurrence at "one hour" after the preceding denial, and applies to it the statement of 58^a, "after a little while."

[2] As Mark xiv. 30^b was inserted before at xlv. 27^b, Tatian probably meant this for the rest of Luke xxii. 61, adding the word "twice" from Mark xiv. 72.

[3] A mistake for Mark xiv. 56^b; see ver. 26 below.

49 28 Answerest thou nothing to what these wit- Mt. 26 62[b]
29 ness against thee? But Jesus held his Mk. 14 61[a]
30 peace, and answered him nothing. And Lu. 22 66[b]
they led him up into their temple, saying
31 unto him, If thou art the Messiah, tell us. „ 67
He[1] said unto them, If I tell you, ye will
32 not believe me: and if I ask you, ye will „ 68
33 not answer me a word, nor let me go. And Mt. 26 63[b]
the high priest answered, and said unto him,
I adjure thee by the living God, that thou
tell us whether thou be the Messiah, the
34 Son of the living God. Jesus said unto „ 64[a]
35 him, Thou hast said *it*, because I am. They Lu. 22 70
all said unto him, Art thou then the Son of
God? Jesus saith, Ye say *it*, because I am;
36 I say unto you, Henceforth ye shall see the Mt. 26 64[b]
Son of man sitting at the right hand of
power, and coming on the clouds of heaven.
37 Then the high priest rent his coat, saying, Mk. 14 63[a]
38 He hath spoken blasphemy. And they all { Mt. 26 65[b] / Lu. 22 71 }
said, Why do we still seek for witness? we
have now heard the blasphemy from his
39 mouth. What think ye? They all answered, { Mk. 14 64[b] / Mt. 26 66[b] }
40 and said, He is worthy of death. Then Mk. 14 65[a]
some of them came near, and spat into his
face, and struck him, and mocked him. Lu. 22 63[b]
41 And the soldiers,[2] smiting his cheeks, said, Mk. 14 65[b]
Prophesy unto us, Messiah, who is he that Mt. 26 68[b]
42 struck thee? And many other things spake Lu. 22 65
they against him, blaspheming.
43 And the whole council of them rose up, Jn. 18 28[a]
and took Jesus, and brought him bound
into the Praetorium;[3] and delivered him up Mk. 15 1[b]
44 to Pilate the governor: and they themselves Jn. 18 28[b]
entered not into the Praetorium, that they

[1] The Arabic and Vulgate begin ver. 67 here.

[2] Rather the officials attending upon the high priest; cf. the passages here harmonised. The mocking by soldiers is inserted from S. Matthew and S. John at l. 38, etc.

[3] Arabic, Dîwân.

might not be found unclean, when they ate
49 45 the passover. Now Jesus stood before the Mt. 27 11[a]
governor: and Pilate went out unto them Jn. 18 29
outside, and said unto them, What accusa-
46 tion have ye against this man? They „ 30
answered, and said unto him, If he had
not done evil, we should not have delivered
47 him up unto thee. We found this man Lu. 23 2[b]
subverting our people, and forbidding to give
tribute to Caesar, and saying that he him-
48 self is the king, the Messiah. Pilate said Jn. 18 31
unto them, Take him yourselves then, and
judge him according to your law. The Jews
said unto him, We have no authority to put
49 any man to death: that the word might be „ 32
fulfilled, which Jesus spake, when he signified
by what manner of death he was about to
die.
50 And Pilate entered into the Praetorium, „ 33
and called Jesus, and said unto him, Art thou
51 the King of the Jews? Jesus saith unto „ 34
him, Sayest thou this of thyself, or did
52 others tell it thee concerning me? Pilate „ 35
said unto him, Am I a Jew? The sons of
thine own nation and the chief priests delivered thee unto me: what hast thou done?
53 Jesus said unto him, My kingdom is not of „ 36
this world: if my kingdom were of this
world, my servants would certainly fight,
that I should not be delivered to the Jews:
54 now is my kingdom not from hence. Pilate „ 37
said unto him, Then thou art a king? Jesus
saith unto him, Thou sayest *it*, because I am
a king. And for this cause have I been
born, and for this am I come into the
world, that I should bear witness unto the
truth. And every one that is of the truth
55 heareth my voice. Pilate said unto him, „ 38[a]
And what is truth?
And when he had said this, he went out

50 1 again unto the Jews. And Pilate saith unto Lu. 23 4
the chief priests and the multitudes, I have
2 found nothing against this man. But they „ 5
cried out, and said, He stirreth up our people
with his teaching in all Judaea, beginning
3 from Galilee even unto this place. But Pilate, „ 6
when he heard the name of Galilee, asked,
4 Is this man a Galilaean? And when he „ 7
knew that he was under Herod's jurisdiction,
he sent him unto Herod, for he was at
Jerusalem in those days.
5 Now Herod, when he saw Jesus, was ex- „ 8
ceeding glad: for he was of a long time
desirous to see him, because he had heard
many things about his deeds; and he ex-
6 pected to see some sign from him. And he „ 9
questioned him in many words; but Jesus
7 answered him nothing. And the scribes and „ 10
the chief priests stood, accusing him violently.
8 And Herod with his attendants set him at „ 11
nought, and after he had mocked him, he
arrayed him in a scarlet robe, and sent him
9 to Pilate. And Pilate and Herod became „ 12
friends on that day: for before there was
enmity between them.
10 And Pilate called together the chief „ 13
11 priests and the rulers of the people, and „ 14
said unto them, Ye brought unto me this
man, as one that perverteth your people:
and I examined him before you, and found
no fault in this man out of all the things
12 whereof ye accuse him: nor did Herod also: „ 15
for I sent him unto him; and he hath done
13 nothing whereby he deserveth death. I will „ 16
therefore chastise him, and release him.
14 The whole multitude cried out, saying, „ 18
Away with him from us, away with him.
15 And the chief priests and elders accused Mk. 15 3
16 him of many things. And when he was Mt. 27 12
accused by them, he answered not a word,

50 17 Then saith Pilate unto him, Hearest thou Mt. 27 13
not how many things they witness against
18 thee? And he did not answer him even „ 14
with one word: and Pilate marvelled thereat.
19 And when the governor was sitting upon „[1] 19
the place of judgment, his wife sent unto him,
saying unto him, Take heed that thou hurt
not that righteous man: for I have suffered
many things this day in my dream because
of him.
20 Now at every feast the governor was „ 15
wont to release unto the people one prisoner,
21 whom they would. And there was in their „ 16
prison a notable prisoner, who was called
22 Barabbas. When therefore they were „ 17[a]
gathered together, Pilate said unto them,
23 Ye have a custom that I should release Jn. 18 39
unto you a prisoner at the passover: will
ye that I release unto you the king of the
24 Jews? And they all cried out, and said, „ 40
Do not release unto us this man, but release
unto us Barabbas. Now this Barabbas was
25 a robber, who for insurrection and murder Lu. 23 19
done in the city had been cast into prison.
26 And all the people cried out, and began to Mk. 15 8
ask *him* to do unto them even as custom
27 allowed. And Pilate answered, and said unto „ 9[a]
them, Whom will ye that I release unto you? Mt. 27 17[b]
Barabbas, or Jesus, which is called Messiah,
28 the King[2] of the Jews? For Pilate knew „ 18
that envy had moved them to deliver him up.
29 Now the chief priests and the elders besought „ 20
the multitudes that they should ask for the
release of Barabbas, and destroy Jesus.
30 The governor answered, and saith unto them, „ 21
Which of the two will ye that I release

[1] Chronological order is not affected by the displacement of this verse from its setting; whilst greater continuity is given to the combined narrative which follows.

[2] Cf. Mark xv. 9.

50 31 unto you? They said, Barabbas. Pilate Mt. 27 22[a]
said unto them, What then shall I do con-
cerning Jesus, which is called Messiah?
32 They all cried out, saying, Crucify him. Mk. 15 13
33 And Pilate spake unto them again, for he Lu. 23 20
34 desired to release Jesus; but they cried out, „ 21
saying, Crucify, crucify him, and release
35 unto us Barabbas. And Pilate said unto „ 22
them the third time, What evil hath this
man done? I have found no cause deserving of death in him: I will chastise him
36 and release him. But they were the more „ 23
urgent with a loud voice, demanding that
he should crucify him. And their voice,
and the voice of the chief priests prevailed.
37 Then Pilate released unto them Barabbas, {Mk. 15 15[a] Lu. 23 25[a]}
who for insurrection and murder had been
cast into prison, whom they asked for;
but Jesus he scourged.[1] Mt. 27 26[b]
38 Then the soldiers of the governor took „ 27
Jesus, and brought him into the Praetorium,
and gathered unto him the whole band.
39 And they stripped him, and clothed him „ 28
40 in a scarlet cloke, and arrayed him in a Jn. 19 2
purple garment; and plaited a crown of
41 thorns, and put it on his head, and a reed Mt. 27 29[b]
in his right *hand;* and, mocking and de-
riding him, they kneeled down before him,
and did obeisance, saying, Hail, King of
42 the Jews! And they spat into his face, „ 30
and took the reed from his hand, and smote
43 his head, and they struck his cheeks. And {Jn. 19 3[b] „ 4}
Pilate went out again, and said unto the
Jews, I bring him out to you, that ye may
know that I find no cause for his condemna-
44 tion. Jesus therefore went out, wearing the Jn. 19 5
crown of thorns and the purple garment.
Pilate said unto them, Behold, the man!

[1] The last clause of this verse is omitted, and its equivalent is supplied from S. John at li. 6.

50 45 And when the chief priests and the officers Jn. 19 6
saw him, they cried out, saying, Crucify him,
crucify him. Pilate said unto them, Take
him yourselves, and crucify him: for I find
46 no cause in him. The Jews said unto him, " 7
We have a law, and according to our law he
is deserving of death, because he made him-
47 self the Son of God. And when Pilate " 8
heard this saying, he was the more afraid;
48 and he entered into the judgment-hall[1] again, " 9
and said unto Jesus, Whence art thou?
49 But Jesus answered him not a word. Pilate " 10
said unto him, Speakest thou not unto me?
knowest thou not that I have power to
release thee, and have power to crucify
50 thee? Jesus saith unto him, Thou wouldest " 11
have no power against me, except it were
given thee from above: therefore he that
delivered me unto thee hath a greater sin
51 than thy sin. And because of this word " 12
Pilate wished to release him: but the Jews
cried out, If thou release him, thou art not
Caesar's friend: for every one that maketh
himself a king opposeth Caesar.

51 1 And when Pilate had heard this saying, " 13
he brought Jesus out, and sat down on the
tribunal,[2] at the place called The Pavement,
2 but in Hebrew it is called Gabbatha. Now " 14
that day was the Friday[3] of the passover:
and it was about the sixth hour; and he
said unto the Jews, Behold your king!
3 But they cried out, Away with him, away " 15
with him, crucify him, crucify him. Pilate
said unto them, Shall I crucify your king?
The chief priests said unto him, We have
4 no king but Caesar. And when Pilate saw Mt. 27 24
that he prevailed nothing, but rather that a
tumult increased, he took water, and washed

[1] Arabic, "riwâḳ." [2] Arabic, mimbar.
[3] Or, "assembly."

his hands before the people, saying, I am
innocent of the blood of this righteous man:
51 5 see ye *to it*. And all the people answered, Mt. 27 25
and said, His blood *be* on us, and on our
6 children. Then Pilate commanded that Jn. 19 16a
consent should be given to their petition,
and he delivered Jesus up to be crucified
according to their wish.
7 Then Judas the betrayer, wher he had Mt. 27 3
seen Jesus condemned,[1] went away, and gave
back the thirty pieces of silver to the chief
8 priests and elders, saying, I have sinned in „ 4
that I betrayed innocent blood. They said
unto him, What is that to us? see thou *to it*.
9 And he cast down the money in the temple, „ 5
and departed; and he went away, and
10 hanged[2] himself. And the chief priests took „ 6
the money, and said, We have no right to
put it into the ark of offerings, for it is the
11 price of blood. And they took counsel, and „ 7
bought with it a potter's field for the burial
12 of strangers. Wherefore that field was „ 8
called, The field of blood, unto this day.
13 Then was fulfilled that which was spoken „ 9
through the prophet,[3] saying, I took the
thirty pieces of silver for the price of the
great *one*, which was fixed by the children of
14 Israel; and I paid them for the potter's „ 10
field, as the Lord commanded me.
15 And the Jews took Jesus, and went away {Jn. 19 16b, Mk. 15 20b}
to crucify him: and when he had taken up Jn. 19 17a
16 his cross and gone out, they took off from Mt. 27 31b

[1] Or, "assailed." Judas could scarcely have had this interview with the chief priests before the condemnation by Pilate. Tatian's displacement here would seem therefore to be an improvement.

[2] As Ephraem refers to the account in Acts i. 18, it has been thought that his copy of the *Diatessaron* contained part of that verse, which was afterwards omitted. At the close of the present verse he adds, "and died."

[3] Omitting "Jeremiah," as the Peschito does; "Jeremiah" is a mistake in our Gospel for Zechariah.

him the purple[1] and scarlet garment, with
which he was clothed, and clothed him with
his own garments.
51 17 And as they were going away with him, Mt. 27 32[a]
they found a man of Cyrene, coming from
the country, Simon by name, the father of Mk. 15 21[b]
Alexander and Rufus; him they impressed, Mt. 27 32[b]
18 that he might bear the cross of Jesus. And Lu. 23 26[b]
they took up the cross, and laid it on him,
that he might bear it, and come after Jesus.
And Jesus went on with his cross behind
him.
19 And there followed him much people, „ 27
and women who lamented and were excited
20 on account of Jesus. But Jesus turning „ 28
unto them said, Daughters of Jerusalem,
weep not over me, weep over yourselves, and
21 over your children. The days will come, in „ 29
which they shall say, Blessed are the barren,
and the wombs that bare not, and the
22 breasts that gave not suck. Then shall they „ 30
begin to say to the mountains, Fall on us;
23 and to the hills, Cover us. For if they do „ 31
thus in the green tree, what shall be done in
the dry?
24 And they brought with Jesus two others „ 32
25 of the malefactors to be put to death. And „ 33[a]
when they were come unto the place which
is called, The skull, and is called in Hebrew Jn. 19 17[c]
Golgotha: there they crucified him. With Lu. 23 33[b]
him they crucified those two malefactors,
one on the right and the other on the left.
26 And the scripture[2] was fulfilled, which said, Mk. 15 28
27 He was reckoned with transgressors. And „ 23[a]
they gave him wine to drink and myrrh,
and vinegar mingled with gall; and when Mt. 27 34[b]

[1] Cf. Mark xv. 20.

[2] As a comment of the evangelist himself, Tatian considered himself at liberty to remove this verse, from its position in S. Mark, to a more convenient situation.

he had tasted it, he would not drink; and he received it not. Mk. 15 23b

51 28 And the soldiers, when they had crucified Jesus, took his garments, and divided them into four parts, to each band of soldiers a part. Now his coat was without seam, Jn. 19 23
29 woven from the top throughout. They said therefore one to another, Let us not divide it, but cast lots for it, whose it shall be. And the scripture was fulfilled, which saith, " 24

They parted my garments among them;
And for my vesture did they cast lots.

30 This the soldiers did; and they sat, and Mt. 27 36
31 kept guard over him there. And Pilate wrote on a tablet the cause of his death, and put it on the wood of the cross above his head. And there was written thus in it: THIS IS JESUS OF NAZARETH, THE Jn. 19 19
32 KING OF THE JEWS. And this board read many of the Jews: for the place where Jesus was crucified was nigh to the city: and it was written in Hebrew, in Greek, and " 20
33 in Latin. The chief priests therefore said to Pilate, Write not, The King of the Jews; but, He who said, I am King of the Jews. " 21
34 Pilate said unto them, What is written, is " 22
35 written. And the people stood beholding. Lu. 23 35a
And they that passed by railed on him, Mt. 27 39
36 wagging their heads, and saying, Oh! thou that destroyed the temple, and buildest it Mt. 27 40a / Mk. 15 29b
again in three days! save thyself, if thou art the Son of God, and come down from Mt. 27 40b
37 the cross. In like manner also the chief priests, and scribes and elders, and the Pharisees mocked him, and laughed to each " 41
38 other, saying, The saviour of others cannot " 42
39 save himself: If he is the Messiah, the Lu. 23 35b
chosen of God, and the King of Israel; let him now come down from the cross, that Mt. 27 42b
40 we may see, and believe on him. Having " 4

trusted in God, let him deliver him now, if
he hath pleasure in him: for he said, I am
51 41 the Son of God. And the soldiers also Lu. 23 36
mocked him, coming to him, and offering
42 him vinegar, saying unto him, If thou art „ 37
43 the King of the Jews, save thyself. In like Mt. 27 44
manner the robbers also that were crucified
with him reproached him.

44 And one of the two criminals which were Lu. 23 39
crucified with him railed on him, saying, If
thou art the Messiah, deliver thyself, and
45 deliver us also. But his companion rebuked „ 40
him, saying unto him, Dost not even thou
fear God, seeing thou art in the same con-
46 demnation? We indeed justly, and even as „ 41
we have deserved, and according as we have
done are we rewarded: but this man hath
done nothing really deserving of blame.
47 And he said unto Jesus, Lord, remember me „ 42
48 when thou comest into thy kingdom. Jesus „ 43
said unto him, Verily I say unto thee, To-
day shalt thou be with me in Paradise.[1]

49 Now there stood by the cross of Jesus his Jn. 19 25
mother, and his mother's sister, Mary, who
is named[2] after Cleophas, and Mary Magda-
50 lene. And Jesus saw his mother, and the „ 26
disciple, whom he loved, standing by, and
said unto his mother, Woman, behold, thy
51 son! And he saith to the disciple, Behold, „ 27
thy mother! And from that hour the disciple took her unto himself.

52 Now from the sixth hour darkness covered Mt. 27 45a
the whole land until the ninth hour; and {Lu. 23 44b, „ 45a}
53 the sun was darkened. And at the ninth Mk. 15 34
hour Jesus cried with a loud voice, saying,
Jâil, Jâili,[3] why hast thou forsaken me? that

[1] Ephraem has, "in the garden of delight." The Curetonian Syriac has, "in the garden of Eden;" and "Eden" means "delight."

[2] Or, "kinswoman of." Cf. lii. 36.

[3] Really Îl Îli, since Ja is Arabic for O.

is, My God, my God, why hast thou forsaken
51 54 me? And some of them that stood there, when Mt. 27 47
they heard it, said, This man calleth Elijah.
52 1 After these things Jesus, knowing that Jn. 19 28
all things were accomplished, and that the
scripture might be accomplished, said, I
2 thirst. Now there was set *there* a vessel „ 29[a]
full of vinegar: and in that hour one of Mt. 27 48[a]
them ran, and took a sponge, and filled it
3 with the vinegar, and fastening it to a reed, Mk.[1] 15 36[b]
held it near his mouth to give him to drink.
4 And when Jesus had received the vinegar, Jn. 19 30[a]
5 he said, Everything is finished. But the Mt.[2] 27 49
rest said, Let *him* be; let us see whether
6 Elijah cometh to deliver him. And Jesus Lu. 23 34[a]
said, My[3] Father, forgive them; for they
7 know not what they do. And Jesus, crying „ 46[a]
again with a loud voice, said, My Father,
into thy hands I commend my spirit. This
he said; and he bowed his head, and gave Jn. 19 30[b]
up his spirit.
8 And straightway the face of the door of Mt. 27 51
the temple was rent in twain from top to
bottom; and the earth did quake; and the
9 rocks were rent; and the tombs were opened; „ 52
and the bodies of many saints that slept
10 rose up, and went forth; and after his „ 53
resurrection they entered into the holy city,
11 and appeared unto many. Now the centurion[4] „ 54[a]

[1] Or Matt. xxvii. 48 continued.

[2] A marginal note opposite this verse, in an eleventh century MS., No. 5647 in the British Museum, says that in the historical Gospel of Diadorus and Tatian there followed the words, "but another took a spear and pierced his side, and there came out water and blood." Cf. John xix. 34. As no such person or Gospel is known, Diadorus may be a mistake for *Diatessaron*. Cf. lii. 17.

[3] Tatian puts this saying later than S. Luke, and connects it less directly with the Roman soldiers, thus making it applicable to all His persecutors, and uttered when He had endured everything. Tatian's object may, in part, have been to group together the sayings from the cross.

[4] Omitting Mark xv. 39: "which stood over against him," and "that he so cried out, and gave up the ghost."

and they that were with him guarding
Jesus, when they saw the earthquake, and
the things that were done, feared exceed-
52 12 ingly, and glorified God, saying, This man Lu. 23 47[b]
was righteous: and, Truly he was the Son Mt. 27 54[b]
13 of God. And all the multitudes that were Lu. 23 48
come together to the sight, when they beheld
what had happened, returned smiting their
breasts.[1]
14 Now the Jews, because it was the Friday, Jn. 19 31
said, Let not these bodies remain on the
wood, for it is the dawn of the sabbath: for
that sabbath day was a great day. They
asked therefore of Pilate that they might
break the legs of them that had been
15 crucified, and take them away. The soldiers " 32
therefore came, and brake the legs of the
first, and of the other which was crucified
16 with him: but when they came to Jesus, " 33
they saw that he was dead already; and
17 they brake not his legs: howbeit one of the " 34
soldiers with a spear pierced his side, and
straightway there came out blood and water.
18 And he that hath seen hath borne witness, " 35
and his witness is true: and he knoweth
that he saith true, that ye also may believe.
19 These things came to pass that the scripture " 36
might be fulfilled, which saith, A bone shall
20 not be broken in him: and also the scrip- " 37
ture which saith, They shall look on him
whom they pierced.
21 And all the acquaintance of Jesus stood Lu. 23 49[a]
afar off, and the women that had come with

[1] Ephraem here has, "Woe was it, woe was it to us: this was the Son of God!"

The Curetonian Syriac here adds, "and saying, Woe to us, what is this! Woe to us for our sins!" One Latin Codex has a similar reading. A very interesting discussion of the original form of this passage in the *Diatessaron* will be found in Mr. Rendel Harris's Essay, pp. 34, 35. Cf. also Professor Robinson, *The Gospel according to Peter*, pp. 22, 23.

him from Galilee, who were those who were   Mk. 15 41[b]
52 22 following him, and ministering unto him : of   Mt. 27 56[a]
whom one was Mary Magdalene, and Mary   Mk. 15 40[b]
the mother of James the less and of Joses,
and the mother of the sons of Zebedee,   Mt. 27 56[c]
23 and Salome, and many other women which   { Mk. 15 40[c] ; " 41[c] }
had come up with him unto Jerusalem;
and they saw these things.   Lu. 23 49[b]
24 And when the evening of the Friday was   Mk. 15 42
come, on account of the entrance of the
25 sabbath, there came a man named Joseph,   Lu. 23 50
rich *and* a councillor, of Arimathaea, a city
of Judaea, who was a good man and upright,
and a disciple of Jesus, who concealed him-   Jn. 19 38[b]
26 self, being afraid of the Jews; but he had   Lu. 23 51
not consented to the counsel and deeds of
the accusers, and was looking for the kingdom
27 of God. This man then came, and went in   Mk. 15 43[b]
unto Pilate, and requested of him the body
28 of Jesus. And Pilate marvelled how he   " 44
had already died. And calling unto him the
centurion, he asked him about his death
29 before the *usual* time. And when he had   " 45[a]
learned it, he commanded him to deliver up   Mt. 27 58[b]
30 his body to Joseph. And Joseph bought a   Mk. 15 46[a]
clean linen cloth, and took down the body
of Jesus, and wound him in it. They came   Jn. 19 38[d]
31 therefore, and took it away. And there   " 39
came unto him also Nicodemus, who had
before come to Jesus by night, bringing with
him a mixture of myrrh and aloe, about a
32 hundred pounds. So they took the body of   " 40
Jesus, and wrapped it in linen cloths and
spices, as the custom of the Jews is to bury.
33 Now in the place where Jesus was crucified   " 41
there was a garden; and in the garden a
new tomb hewn out in the rock, wherein no
34 man had ever yet been laid. There then,   " 42
because the sabbath had entered in, and
because the tomb was nigh at hand, they

52 35 left Jesus: and they rolled a great stone, Mt. 27 60b
and thrust it to the door of the tomb, and
36 departed. And Mary Magdalene and Mary Mk. 15 47a
named[1] after Joses came after them unto
37[2]the tomb, and sat down over against the Lu. 23 55b
tomb, and saw how they brought in and
38 placed the body there. And they returned, " 56a
and bought spices and ointments, and turned Mk. 16 1b
back that they might come and anoint it.
39 But on the day which was the day of the Lu. 23 56b
sabbath, they left off because of the commandment.
40 Now the chief priests and the Pharisees Mt. 27 62b
41 came together unto Pilate, and said unto " 63
him, Sir, we remember that that misleader
said, while he was yet alive, After three
42 days I will rise again. And now be before- " 64
hand in guarding the sepulchre until three
days, lest haply his disciples come and steal
him by night, and they will say unto the
people, He is risen from the dead: and the
last error will be worse than the former.
43 He said unto them, Have ye not a guard? " 65
go your way, guard it as ye know *how*.
44 And they went, and made the sepulchre sure, " 66
and sealed the stone, together with the guards.
45 Now on the evening of the sabbath which " 28 1a
is the dawn of the first *day*, at very early Lu. 24 1b
46 dawn, behind the rest came Mary Magdalene Mt. 28 1b
and the other Mary and the other women to
see the sepulchre, carrying with them the Lu. 24 1c
47 spices which they had prepared. And they Mk. 16 3
said among themselves, Who shall remove
for us the stone from the door of the tomb?
48 for it was exceeding great. And when they {Mk. 16 4b / Mt. 28 2a}
said so, a great earthquake took place; and

[1] Or, "kinswoman of." Cf. li. 49.

[2] The second leaf missing from the Vatican MS. seems to have extended from this verse to liii. 4 inclusive, this passage being obtained from the Borgian MS. only.

an angel descended from heaven, and came
and rolled away the stone from the door.
52 49 And they came and found the stone removed Lu. 24 2
from the tomb, and the angel sitting upon Mt. 28 2b
50 the stone. And his appearance was as " 3
lightning, and his raiment white as snow:
51 and for fear of him the guards were terrified, " 4
52 and became as dead men. And when he Lu. 24 3
was gone away, the women entered the tomb,
53 and found not the body of Jesus: but they Mk. 16 5b
saw there a young man sitting on the right
side, arrayed in a white robe; and they
54 were amazed. And the angel answered, and Mt. 28 5
said unto the women, Fear not ye: for I
know that ye seek Jesus of Nazareth, which
55 hath been crucified. He is not here; for " 6
he is risen, even as he said. Come and see
53[1] 1 the place where our Lord was laid. And Lu. 24 4
while they were perplexed thereabout, be-
hold, two men stood above them in dazzling
2 apparel; and as they were seized with terror, " 5
and bowed down their faces to the earth,
they said unto them, Why seek ye the living
3 *one* among the dead? He is not here; he " 6
is risen: remember what he spake unto you
4 when he was yet in Galilee, saying, The Son " 7
of man is going to be delivered up into the
hands of sinners, and to be crucified, and to
5 rise again the third day. But[2] go quickly, Mt. 28 7a
and tell his disciples and Cephas, that he is
risen from the dead; and lo, he goeth before
6 you into Galilee; and there shall ye see Mk. 16 7b
him, where he said unto you; lo, I have Mt. 28 7c
7 told you. And they remembered his words; Lu. 24 8

[1] The marks of division for this new chapter are omitted from the Borgian MS., whilst the passage is absent from the Vatican MS.

[2] In S. Matthew these words are a continuation of lii. 55, and spoken by an "angel," called by S. Mark a "young man;" but here they are spoken by "two men." Cf. liii. 1. Modern harmonisers have felt the same difficulty as Tatian did.

and they departed quickly from the tomb Mt. 28 8
with joy and great fear, and hastened and
53 8 went their way running; for perplexity and Mk. 16 8b
quaking had come upon them: and they
said nothing to any one; for they were
9 afraid. But Mary ran, and came to Simon Jn. 20 2
Cephas, and to that other disciple, whom
Jesus loved, and said unto them, They have
taken away our Lord out of the tomb, and I
10 know not where they have laid him. Simon „ 3
therefore went forth and that other disciple,
11 and they came to the tomb. And they ran „ 4
both together: and that disciple hastened
and got before Simon, and came first to the
12 tomb; and looking[1] in, he saw the linen „ 5
13 cloths laid; yet entered he not in. After „ 6
him came Simon, and he entered into the
14 tomb; and saw the linen cloths laid, and the „ 7
napkin, that had been wrapped about his
head, was not with the linen cloth, but
rolled up and laid on the opposite side in a
15 certain place. Then entered in that disciple, „ 8
which had come first to the tomb, and he
16 saw, and believed. For as yet they knew „ 9
not from the scriptures, that the Messiah
was going to rise again from the dead.
17 And those two disciples went away unto „ 10
their own place.
18 But Mary was standing near the tomb „ 11
weeping: so, as she wept, she looked for-
19 ward[2] into the tomb; and she saw two „ 12
angels in white sitting, one on the side of
his cushion, and the other on the side of his
feet, where the body of Jesus had been laid.
20 And they said unto her, Woman, why weepest „ 13
thou? She said unto them, They have
carried away my Lord, and I know not

[1] Omitting "stooping down;" according to Tatian no stooping was necessary; cf. ver. 18.

[2] No stooping, cf. ver. 12.

53 21 where they have laid him. While saying Jn. 20 14
these *words*, she turned herself back, and
saw Jesus standing, and knew not that it
22 was Jesus. Jesus said unto her, Woman, „ 15
why weepest thou? whom seekest thou?
And she, supposing him to be the gardener,
said, Sir, if thou hast taken him, tell me
where thou hast laid him, that I may go,
23 and take him away. Jesus said unto her, „ 16
Mary. And she turned herself, and said
unto him in Hebrew, Rabboni, which is
24 interpreted The Teacher. Jesus said unto „ 17
her, Touch me not; for I am not yet ascended
to my Father: go unto my brethren, and
say unto them, I ascend unto my Father
and your Father, my God and your God.
25 And on the first day, *the day* whereon he Mk. 16 9
rose, he appeared first to Mary Magdalene,
from whom he had cast out seven devils.
26 And some of the guards[1] came into the Mt. 28 11[b]
city, and told unto the chief priests all the
27 things that had happened. And when they „ 12
were assembled with the elders, and had
taken counsel, they gave no little money
28 unto the guards, saying unto them, Say ye, „ 13
His disciples came by night, and stole him
29 away, while we slept. And if the governor „ 14
hear this, we will answer with him, and
30 make you safe from blame. And when they „ 15
had taken the money, they did as they had
taught them: and this saying was spread
abroad among the Jews, *and continueth* until
this day.
31 And then came Mary Magdalene, and told Jn. 20 18

[1] The guards would naturally go to report at the same time as the women. It is therefore, *historically*, a matter of indifference which fact is related first. But it was convenient to Tatian to group the appearance of the Saviour to the women on their way with a series of His other appearances not reported by S. Matthew. To do this he naturally related the proceedings of the guard first.

the disciples, that she had seen our Lord;
and that he had said these things unto her.
53 32 And as those women were going on the Mt. 28 8[b]
33 way to tell the disciples, Jesus met them, „ 9
saying, All hail! And they came, and took
34 hold of his feet, and worshipped him. Then „ 10
said Jesus unto them, Fear not: but go, tell
my brethren to go into Galilee, and there
35 shall they see me. And those women re- Lu. 24 9
turned, and told all these things to the
eleven, and to the rest of the disciples, and Mk. 16 10[b]
to them that had been with him; for they
36 were sad and weeping. And they were Lu. 24 10
Mary Magdalene, and Joanna, and Mary the
mother of James, and the rest of those that
were with them: and these were they that
37 spake unto the apostles. And they, when Mk. 16 11
they had heard them saying that he was
alive, and had appeared unto them, believed
38 not. And these words were in their eyes as Lu. 24 11[a]
the words of madness.
39 After these things he was manifested unto Mk. 16 12[a]
two of them on that very day, and as they Lu. 24 13[b]
were going to a village named Emmaus,
which was at a distance of threescore fur-
40 longs from Jerusalem, and were talking with „ 14
each other of all these things which had
41 happened. For while they communed and „ 15
questioned together, Jesus came, and arrived
even unto them, and walked with them.
42 But their eyes were holden, that they should „ 16
43 not recognise him. And he said unto them, „ 17
What communications are these that ye
address one to another, as ye walk, and
44 are sad? One of them, whose name was „ 18
Cleophas, answered, and said unto him, Art
thou alone a stranger to Jerusalem, since
thou hast not known the things which are
45 come to pass in it in these days? He said „ 19
unto them, What hath happened? They

said unto him, Concerning that Jesus who
was from Nazareth, which was a prophet,
and mighty in speech and deeds before God
53 46 and all the people, whom the chief priests Lu. 24 20
and elders delivered up for condemnation to
47 death, and crucified him. But we thought „ 21
that he was going to deliver Israel. And
all these things came to pass three days ago.
48 Yet certain women also of our company told „ 22
49 us, that they had gone to the tomb; and „ 23
when they found not his body, they came,
and said, that they had seen angels there,
50 which said of him, that he was alive. And „ 24
certain also of our company went to the
tomb, and found it even so, as the women
said, except that they did not see him.
51 Then said Jesus unto them, O destitute of „ 25
understanding, and of a heavy heart to
52 believe! Was[1] it not in all the sayings
of the prophets that the Messiah must suffer „ 26
these things, and enter into his glory?
53 And beginning from Moses and all the „ 27
prophets, he interpreted concerning himself
54 to them out of all the scriptures. And they „ 28
drew nigh unto the village, whither they
were going: and he made them suppose that
he was about to go into a more distant
55 neighbourhood. And they constrained him, „ 29
saying unto him, Abide with us: for the
day hath already declined towards darkness.
56 And he went in to stay with them. And „ 30
when he reclined with them *to meat*, he took
bread, and blessed it, and brake, and gave to
57 them. And straightway their eyes were „ 31
opened, and they recognised him; and he
58 vanished from them. And they said one to „ 32
another, Was not our heart heavy within us,
while he conversed with us in the way, and

[1] The change of reading makes it difficult to end the verse at the usual place.

53 59 interpreted to us the scriptures? And they Lu. 24 33
rose up the same hour, and returned to
Jerusalem, and found the eleven gathered
together, and them that were with them;
60 and they said, the Lord is really risen, and „ 34
61 hath appeared to Simon. But they rehearsed „ 35
the things that had been done in the way,
and how they recognised him, when he brake
the bread; neither believed they these things. Mk. 16 13b
54 1 And whilst they were talking, and the { Lu. 24 36a; Jn. 20 19
evening of that day was come, which was
the first day, and the doors were shut where
the disciples were, for fear of the Jews, Jesus
came and stood in the midst of them, and
2 said unto them, Peace be with you; it is I, Lu.[1] 24 36b
be not afraid. And they were disquieted „ 37
and affrighted, and supposed that they saw
3 a spirit. Jesus said unto them, Why are ye „ 38
troubled? and why do reasonings arise into
4 your hearts? See my hands and my feet, „ 39
that it is I myself: feel me, and know that
a spirit hath not flesh and bones, as ye see
5 me have. And when he had said this, he „ 40
shewed them his hands and feet and side.[2]
6 And while they still disbelieved for joy and „ 41
astonishment, he said, Have ye here anything
7 to eat? And they gave him a piece of a „ 42
broiled fish and honey. And he took it, „[3] 43
and did eat before them.
8 And he said unto them, These are the „ 44
words which I spake unto you, when I was
with you, how that all things must needs be
fulfilled, which are written in the law of
Moses, and the prophets, and the psalms,
9 concerning me. Then opened he their mind, „ 45
that they might understand the scriptures;

[1] The words, "it is I, be not afraid," are a part of this verse in several MSS including the Peschito and the Harclean, but not the Curetonian, Syriac.

[2] Cf. John xx. 20.

[3] This is the whole of our ver. 43; but the Vulgate has more in the verse.

54 10 and he said unto them, Thus it is written, Lu. 24 46
and thus it behoved the Messiah to suffer,
and to rise again from the dead the third
11 day; and that repentance unto remission of „ 47
sins should be preached in his name unto
all the nations: but the beginning shall be
12 from Jerusalem. And ye shall be[1] witnesses „ 48
of this. And I will send forth the promise „ 49[a]
13 of my Father unto you. The disciples, when Jn. 20 20[b]
14 they heard this, were glad. And Jesus said „[2] 21
unto them again, Peace be with you: as the
Father hath sent me, I also send you.
15 When he had said this, he breathed on „ 22
them, and said unto them, Receive ye the
16 Holy Spirit: if ye forgive any one's sins, „ 23
they shall be forgiven him; if ye retain
any one's *sins*, they shall be retained.
17 But Thauma, one of the twelve, who is „ 24
called Thoma,[3] was not there with the
18 disciples, when Jesus came. The disciples „ 25
therefore said unto him, We have seen our
Lord. He said unto them, Except I see in
his hands the prints of the nails, and put
my fingers upon them, and thrust my hand
into his side, I will not believe.
19 And after eight days, on the next first *day*, „ 26
again the disciples were assembled within,
and Thauma with them. And Jesus came,
the doors being shut, and stood in the midst,
and said unto them, Peace be with you.
20 And he said to Thauma, Reach hither thy „ 27
finger, and see my hands;[4] and put forth
thy hand, and spread it upon my side: and

[1] Or, "are." [2] Part of this verse is repeated in lv. 5.

[3] Cf. xxxvii. 61 n. for the Arabic forms: these have no meaning in Arabic; but they are transliterations of the regular Syriac words for "Thomas" and "Twin," *i.e.* Didymus.

[4] There is no mention of nails in the *feet* either here or in S. John. Ephraem distinctly implies in his remarks (Moes. p. 248) that the hands only were pierced by nails. And in *The Gospel according to Peter*, in describing the removal of our Lord from the cross, it says, "they drew out the nails from the hands,'

54 21 be not faithless, but believing. Thauma Jn. 20 28
answered, and said unto him, My Lord, and
22 my God. Jesus said unto him, Now because „ 29
thou hast seen me, thou hast believed:
blessed *are* they that have not seen, and *yet*
have believed.
23 And many other signs did Jesus in the „ 30
sight of his disciples, which are not written
24 in this book: but these are both written, „ 31
that ye may believe on Jesus, the Messiah,
the Son of God; and that believing ye may
have eternal life in his name.
25 And after these things Jesus shewed him- „ 21 1
self again to his disciples at the sea of
Tiberias; and he manifested himself to them
26 on this wise. There were together Simon „ 2
Cephas, and Thauma, who is called Thoma,
and Nathanael, who was of Cana of Galilee,
and the sons of Zebedee, and two others of
27 his disciples. Simon Cephas said unto them, „ 3
I go to catch fishes. They said unto him,
We also come with thee. And they went
forth, and went up into the boat; and that
28 night they caught nothing. But when „ 4
morning came, Jesus stood on the seashore:
but the disciples knew not that it was
29 Jesus. Jesus therefore said unto them, „ 5
Children, have ye anything to eat? They
30 said unto him, No. He said unto them, „ 6
Cast your net on the right side of the ship,
and ye shall find. They cast therefore;
and they were unable to draw the net for
the multitude of fishes, that were come into
31 it. And that disciple, whom Jesus loved, „ 7
said unto Cephas, This is our Lord. And
Simon, when he heard that it was our Lord,
took up his coat, and girded it up to his
loins (for he was naked), and cast himself
into the sea, that he might come to Jesus.
32 But the other disciples came in the ship „ 8

(for they were not far from land, but about
two hundred cubits off), dragging the net
54 33 *full* of fishes. And when they went up Jn. 21 9
unto the land, they saw live coals laid, and
34 a fish laid thereon, and bread. Jesus said „ 10
unto them, Bring of these fish, which ye
35 have now caught. Simon Cephas therefore „ 11
went up, and drew the net to land, full of
great fishes, a hundred and fifty and three:
and with so great a weight, the net was not
36 rent. Jesus said unto them, Come, *and* sit „ 12
down. And no one of the disciples dared
to ask, who he was, knowing that it was our
Lord: yet he did not appear unto them in
37 his own form.[1] And Jesus came and took „ 13
the bread and the fish, and gave unto them.
38 This is the third time that Jesus was mani- „ 14
fested to his disciples, since he had risen
from the dead.
39 So when they had broken their fast, „ 15
Jesus said to Simon Cephas, Simon, son
of Jonah, lovest[2] thou me more than these?
He said unto him, Yea, Lord; thou knowest
that I love thee. Jesus said unto him, Feed
40 my lambs for me. He said to him also „ 16
again, Simon, son of Jonah, lovest thou me?
He said unto him, Yea, Lord; thou knowest
that I love thee. He said unto him, Feed
41 my rams for me. He said unto him also „ 17
the third time, Simon, son of Jonah, lovest
thou me? And Cephas, being grieved because he said three times, Lovest thou me?
said unto him, Lord, thou knowest[3] all
things; thou knowest that I love thee.

[1] Tatian seems to have based this addition upon Mark xvi. 12, "in another form." Cf. xxiv. 3.

[2] In the Arabic no distinction is drawn throughout this passage corresponding to the ἀγαπᾷν and φιλεῖν of the Greek.

[3] Or, "recognisest;" a different Arabic word from that rendered "knowest" in other parts of this narrative.

Jesus said unto him, Feed my sheep for
54 42 me. Verily, verily, I say unto thee, When Jn. 21 18
thou wast young, thou girdedst thyself, and
walkedst whither thou wouldest: but when
thou art old, thou shalt stretch forth thy
hands, and another shall gird thee, and
43 bring thee whither thou willest not. This „ 19
he said unto him to signify by what manner
of death he was going to glorify God. And
when he had spoken this, he saith unto him,
44 Come after me. But Simon Cephas, turning „ 20
about, saw the disciple whom Jesus loved
following him—that one which leaned back
on the breast of Jesus at the supper, and
said, Lord, who is he that shall betray thee?
45 When therefore Cephas had seen him, he „ 21
said to Jesus, Lord, and this man, what
46 shall be concerning him? Jesus said unto „ 22
him, If I will that he tarry till I come,
47 what *is that* to thee? follow thou me. And „ 23
this saying was spread abroad among the
brethren, That disciple will not die: and
Jesus said not, that he should not die; but,
If I will that he tarry till I come, what *is*
that to thee?
48 This is that disciple which beareth witness „ 24
of these things, and wrote them: and we
know that his witness is true.
55 1 But the eleven disciples went into Galilee, Mt. 28 16
unto the mountain where Jesus had appointed
2 them. And when they saw him, they wor- „ 17
shipped *him:* but some of them doubted.
3 And as they sat there, he appeared again Mk. 16 14
unto them, and upbraided them with their
lack of faith and hardness of heart, because
they believed not them, which had seen that
4 he was risen again. Then saith Jesus unto Mt. 28 18[b]
them, All authority hath been given unto
5 me in heaven and on earth: for even as my Jn.[1] 20 21[b]

[1] Repeated from liv. 14.

Father sent me, so I also send you. Go ye Mk. 16 15[b]
therefore into all the world, and preach my
55 6 gospel to every creature; and teach all the Mt. 28 19[b]
nations, and baptize them in the name of
the Father and of the Son and of the Holy
7 Spirit: teaching them to observe all things „ 20
that I commanded you: and lo, I am with
you all the days unto the end of the world.
8 For he that believeth and is baptized shall Mk. 16 16
be saved; but he that disbelieveth shall be
9 condemned. And these signs shall follow „ 17
them that have believed on me: in my
name shall they cast out devils; and they
10 shall speak with new tongues; they shall „ 18
take up serpents; and if they drink a deadly
poison, it shall not hurt them; they shall
lay hands on the sick, and they shall recover.
11 But tarry ye in the city of Jerusalem, until Lu. 24 49[b]
ye be endued with power from on high.
12 And our Lord Jesus, after he had spoken Mk. 16 19[a]
unto them, led them out unto Bethany: and Lu. 24 50
he lifted up his hands, and blessed them.
13 And while he blessed them, he was separated „ 51
from them, and ascended into heaven, and Mk. 16 19[c]
14 sat down at the right hand of God. And Lu. 24 52
they worshipped him, and returned to Jeru-
15 salem with great joy; and they were con- „ 53
tinually in the temple, praising and blessing
God. Amen.
16 And they went forth from thence,[1] and Mk. 16 20
preached everywhere, the Lord helping them,
and confirming their sayings with the signs
which they did.
17 And there are also many other things Jn. 21 25
which Jesus did, the which if they should
be written one by one, according to my
opinion even the world itself would not
contain the books that must be written.

[1] "From thence" is added in connection with "Jerusalem," which was mentioned in ver. 14.

CONCLUDING NOTE IN THE BORGIAN MS.

THE Gospel is concluded, which Tatian compiled out of the four Gospels of the four holy apostles the blessed evangelists, on whom be peace, and which he named *Diatessaron*, that is, That which is composed of four. The excellent and learned presbyter, Abû-l-Faraj Abdullah Ibn-at-Tayyib, with whom may God be pleased, translated it from Syriac into Arabic, from a copy written by the hand of Gubasî ibn Alî Al-mutayyib, a disciple of Ḥunain ibn Ishak, on both of whom may God have mercy. Amen.

Gorgias Reprint Series

1. J. B. Segal, *Edessa 'The Blessed City'* (2001, based on the 1970 edition).
2. J. Hamlyn Hill, *The Earliest Life of Christ: The Diatessaron of Tatian* (2001, based on the 1910 2nd abridged edition).
3. Joseph Knanishu, *About Persia and Its People* (2001, based on the 1899 edition)
4. Robert Curzon, *Ancient Monasteries of the East, Or The Monasteries of the Levant* (2001, based on the 1849 edition)
5. William Wright, *A Short History of Syriac Literature* (2001, based on the 1894 edition)
6. Frits Holm, *My Nestorian Adventure in China, A Popular Account of the Holm-Nestorian Expedition to Sian-Fu and Its Results* (2001, based on the 1924 edition)
7. Austen Henry Layard, *Nineveh and Its Remains: an account of a visit to the Chaldean Christians of Kurdistan, and the Yezidis, or devil-worshipers; and an inquiry into the manners and arts of the ancient Assyrians*, Vol. 1 (2001, based on the 1849 edition)
8. Austen Henry Layard, *Nineveh and Its Remains*, Vol. 2 (2001, based on the 1849 edition)
9. Margaret Gibson, *How the Codex Was Found, A Narrative of Two Visits to Sinai From Mrs. Lewis's Journals 1892-1893* (2001, based on the 1893 edition)
10. Richard Davey, *The Sultan and His Subjects* (2001, based on the 1907 edition)
11. Adrian Fortescue, *Eastern Churches Trilogy: The Orthodox Eastern Churches* (2001, based on the 1907 edition)
12. Adrian Fortescue, *Eastern Churches Trilogy: The Lesser*

Eastern Churches (2001, based on the 1913 edition)

13. Adrian Fortescue, *Eastern Churches Trilogy: The Uniate Eastern Churches: the Byzantine Rite in Italy, Sicily, Syria and Egypt* (2001, based on the 1923 edition)
14. A. V. Williams Jackson, *From Constantinople to the Home of Omar Khayyam: Travels in Transcaucasia and Northern Persia for Historic and Literary Research* (2001, based on the 1911 edition).
15. Demetra Vaka, *The Unveiled Ladies of Stamboul* (2001, based on the 1923 edition)
16. Oswald H. Parry, *Six Months in a Syrian Monastery: Being the Record of a Visit to the Head Quarters of the Syrian Church in Mesopotamia with Some Account of the Yazidis or Devil Worshipers of Mosul and El Jilwah, Their Sacred Book* (2001, based on the 1895 edition).
17. B. T. A. Evetts, *The Churches and Monasteries of Egypt and Some Neighbouring Countries, Attribted to Abû Sâlih the Armenian* (2001, based on the 1895 edition)
18. James Murdock, *The New Testament, Or the Book of the Holy Gospel of Our Lord and Our God Jesus the Messiah, A Literal Translation from the Syriac Peshita Version* (2001, based on the 1851 edition)

Printed in the United States
4225

9 780971 309722